THE SWORD OF DISCERNMENT.

DOUG McPHILLIPS

My Camino Guide Book

Shoes are optional.

Soak-up the sun.

Build sandcastles in the air.

Enjoy new friendships.

Listen to others.

Spend some time alone.

Rest. Relax. Renew.

Enjoy the fresh air.

Smile. Laugh. Sing. Dance.

Live in the moment.

Hear the sound of your walking feet.

Become in tune with you.

For all those pilgrims who have arrived
and the pilgrims still on their Camino.

TABLE OF CONTENTS

THE INTRODUCTION		Page	5.
CHAPTER 1.	The Camino Way	Page	17.
CHAPTER 2.	St. Jean to Pamplona.	Page	29.
CHAPTER 3.	Resilience.	Page	41.
CHAPTER 4.	Lessons from the dead.	Page	51.
CHAPTER 5.	Like ships on the night.	Page	61.
CHAPTER 6.	From darkness to light.	Page	83.
CHAPTER 7.	Lessons from the living.	Page	89.
CHAPTER 8.	Pilgrim's Tramp.	Page	103.
CHAPTER 9.	The Dancing Queen.	Page	113
CHAPTER 10.	Pilgrim's Progress.	Page	125.
CHAPTER 11.	Gauvas' Advise.	Page	149.
CHAPTER 12.	The Road to Leon.	Page	157.
CHAPTER 13.	Playing the child's game.	Page	167.
CHAPTER 14.	When Irish eyes are smiling.	Page	181.
CHAPTER 15.	Strange happenings.	Page	195.
CHAPTER 16.	Dreams & Realities.	Page	207
CHAPTER 17.	Old Symbols & New Signs.	Page	225.
CHAPTER 18.	Santiago!	Page	235.

"Let no-one say the past is dead.

The past is all about us and within

Haunted by tribal memories,

I know this little now.

This accidental presence is the all of me whose long making is so much of the past."

                      Oodgeroo Noonaccual.

(Engraved in the floor at the International Airport, Sydney, Australia.)

Lessons of the Dreamtime.

The practice of Shamanism uses a meditative state of mind to make contact with the spiritual world and reach a state of ecstatic trance. This altered state is an individual journeying in an ever-changing drum rhythm of tunnel-like imagery, in which the Shaman experiences sensations and communications that go beyond the usual senses. In this altered state, the Shaman converses with plants, animals and people in the spirit of the heavens and those in between and below the earth. In the Australian indigenous culture, the world was created during The Dreamtime. Aborigines who take their Dreamtime journey describe how their ancestral spirits formed the land and how the relationship between the peoples' spirits changed to become stars, trees, hills, landscapes, animals and creatures which came from the sea; in fact, every living thing that roamed the earth millions of years ago came from The Dreamtime.

Aborigines have always honoured the sacred earth, the universe and the natural world, learned through their Dreaming and told to the listener in tales of myth and legend. An aborigine on Dreamtime walkabout dances at corroboree ceremonies and sings songs on Dreaming tracks in order to bring spirit ancestors to life and gain access to Dreaming. Any new journey, either inward or outward, may enlighten the traveller and breathe a perspective for living that may not have been considered had not the journey been taken in the first place. Such a journey of the spirit, consciously or unconsciously, has been taken by pilgrims throughout history who have walked The Camino to Santiago.

It is said The Camino – or The Way – lies directly under The Milky Way and follows key ley (energy) lines that reflect the energy from the stars above. In Eastern philosophies, the spiritual life-force (prana) is inextricably linked with the life-force of the sun and especially strong along lines of energy called ley lines. This is in turn linked to the energies conducting within our own galaxy, other galaxies and the star systems. The Camino that follows the earth's ley lines begins in France, at St. Jean-Pied-de-Port, and makes its way east to west across The Pyrenees to the famous cathedral called Santiago de Compostela, in Santiago, where the remains of St. James the Greater, the apostle of Jesus are said to be interred.

The challenge of walking 800 km, to seek spirituality through inner contemplation, let-go of burdens, look for a new direction, figure something out, to follow ley lines, or to just plain surrender to the journey, is an individual experience which has motivated pilgrims who have tramped this pathway to Santiago for thousands of years. The knowledge and understanding of our lives, the history of conflict, loneliness, confusion, hatred and separation from ourselves and from our God are often masked in the life we lead on a day-to-day basis. It is our moral obligation to continue to search our nature; otherwise we are living only half-lives. The Camino de Santiago is a step back in time to a religious and cultural experience which may well be a near-death experience – through mental, physical and cultural insights – that takes the pilgrim back in time in order to move forward again. Alternatively, just accept the reality of the thing, experience the historic influence on this ancient path; feel the legend of the people and the religious heritage that is the foundation stone of what is Spain today.

Dreamtime

Awakened to The Dreamtime,
wonder in a daze,
called by the love sound cicada
and a far-off kookaburra!

Dazed in a sunlight blaze
of where it all began
telling a Dreamtime tale
of universe and man.

Viewing the seep of silver sky,
coloured rainbow too,
caught in the tale of serpent fire
and the distant sound of a bird.

Swimming with fish to feel their fear,
sliding with a crocodile.
slithering and hissing like a snake,
watching the pale moon rising!

Dreaming an ancient story
tribesmen must respect,
one man's painted dream
imagined in the telling,
or playing an instrument!

Feeling the dry earth on my feet,
hearing the drum in my heart,
seeing through ancient eyes,
beginning and end at the start!

Yes! We are the music makers,
we are the makers of dreams,
wandering by lone sea breakers,
sitting by desolate streams.

World losers and world forsakers,
on whom the pale moon gleams;
we are the movers and shakers
of the world forever, it seems!

The Unique Spirit of Being Australian

Indigenous people inhabited this continent for more than 50,000 years, living a nomadic existence, understanding "the spirit of the land" and how to survive. The white man, our forefathers, claimed the land of Australia as a penal colony in 1788 and, up until the gold rush of the 1850s, a swell of settlers arrived from all points of the compass.

The nation of Australia has grown during the past two hundred years, through droughts, floods, fires, economic depression, wars and civil unrest. The strength of the nation has been its multi-cultural heritage and its spirit, learned from the original native inhabitants and from the many pioneers of the land who developed the nation "on the sheep's back" and the cattle industry long before our latter mining-boom years of wealth.

In turbulent times of natural and unnatural disasters, many if our inhabitants travelled the outback as drifters, seeking work. These heroes of the bush, called "sundowners", slept out under the stars when they could not find shelter. Many were of European and Asian descent and just as many were Aboriginal. They worked for meagre pay, often settling for a meal and a bed in exchange for odd jobs on farms, for shearing sheep or taking cattle on drives across our wide brown sunlit land. The phrase "on the wallaby trail" was coined for those who followed the kangaroo tracks for food and water. "Humping a bluey" became the vernacular term for men on the bush tracks seeking work around the country while carrying all their scant possessions in a knapsack (a "bluey"). Apparently, a red-headed Dutchman (red-headed people are called "blue" irrespective of their name) came to Australia seeking work after his wife, Matilda, died. He carried his food box, known as a tucker box, in his knapsack, which he named Matilda, after his wife. The poet of the time, Andrew "Banjo" Patterson, wrote a song about the Dutchman which was, and still is, sung as Waltzing Matilda! Australia has grown from its foundations in the culture of rebellious heroes that makes us unique as a nation, to one still in search of a collective identity. Whilst we have many examples of individuals who helped shape our nation, we are nevertheless influenced in a modern world by the concept of International Multiculturalism, although still admiring individualism. We are still young as a nation and still on a major learning-curve, both individually and collectively, in an ever-changing world, both at home and abroad.

We are a nation of individuals who are somewhat laid-back, conscious of our part in the modern world, but to some extent still searching for the illusion of our identity. Yes, we have a uniqueness in our humour, challenges in our cultural differences, strong belief in our political viewpoints, concern for our fellow man and a fight-for-the-underdog attitude towards most things. We are intolerant of those who appear to stick their heads above the crowd, and more likely to support the underdog, whilst still congratulating the winner. Most international travellers have an image of Australians as casual, easy-going and relaxed types. Our undying slogan, "She'll be right, mate", sums-up our view of the world – an acceptance of whatever happens in life. This may be true to some degree and certainly applied historically, but we are now in the fast lane of change as a modern economy and on a steep learning-curve towards identity as a modern-day people.

Modern-day Australians, unlike their forefathers, travel the world for business and pleasure more than ever. We have not lost the spirit of adventure and will always fight for a good cause if we believe in it. We are geographically isolated from the majority of the world's population but constantly meet the challenges of communication with other nations, Australians, in the main, are still looking for a catalyst of what it means to be "us". Perhaps it is why we travel to foreign lands, in the hope that we make some connection with who we are and what we are all about. Perhaps it is why our Aboriginal brothers go walkabout, to experience The Dreamtime. There is no doubt in my mind that the unique experience of my adventures stems from my upbringing, my ancestral blood connection to Britain, Ireland, Germany, France and French Canada, and from my own search for the meaning of life.

The trials and tribulations of my life as an Australian, my understanding of the walkabout of my Aboriginal brothers, the historical adventures of my kin and those of other Australians, have led me far and wide and, ultimately, to The Camino de Santiago, along which many of the burdens of life I have laid down. My Camino has opened-up for me a renewal of life and a new zest for living, and I trust that this journey of the spirit helps you in yours, be you an adventurer like me from down-under or another atlas-eater from some other distant shore.

Enter the Dragon, the Sword and the Awakening

I had come to a mystical side of myself that could not be expressed in words or through worldly deeds; a cause that could be fulfilled only by the spirit that was central to the candle that burned within - a candle that to me was a symbol of life itself, a flame that burned at a deep level, projecting light into the darkness. And in the flickering awareness I could almost hear a message: "Exist; stay alive; survive". Here, for the first time, I was learning about my true nature, aware of my body, my mind and the true spirit within. I had come from a darkness and had tried to clutch too tightly to the past when my worldly claims engulfed me. Yet here I was now, surrendering my all, falling moment by moment into that surrendering and risking falling into the unknown; falling into the fearful dragon's mouth of self-acceptance, with the fear of falling into a pit of darkness where the dragon lived, where there was no light, only darkness, of weeping and gnashing of teeth.

It was there that I had fallen part of the way previously, when I lost all that I thought life was about. Wife, children, friends, business and wealth had left me, and it was then that I had turned to other lovers; lovers who brought me their pain in my pain, comfort in my agony, illusion in their mystic lover-rites. I'd had a sense of the Goddess for a brief moment, only to find disenchantment and, once more, illusion. A cover of the inner truth that I was seeing clearly now for the first time in my life. I had turned to regain the respect of my children only to find that they had moved on, as was their right, and all I could do now was to be there for them in the event of their fall; be there now, in a sober mind. I had struggled to regain the wealth that I once possessed, only to find that apart from the need for food, clothing and shelter, the pursuit of wealth was of little comfort to me. I felt apart from the world I once knew and was coming to realise that my heart no longer craved for anything that was once my sure-fire way of enthusiasm for living.

I had taken an inner-truth of honesty to myself; an open-mindedness and a willingness to grow; a willingness not to worry; of acceptance; of belief in living with whatever comes my way. I began to relax then, to allow the coil of the wound-up spring within me to slowly unwind, let-go and trust in God without definition. I knew it was not the old ways of strength, enthusiasm, leadership and dogma that would project me like an arrow towards some designated target. Rather, it was to be a slow road, one day at a time, moment to moment to moment, using the spiritual thread of the coiled spring to unwind, unravel and let-go in order to achieve inner calm. I was learning to use no force, to let the force within take hold, allowing time to heal and grow, I knew I needed to go with the grain, as an artist working with wood, in time, knows. Often in the past I had run against the grain and the result was splintered wounds. I was running now with the flow of the inner river and was going with the current in open water. I knew that once I understood and accepted the drift of it, a gentle movement of the rudder would keep me on course!

I was coming to a vacuum and was surrendering and letting it sink into the marrow of my bones. I knew that it was time once again to fall into the bottomless pit where the dragon lived; to descend into the dragon's mouth, in my mind, and there I would find a lotus flower. There, falling into the hell of the bottomless pit, I would reach a vacuum of nothingness (no-thing-ness). It would be in that state that the dragon would turn into a lotus flower of creative ideas – the womb of rebirth.

On previous falls into the pit I had taken a parachute of meaningless clutched possessions and wild ego notions; a crutch to lessen the impact of the fall. The residual inner nervous tension had remained, and so this time I was going without a parachute, without forethought, without a plan. I knew that I had to surrender to win; to give way to keep; to surrender to get well; to die to live! So the new life of the inner spiritual was unfolding. I was learning to let-go and allow the inner core of my being to take hold of something from nothingness. It was where I now believed the universe began: that something that was my God. I discovered within myself a way of cutting through to the reality of everything that comprised my life, and an enlightened ability to judge and act with wisdom; discovered, symbolically, a Sword of Discernment, a tool to carry as my staff of action, my brand of reason. I had a choice now: to use my Sword of Discernment like a knight of old, to just go with the flow, nice and easy, and accept with free will whatever comes along; to use my inner Sword of Discernment with wisdom and understanding whenever and wherever I may think fit; to pursue or not to pursue in consideration of who and what I was beginning to realise I was, am and will be; the right to act or not to act according to the dictates of my consciousness, of my heart and the beauty that lived within me.

I determined to adopt an accord of consciousness with every human being with whom I would come in contact on my outward and inward journey: a journey of understanding; a journey of nature being both cruel and kind; of being as vigilant as a female serpent within my inner being on the pathways of my life, and as innocent as a dove. A freedom nothing bar death could take from me – my freedom of choice for living. I knew within my heart of hearts there existed a Sword of Discernment and I longed for an outward expressive symbol of this inner need and courage. I would venture forth, to let-go of my inner turmoil and take a journey of the spirit – my spiritual heart expressed in a real symbol. I could think of no better way than the way of St. James, the apostle, whose symbol was a real Sword of

Discernment; the sacrificial cross of St. James, the fleury fitch, whose sword blade signifies the sword of a warrior. I would follow the path of St. James. The Moor-slayer, on The Camino Way, where I would lay-down my burdens and walk the traditional Way that so many pilgrims had walked before me.

I felt that I knew the outward expression of that which I sought would manifest into the sword of St. James. Like the Spanish who fought and conquered the Moors so many centuries ago, their vision of the Saint on a white steed advancing before them holding aloft a fiery red sword of Santiago leading their charge and taking them to victory, I, likewise, would venture forth on the road to Santiago, leading ever onward with a courageous cry, to the quest that pierced my heart.

I would walk The Camino de Santiago! Whilst I would seek a symbolic sword as proof of my journey, I knew that my Sword of Discernment would be more than merely a sword. I knew I would express in words the cry of my heart, the link that I had to my past journey. My current turmoil would be in my spiritual quest. I would venture forth with hope and confidence despite the dark night of the soul. I was not yet to know the events that would unfold as a result of walking my Camino. The thought of a new dawning after the long night gave me courage to step forth. The night is darkest just before the dawning and, despite the sword that pierced my soul, I ventured forth.

CHAPTER 1

THE CAMINO WAY.

The Association of James as the patron saint of Spain has no basis in the bible, but exists only in the realm of tradition, oral history, legend and myth. The story goes that St. James preached that faith without works is dead, meaning that actions speak louder than words. Apparently he was not very successful, recruiting only seven disciples during his seven years of preaching in Spain. The last we hear of James is in the biblical account of his martyrdom at the hands of Herod Agrippa in Rome, in about 44 CE (Acts 22:12).

The legend says that James' body was transported to Spain on a stone ship without oars or sail, Viking-style, carried by angels and the wind. The ship landed at Iria Flavia (present-day Padron), and James' disciples met the ship there and carried his body to a nearby hill where he was buried. The body of James appears to have been forgotten for the next seven-and-a-half centuries, until 813. It is written that a Christian hermit named Pelayo saw, on Mount Libredon, a shining light which led him to James' grave and the remains of two of James' disciples, Atanasio and Teodoro. The bishop authenticated the relics and, to honour the Saint, King Alfonso II built a chapel which drew a modest number of pilgrims. The Cathedral de Santiago was commenced in 1075 and completed in 1120. It is reported that below the main altar in the cathedral the remains of St. James are encased in a tomb, and pilgrims have flocked there since Medieval times to pay homage. The Camino de Santiago has been, for pilgrim travellers, a long but tireless journey; they come from France, Germany, Portugal and many other European nations and from within Spain itself to pay homage to St. James and to seek indulgences.During the peak of Santiago's attraction as a place of pilgrimage, in the Middle Ages, from the 9th to the 16th century, two million pilgrims – approximately five thousand per day – came to visit the Saint's burial place. The Reformation in Europe and the Spanish war with England saw the decline of Santiago as a place of pilgrimage.

The scallop shell remains the symbol of the Camino, its outer shell representing the many routes that lead to Santiago. The shell has been used for centuries to denote that an individual displaying it is on a pilgrimage and is protected.

Historically, the Knights Templar of the Order of St. James, whose symbol is a red sword, protected pilgrims on The Camino Way against thieves and vagabonds. The Camino de Santiago may seemingly be a Christian experience, but many people of other faiths, or of no faith at all, walk the path, as they did also in Medieval times. A myth about the modest shrine of St. James recounts the battle of Clavijo, where the Spanish fought the Muslim invaders. James is said to have appeared, arriving on a white horse with the sword of the Templars above his head, leading the Spanish into battle. The image of St. James was a convenient motif to draw Christian support to the frontier of the Muslim-Christian battle and to bolster financial support for the Christian domination of Iberia.

It is said that the Christian soldiers scattered some of James' ashes during the battle, whilst the Muslims had a mummified arm of Mohammed in a cloth as a guiding symbol. Although the fact that the legend lives on that James appeared on the battle field at Clavijo, it seems to be a direct consequence of the Christians regaining the upper-hand in Spain, but is merely a story. In fact St. James, as the best of scholars seem to agree, never came to Spain. There is no earthly reason why his body should have been brought to Galicia and nothing is suggested in the Acts of the Apostles in the bible, where his death is recorded. James died several centuries before Islam was conceived, probably never mounted a horse in his life and certainly never slew a

Muslim. There is no earthly reason why Santiago should be a place of pilgrimage, although it is.

To Bring a Sword.

"Think not that I come to bring peace on earth; I came not to bring peace but to bring a sword." This is one of Jesus' most controversial statements and was never meant to be taken literally. In fact, when Peter took a sword and cut off the ear of one of the soldiers who came to take Jesus from the garden of Gethsemane, Jesus, it is written, rebuked him and told him to put away the sword. He had also stated, according to the bible, "He who lives by the sword will die by the sword." Jesus was reportedly The Prince of Peace, yet His words relating to the sword were intended to emphasise its use only figuratively. That Jesus used a Sword of Discernment is perhaps more accurate, as He was pointing out to His followers that following Him was not an easy route. It is historically written that His way was not to be the way of the world, but a heavenly way of the spirit. He would divide and conquer with a Sword of Discernment, using His inner power and energy for the good of mankind. Where there was no peace, He would divide the people using His Sword of Discernment, dividing son and father, daughter and mother, to achieve His purpose as The Prince of Peace.

Yes, it was a choice to use a Sword of Discernment as in the stories of Jesus, with wisdom and courage, that strengthened this story-teller's resolve to traverse The Way to Santiago. It would be a journey of his own spirit, of letting-go the experiences of his life and the lives of those he loved; a journey of letting-go of his family, his friends, lovers and acquaintances - those with whom he had experienced his life journey so far.

He wished to return briefly, if only in heart and mind, to recall the influences and experiences he had learned on his life ways. He yearned to revisit and experience the lessons from those who had passed and were now dead and, equally, revisit and learn lessons from the living. To relieve, then let-go of the pain and suffering with which he had not fully come to terms and which cried out within him for release.

The belief he once had as a child had been lost somewhere along the way. Perhaps he could return to the religion of his childhood and renew his faith. He needed to revisit, to learn for himself that he no longer really believed in the old ways of his Catholic teaching. He needed to know if he could return to following the Christ of the bible, or to a new-found spirituality. He would follow the Way of St. James in pursuit of a symbol, of a Sword of The Order of Santiago, a Sword of The Knights Templar, whose job it once was to protect the pilgrims along the route of the Camino de Santiago; a sword that would be an outward expression of his inward discernment. He knew that any sword in a souvenir store on the Camino would be adequate to allow him to complete his wishes.

However, deep within himself, he knew that he had to do it like the pilgrims of old, to find an outward symbol or expression of his inner discernment. It was more than just a toy sword from a shop that he was determined to find. It was to be more like the fulfilment of something that was buried deep within, that could not be solved by anyone but himself. A quest for the sword, not unlike a Godly purpose - that was partly why he had been born to this earth. He had so much to learn, so much to recall, to renew, to let-go of. He was now totally committed to walking the road to Santiago, to find a symbol either during or at the end of his journey.

Once he had fallen into the dragon's mouth of his inner purpose, he believed he would evolve and rise up like a phoenix from the ashes, with an outward expression of creative ideas. He did not know how or where it would happen, but the Sword of Discernment he would have. The key to his quest for the future he would find. He would have his symbolic sword, carry it like a knight of old, always ready to unsheathe it and deal with his inner enemies, to protect and guide those he loved, to be there for them, always. Firstly, though, he had to conquer fear and fall into the dragon's mouth and see what would evolve. He was ready to walk The Way. He knew he was ready to walk The Camino de Santiago.

****

Pride Cometh Before a Fall. The British Airways flight to Paris via London was packed and I was fortunate that they allowed me to carry on my backpack and tent, as they were well over the weight limit and should have attracted excess baggage costs. I was pleased to be seated and able to rest a little. It had not been a good night's sleep at the Novotel Mencken Airport. The hotel was faultless and a nice place to stay for a short visit, but I was simply due for a good sleep and excited about the next leg of my journey and The Camino.

A week of wedding celebrations in Grafenau, Bavaria; a rail journey and sight-seeing in Prague, in the Czech Republic for a few days; a train trip to Munich for 24 hours – all had taken their toll on me, especially since I had been lugging my heavy backpack around, and this extra burden was very tiring. I was landing at London Airport only ten minutes before my connecting flight to Paris, and voiced my concern to the stewardess, who assured me that a third of the passengers also had limited time to catch their ongoing flights, but all would be well.

I was amazed that British Airways had lined me up with a concierge who quickly dispensed with red-tape, and I was on the plane to Paris with minutes to spare. Landed safely at Charles de

Gaulle Airport and quickly boarded a bus to the city. The traffic congestion and the slow pace of the bus became a little frustrating, so I got off and made my way to the Metro, changing trains where needed, and alighted a couple of streets short of Hotel Welcome, on the Rue de Seine, where I had stayed the year before. I was feeling proud of the fact that I had mastered the transport system at one fell swoop, having been in Paris for only a couple of days in the past. I thought I was pretty smart.

This pride was very short-lived. As I entered the hotel foyer with sunglasses still on from the glare outside I caught my foot on the only step that the hotel has and was launched like a rocket, propelled forward with the heavy weight of my backpack adding to the speed of trajectory! I landed flat on my face and, for a brief moment, lost consciousness. The bloody mess on the hotel foyer's recently-polished marble tiles, resulting from the large cut above my left eye, must have been an annoyance for the concierge. However, that was not my main concern and the concierge didn't show any sign of emotion, but merely went and got a clean cloth and some disinfectant and assisted in cleaning-up the mess. My glasses had become embedded in my face, and the bridge of my nose and both eyes had already turned a nasty shade of purple. The thought of my sobriety and awareness made me laugh: "Surrender to get well; suffer to win." Yes, my Camino certainly started in Paris. I did not feel much like sightseeing so I settled for a shower and a brief cat-nap before finding a pleasant sidewalk café where, despite having a headache, I ate a hearty meal. I took a stroll by the River Seine, looked at the tourist sites and resolved to get up early in the morning and take some photos near the river. I awoke early and went for a walk through the back streets around The Latin Quarter and found a small café, enjoying coffee and a croissant before heading to the river for some early morning sunrise photo shots.

The taxi fares are relatively cheap in Paris, so I made an early start to the main rail station for the train's six-hour trip to St. Jean-de-Pied at the base of The Pyrenees where my official Camino would start. I had already decided to go with the flow and just handle whatever came up. I hadn't planned a thing, nor viewed a map of the walk. I had only downloaded a list of the villages along the Way and the distances between them. This, of course, would prove to have been foolhardy, as I came to experience a couple of days later. I had realised that a good part of the purpose of my journey was to recall and let-go of a lifetime of events that had shaped my life to date. So I turned my mind from the pain and discomfort resulting from my fall and began to write in my journal.

I began to recall my country days and my early mornings with Byron, the flying doctor, as the train made its way towards the Spanish border. I used to help Byron on his property, carrying hay and feeding his livestock. I remembered how we did some wild safari steer-jumping, off the bonnet of his four-wheel drive to bring-down a long-horned beast! That was the fun part, but before we set off to our real jobs during the day we did a lot of heavy work, which kept us fit and healthy. I had flashes of rounding-up cattle with Bruce in the mountains of the New England, on horseback, and sailing with him through the heads of Sydney Harbour; remembering his sad ending, how he disappeared at sea a year prior to this Camino journey. The thoughts of the sea reminded me of the time I had climbed the crow's nest of a Russian ship during a cyclone, between Perth and Singapore, just to get a photo of the bow disappearing in a wave in front of me, drunk as a skunk at the time. Mostly I daydreamed of times with my granddad and his stories of the bush. As the train snaked its way towards The Pyrenees, a theme came to my head, of my childhood days with him. I began to write the lyrics of a song about Granddad and me, and hummed it to the tune of the rocking rhythm of the train.

Little did I know that this song was to be the catalyst for changing my life forever from then on. I put away my journal and began a conversation with a fellow passenger, who came from the village of St. Jean-Pied-de-Port. We were just an hour out of the village and I could see the mountain range looming in the distance. I was nearing the start of my 800 km trek to Santiago, with a vision of letting-go past suffering and a heart looking forward to finding a worthy symbol of a Sword of The Order of the Knights of Santiago.

We arrived at St. Jean-Pied-de-Port to the sound of trumpets and drums. It was Sunday, 21st July, 2013, the one-hundredth anniversary of the village, and the entire population was dressed in period costume for the occasion. It was early evening and the summer sun was still high in the sky as I weaved my way through the busy streets of the little village, guided by my fellow passenger, to my accommodation at the Hotel Itzalpea. Booking this hotel was the only forward planning I had done for my Camino. How was I to know it would prove to be a wise move, considering the celebrations taking place? All of the hotels were booked, so it was lucky I had booked some months before leaving Australia. I thanked my local guide, confirmed my booking with the hotel-keeper and climbed the spiral stairs to my room in the third-floor attic. It was small and clean, with an open-window view across a red terra-cotta roof to The Pyrenees close by.

The mountains were silhouetted as the sun moved behind the vista, but the temperature was still around forty degrees Celsius even though it was 8:00 pm. I took my time having a shower then rested briefly before dressing and finding my way to a local restaurant for a meal. I had a drink and ate my meal at an outside table as the last of the parade and drums faded into the distance. A large fort-like wall across the street encased a group of red-brick houses. The wall, supported by its contact with white concrete buildings, would be something repeated many times in the Basque country into which I was about to venture the very next day.

    A late, final parade of horse-drawn wheel-buckets driven by a small boy caught my eye. This was followed by a bevy of horse-drawn carriages, again led by small boys pulling the reins. The parade ended with children in period costumes, some beating on kettle-drums that echoed through the town and mountain foothills. I ate the last piece of bread that came with the meal and retired to my attic room above the red terra-cotta roof that was the foreground in my final photograph of the day in the evening twilight. I fell asleep looking at the shadow-land of mountains of The Pyrenees - the vision of my initiation to The Camino de Santiago and my spiritual awakening that was to begin the very next day. I fell asleep humming a melody to the Boundary Rider lyrics I had written that very morning.

Boundary Rider

Well I've been a boundary rider
on the wild New England range,
rounding-up range cattle,
driven more across the plains.

Oh! I learned to live the bush way
when I was just a kid,
camping out with my old granddad,
cutting timber's what he did.

I've had my share of hard times,
I've had my share of pain.
if I had my time back over,
probably do it all again.

Killing dingoes when in danger,
cooking rabbit to survive,

staying warm at night's log fire,
sleeping-out when I was five.

Well I crossed the barren desert
and I tramped the hills alone,
made it through some swollen rivers,
wild dust storms and chilly snows.

'Cause I've been an over-lander,
it was the life I'd lived.
if I had my time back over,
probably do it all again.

"Hear the thunder on the mountain,
it's the brumbies on the run.
see the murder of the black crows
as they greet the morning sun."

"Feel the gentle chill of first light,
tea and damper's almost done.
breaking camp we long to start out,
saddle-up for boundary run."

Well my granddad was a drover,
'cross the country he did roam,
seeking-out his heart's companion
where he found his heart and home.

Boxed in tents for Jimmy Sharman,
tried to earn a decent quid.
carried swag across the Darling.
seeking work, that's what he did.

He cut timber on the north coast,
drove cattle on the plain,
shore sheep west of Tamworth
in those good old country days.

Panned for gold in old Kalgoorlie,
strut the boards and sang on stage.
did his share of hard-core drinking
in the good old country ways.

Once he sat on his verandah
telling stories to grandkids
of the life he'd left behind him
and the things that he once did.

So I sing this song for Granddad,
in my heart he will remain.
'cause he was a boundary rider
on the wild New England range.

"Hear the thunder on the mountain,
it's the brumbies on the run.
see the murder of the black crows
as they greet the morning sun."

"Feel the gentle chill of first light,
tea and damper's almost done.
breaking camp we long to start out,
saddle-up for boundary run."

There's a child who sat beside him
on the day that he had died.
He came back for a moment

then he rode off with a smile.

Chasing moonbeams in the starlight
somewhere in the sky above,
looking down on boundary riders
with a heart stock-full of love.

Well he'd been a boundary rider
on the wild New England range.
rounded-up range cattle,
driven more across the plains.

He had his share of hard times,
had his fill of pain.
if he had his time back over,
probably do it all again.

"Hear the thunder on the mountain,
it's the brumbies on the run.
see the murder of the black crows
as they greet the morning sun."

"Feel the gentle chill of first light,
tea and damper's almost done.
breaking camp we long to start out,
saddle-up for boundary run."

CHAPTER 2.

St. Jean-Pied-de-Port to Pamplona

The ascent in The Pyrenees to the famous Roncesvalles post is probably the most difficult of the entire French way to Santiago. The "Napoleon Route" starts with a steep climb past country houses before reaching mountain meadows – the cross – which provides the first pause for letting-go of burdens. The Camino changes to spectacular sweeping mountain views merging into woodlands towards the French/Spanish border, and descends to Roncesvalles.

There the Camino de Santiago trail continues through beech and oak woodlands, crosses two mountain passes before descending towards Zubrini, then across the Medieval Rabies Bridge over the river to Arga. The Camino follows the River Arga to Larrasoana, an important stop for pilgrims in Medieval times. The journey towards the famous city of Pamplona becomes busy with pilgrims, as it has done historically. Famous for its Running of the Bulls, the San Fermin Festival, the city of Pamplona attracts pilgrims to its Medieval streets, cathedral, famous food and wine, favourite coffee-houses, and haunts of the writer, Ernest Hemingway, who wrote of the Running of the Bulls.

Starting Out Along The Way, I awoke to the hot morning sun pouring into my attic haven. It was already 8:30 am, the latest I had slept since arriving in Europe three weeks earlier. I quickly showered, repacked my backpack and headed down the spiral staircase to a hearty breakfast. The temperature was already forty degrees Celsius according to the thermometer on the inn-keeper's desk. I paid my hotel bill and made my way outside, but not before filling my water bottles from the water jug on the breakfast table and stuffing another bread roll into my backpack for the journey.

In my haste, I had forgotten to check the attic hide-away, and had left behind the plug for my phone charger. I had no doubt left it in the wall socket when I'd charged my phone the night before. This was to be an inconvenience for the next week or two, as the northern hemisphere's electric power-points have different socket outlets than our Australian ones. So, without the correct phone leads or power-point prongs, a local converter would be a waste of effort.

The brightness of the hot morning sun and the heat rising from the footpath were already causing me discomfort. I made my way along the street, following the walled-in area of buildings flanked by white stucco'd cafes, hotels and an outdoor dining area near a narrow but pretty river scene. I crossed the bridge over the stream in the middle of the village and made my way to a tourist shop and information centre. I was the only person in the shop and there was no shop assistant to attend to my wants. Here, I hoped to find a replica of my Sword of Discernment, to protect me against mythical dangers, give me some constant reminder of the outward expression of my desires for the journey and, I reasoned, something that would denote that I was a pilgrim on a spiritual quest.

The majority of the youth who had walked the Camino over past decades took the journey as a rite of passage to their spirituality. Apparently, only 25% of western-world youth attend some form of Christian worship these days, so a Camino journey for youth who take this road to an inner-world experience made some sense to me. Those of us of older vintage hang about the edges of our hearts' desires, scarred by the world of reality over a lifetime of living within linear rational faith, and find ourselves on The Camino determined to let-go of our long-held burdens, with some hope of either regaining the innocence of the Christian belief of our youth, or hoping to experience a renewal of our former faith. I was of the latter, hoping to let-go of the burdens of my heart and looking to experience some former Catholic doctrine of faith and morals by visits to ancient church buildings and attending religious services along the way.

I was hoping to embrace the passion, wildness and enthusiasm of my youth, in a last-ditch effort to hold on to whatever youth was left in me. This was an intricate part of my search on The Camino, my last hurrah, before I resigned myself to the inevitable realisation of letting-go of the youth that I once was – but was no longer. I recalled that my Scottish mate, Norm, had said to me before I left Australia, "We don't get out of this thing alive mate, so make the most of it." I was examining the dressed dummy in the tourist shop's window; it was surrounded by scallop shells on the window floor. The dummy model wore a felt hat with the front turned up, which would be useless when facing the sunlight. I could see scallop shells had been sewn onto both the hat and the cape which appeared to be thrown over the dummy's shoulder. A shepherd's crook was fastened to the dummy's right hand and a small water-gourd hung from the crook; I recognised that this was the traditional dress of Medieval pilgrims who walked The Camino in penance, as a rite of passage, or inner journey, while letting-go of the outside world.

I wondered how Napoleon felt as he led his army across The Pyrenees on his march south to take over more territory for France. I thought of the French warrior, Charlemagne, with his troops in retreat from the Moors, and the death of his nephew, Roland, along this pathway I was about to walk. I thought, too, of the journey of Francis of Assisi on his spiritual striving for simplicity as he walked his Camino Way; the route taken by Isabella of Castile in charitable giving, on her Camino. I knew that, within the day, I would walk the pathways of these historic figures, and of the more modern ones: Pope John XXIII; Shirley MacLaine, the actress; and Martin Sheen who, before acting in the movie "The Way", walked this path to be more in touch with the role he played in the film. My daydream was interrupted by the shopkeeper, who seemed to appear from nowhere, enquiring if I had a scallop shell to wear as a sign, so that fellow pilgrims would recognise that I, too, was a pilgrim. I declined the purchase, but was advised that she did have a wooden sword for sale. I also declined the offer of a map, preferring to let-go and allow nature to take its course. I was aware of the scallop shell insignia and the yellow arrows to guide me, as I started out on my Camino Way.

"It isn't the mountains ahead to climb that wears you out,
It's the pebble in your shoe."

Muhammed Ali

"Snakes and arrows cannot go where sounds remain forever."

I meandered my way out of the village of St. Jean-Pied-de-Port, already feeling the perspiration trickle down my back in the forty-degree heat. It was mid-morning and I was the only pilgrim heading to the foothills of The Pyrenees at that time. The yellow arrow pointing the way – the ultimate sign-post for me and for most pilgrims – appeared on the side of a building as my introduction to The Camino Way.

The Camino scallop shell and yellow markings denote the many roads throughout Europe that ultimately converge as one, not far from the city of Leon. The back of the shell appears like a map, with the ridges all coming to a central point on the edge of the shell. Apart from being the main sign-posting along the route to Santiago, it has another symbolic meaning: it is said that when you turn the shell over, it resembles an open hand of kindness. Most of what I was to encounter on my Camino would prove to me that the shell carried on pilgrims' backpacks to denote that were on a pilgrimage should have been worn inside-out. If pilgrims knew in advance, they may have considered it a symbolic gesture, or invitation if you will, to show mercy to the many beggars and unemployed youth encountered in the cities and villages on the journey to Santiago.

The sign-posting Camino shells have been set up meticulously in large numbers throughout the route to Santiago and care must be taken to correctly interpret the meaning of their direction. I had read about the Camino shell-signage and knew that if the lines of the shell-point faced left or right, then you turned left or right. Equally, if the shell pointed upwards, you continued walking in the direction you were already on, straight ahead. My first Camino shell pointed straight ahead and stood on a slight slope near a freshly-ploughed field of hay. The aroma in the air indicated that the field had been recently ploughed, and the farmer stood nearby, bending over the engine of his tractor, probably trying to figure out why it had suddenly stopped. I looked at the scene before returning my gaze to the scallop shell sign and, looking down at its base, was surprised to see a dead black snake curled there.

It was an asp, the same as described in the stories of Cleopatra's death. I knew, from the history of snakes, that this was a particularly venomous reptile and that death by a heart attack could occur very quickly after being bitten. I felt this was some sort of medical omen, and thought of the medical symbol of a snake. The image of a serpent wrapped around a staff is familiar in the medical field; it decorates pharmaceutical packaging and hospitals alike. At home, in Australia, this medical symbol is used as a badge on car bumpers, signifying a doctor's profession.

The symbol actually has another version: the winged version is known as a caduceus, and the stick that the snake winds around, with two heads facing each other, is actually the staff carried by the Olympian god, Hermes. In Greek mythology, Hermes was a messenger between the gods and humans; this explains the wings. He was also a guide to the underworld, which explains the staff. Hermes was the patron of travellers, making his connection to medicine appropriate because, in older times, doctors often had to travel great distances by foot to visit their patients. It is commonplace to wear gaiters in the bush in Australia, where there are so many venomous snakes, but I never thought for a moment that I might need them in The Pyrenees where, as I found out further along the way, this particular snake lives. I cursed the thought of the dark side of an omen and considered Hermes as the patron of travellers to be a good thing for me. I also had a passing thought of St. Christopher, the Christian version of the patron saint of travellers, who reportedly carried the child Jesus across a swollen river. I remembered the St. Christopher medallion carried by many travellers for a safe journey when I was a child. I had not seen that medallion in decades in any motor vehicle I travelled in, either at home or abroad. I banished those thoughts from my head and felt the swelling of my nose and around my eyes, reliving for a moment my fall in Paris. My Camino had certainly started at the Welcome Hotel on the Rue de Seine and Paris, and not at this first omen of myth or past belief at the first scallop shell of my Camino.

The climb up the ancient well-traversed French Way continued steeply to five hundred metres and, despite the heat, gave me ample photo opportunities of the valley below and beyond to the now-distant view of St. Jean-Pied-de-Port; as I continued my climb, the village slowly vanished behind me.The heavy backpack was already taking its toll, but with determination I continued the climb in the blistering heat. I was beginning to realise that, with a waterproof jacket, ample clothing and a waterproof sleeping-bag, I had no need of the tent for this journey, and regretted that I had not left it behind. Here and there along the track pilgrims had jettisoned unwanted items of clothing, including boots, jackets, hats and towels, and personal memorabilia. Near a point called Orison, eight hundred metres up, I came across a shrine where pilgrims had left rosary beads, sunglasses, caps, bracelets, business cards, an address book, matches and cigarettes. Either this was the first stage of letting-go material possessions, or an indication that some found the going tough and left some of the weight from their backpacks at this popular dumping-ground. The shrine had some Christian religious symbolism and was surrounded by a wrought-iron enclosure, so it was apparently a sign to let-go of something related to material possessions or bad habits. I left a pack of my anti-depression pills, but kept a few. I still had a fear in my heart of going down into the deep pit of depression once again. I had cut down to twelve grams per day, over a twelve-month cycle, without the help of the medical profession, although I had kept my GP informed of my progress in this process, and also informed him about my state of mind.

I now knew the meaning of "Less is more on The Camino", and concluded that it was not a spiritual journey that I was experiencing, but more a journey of the spirit, my own earthly experience of the soul. I stayed at the shrine long enough for a young French girl to catch up with me. We walked on together, talking of our respective lives, the goal of Santiago de Compostela and the prospect of gaining the certificate on completing the journey.

As we climbed, we were passed by men on horseback, quite obviously inexperienced riders as they had difficulty controlling their steeds while waving madly at us, calling "Buen Camino", which was to become a daily familiar greeting on The Way. The young girl decided to stop and eat some lunch and I continued on, walking alone. A group of Italian bike-riders appeared from behind me and they, likewise, struggled up the steep slope and passed me, also giving the now familiar "Buen Camino" greeting. Upon reaching a marker known as Bentarte, at 1,327 metres, I decided to stop and rest for a while, by now knowing that I was running short of water. I drank a small mouthful of the remaining water and ate the bread roll I had taken at breakfast.

Once more, I began to climb again and was really suffering from heat exhaustion and lack of water. The pinnacle was at 1,479 metres, and I thought of Martin Luther King's words as I reached the summit and looked at the valley below. "Well, I don't know what will happen now. We've got some difficult days ahead. But it doesn't matter to me now, because I've been to the mountain top. And I don't mind. Like anybody, I would like to live a long life…and He's allowed me to go up to the mountain. And I've looked over. And I've seen the Promised Land…I am not worried about anything. I am not fearing any man." The road meandered down a ways and then up again to a lookout with a metal sign detailing the road ahead and the topography of the surrounding hills. It was at this point that a young and fit German lad by the name of Ollie appeared at the bend in the road. He too was out of water. We discovered a well nearby, where a tap almost hidden from view relieved our dehydration. We walked together for quite some time and met up with two Irish women, Jacinta and her daughter, Vanessa. Ollie said his "Buen Camino" and walked on. My next sighting of him was to be forty days later, in Santiago. The Irish women were friendly, in the typical Irish manner, and we rounded a bend a little while later to discover a café at the highest point. Here I was able to catch-up on some badly-needed nourishment and a well-earned coffee and rest. The Irish women, after we exchanged pleasantries, returned to the road and I sat a while to write some brief notes in my journal. It seems strange for me to write a journal, as in the depth of my depression, after my divorce and the suicide of my son, Peter, I had expressed my grief by writing poetry. I had actually written a book of poems over a six-month period of rest and recovery. But my poems were more an expression of my grief and pain and were never meant to see the light of day. I always found it easier to express my feelings in poetry, but the journal-writing here was a new thing; except for some free-thinking writing that was advised in therapy, prose had not come naturally to me. The miracle of my Camino was later to prove to me that both were natural talents that I had never previously exposed.

The climb to Lepoeder, on the way to Roncesvalles, was a total of seventeen kilometres and almost 1,500 metres up. It was then a slow-walking steep fall for the next ten kilometres to the cosy Medieval hamlet of Roncesvalles. I looked forward to a shower, a hot meal and, although I had sworn-off alcohol, a glorious non-alcoholic beer, in Spain known ironically as SIN-beer. Walking on a cobblestone pathway under an archway, I encountered the Conventus Hospitalis Roncesvalles for my first stay at an albergue, or pilgrim's hostel or refugio, on The Camino. The volunteer hospitalera greeted me with an official "Hullo" and requested my Crecencial el Peregrino, the passport allowing a pilgrim to use The Camino system of accommodation, and which, when stamped, is documented proof that a pilgrim has completed the journey. It provides right of entry into all albergues on The Camino. The completed passport is necessary for claiming your Compostela certificate, evidence that the entire distance to Santiago has been completed. I purchased my pilgrim's passport from the Hosptalis' desk and the lady kindly noted in it that my entry-point has been St. Jean-Pied-de-Port before adding her official Roncesvalles stamp. I could now officially call myself a pilgrim.

The Albergue stay at the Conventus Hospitalis proved to be one of the better sleeping quarters on my journey to Santiago. After a hearty meal in the company of some Italian bike-riders, who could not understand a word of English, and a drink or two with the two Irish women, I proceeded to my dormitory bunk to sleep. With my weary thoughts of letting-go, handing-over to a power greater than myself, and mixed thoughts of Roland, the nephew of Charlemagne, the French warrior and his final act of breaking his sword in his battle to the death with the giant hero of the Moors, I began to drift into another land and fell asleep.

The flash of lights and things that go bump in the night were just too much for me. I awoke in the dark to the sound of pilgrims stuffing their sleeping-bags into their backpacks, head-lamps occasionally flickering into my half-opened eyes and quiet whispers, signalling that some pilgrims were keen to get an early start on The Way, before the heat of the day took hold. This, I found, was the order of the day on the the Camino, and it really didn't concern me too much. I had just forgotten what it was like, and recalled similar mornings at boarding school during my youth. I was now walking the hallowed ground, with thoughts of Charlemagne and his army marching across The Pyrenees in 778 on his return to France after battling the Muslims in Spain for six years; his nephew, Roland, in charge of the rear guard, being attacked and fighting bravely, breaking his sword on a rock to prevent it falling into the Muslims' hands before being mercilessly slaughtered. I was now walking in this blood-stained valley where Charlemagne returned to find his beloved nephew dead. After about an hour I reached the main pathway to Santiago and, at the junction, was a busy little oasis café. Like so many other pilgrims, I crowded into the small provision store for some fruit, biscuits and milk, as this was the first and only opportunity to eat some breakfast. The food was not very nourishing, but it was better than walking with an empty stomach. There was a notice board above the entry with a sign saying that Ernest Hemingway had stopped to eat at the same spot when he was on his way to Pamplona for the Running of the Bulls celebration.

King Gougia, in the magnum opus of the ancient Chinese of the 5th century CE, was captured by his arch enemy and made to suffer three years imprisonment before given amnesty. Rather than return to his throne, he resolved to eat peasant food and live simply. He slept on a bed of brushwood and licked a gall-bladder every day to taste life's bitterness. It was, for him, a reminder of the shame and humiliation he had suffered in captivity, and he drew strength from it. The memory of that story bolstered my spirits; I believed that I could, for most of the day, live off the mal-nourishment I had just consumed, but did wonder how my energy could be maintained in the now sweltering heat. I also wondered what Hemingway had eaten at this oasis on The Way.

Mission Mountain

There's a track to mission mountain,
it's the pathway of my dreams,
a way along the byway
of valleys, hills and streams.

An oath to Godly purpose
in the spirit plain above,
a reason for my living
on a road to endless love.

There's a track in old Basque country
where I found my way.
With tent, knapsack and tucker-bag
I waltzed the Matilda way.

Walking the Spanish highlands,
on The Camino,
walking the Spanish highlands
on The Camino.

So sweet muse of mission mountain,
the source of light and love,
lead-on this weary traveller
to tramp the path of love.

There is nature's endless wonder,
by valleys, hills and streams,
bringing all now to reality
not just in my dreams.

CHAPTER 3

RESILIENCE.

"……as the battle rolls on,
 the men fall to the ground.
 Their ears ache for the shrill of the horn
 but Roland persists on holding his ground.
'Let us strike a mighty blow
 for our Lord and our God.'
  Song of Roland,
 never knight be so worthy,
  song of Roland,
 ever knight be so worthy."

Shame acts as a depressant and suffering, although painful, gives strength. I was reminded of my good friend Patrick, who often stated, "Pain is good; it makes us strong." Shaking off my sense of a heavy heart and the pain of near-blistered feet, I resolved that on my return home I would live a more simple life, get rid of excess clothing and sell unwanted possessions. However, I thought then and there to buy a new motor vehicle on my return and set my new way of living just right. "Less is more on The Camino" once again crossed my mind.

It proved to be a beautiful day for walking and meeting many more new pilgrims on their own life journeys on their Camino. The pathway, at about 1,000 metres above sea level, remained easy going for the majority of the 23.3 km to Zubiri. There, my plan was for the day to end and to find a peaceful way to relax. The forested walking trails and occasional highway crossings were a welcome change after the Pyrenees crossing of the previous day. The day's trek was often broken by walking through charming little villages and towns, which seemed to ease the burden of thinking about the heaviness of my over-weighted backpack.

I was relieved to take it off about half-way through the day and, whilst resting in the shade of an old oak tree, enjoyed the remainder of the food I had purchased in a café bar in a village I had passed through. Here and there the path that I was taking was marked with red and white striped arrows. As I got closer to Zubiri, the arrows indicating the direction changed to yellow and blue. Then they changed again, rainbow colours slowly melted to more yellow shells and yellow arrows – yellow being the traditional colour of The Camino.

It was dusk when I arrived at Zubiri, but there were no immediate signs of accommodation, so I headed for a café bar for a drink and food, and once again was greeted by the recently-met Irish beauties, Jacinta and her daughter Vanessa. The evening was hot and I stayed for a second drink before bidding them the Camino farewell and continuing along the road to find a room for the night. I could not find anywhere to stay along the pathway, so resolved to keep walking, as there was still plenty of daylight.

The oppressive heat and the now broken blisters on both feet proved to be irritating and painful, and I was beginning to regret that I had not searched a little harder for accommodation in Zubiri. Still, the pathway looked safe enough and I could easily have pitched my tent and made camp for the night. I resolved to soldier on, despite the discomfort of wearing too-thick socks in the hot conditions and the constant movement of feet in my boots rubbing like sandpaper on raw blisters. It occurred to me that I would have been far better-off following the nearby Arga River, meandering along its banks through rural hamlets on a pleasant nature pathway to Pamplona. I figured I would reserve the remaining 21 km to Pamplona for that purpose tomorrow and, despite my discomfort, walked the remaining 6 km of the traditional way to Akerreta to find a bed for the night.

I arrived at an albergue in the centre of town near the river at around 9:00 pm and proceeded to reception after waiting a good ten minutes before the door was opened for me. The male receptionist abruptly demanded my Camino passport, stamped it and waited impatiently while I fumbled for the ten-Euro charge for my bed for the night. He led me up a staircase and, in a mix of Spanish and English, showed me around. He took me to the lockers to secure my backpack, wallet and boots. It took another trip downstairs for a Euro charge for the locker before I had both the front door key and locker key in my possession.

The Albergue was practically empty, so I had a quick shower, changed my clothing and headed off to a nearby bar, which was the only place still open at 9:30 pm in this town. I managed to convince the bartender to provide me with some leftovers from the kitchen, resulting in a bowl of soup and some bread. This place was thick with flies, already heading to the cool indoors. I ate my soup, dipping the remaining bread before eating, despite the flies crawling all over it. I simply didn't care, as it was good to get food into my stomach before falling asleep a few hours later in the Albergue. It had been a long and hard road of inner discovery, but I doggedly resolved to keep on keeping-on. It was a pain-filled climax to the end of a day of walking 30 km.

I awoke early at the Akerreta albergue to the pain of severely blistered feet and a torn toe-nail. I decided to be my own doctor, and made my way to the town's pharmacy, purchased some more band-aids and hobbled my way back to a bench seat in the town square. There I began to hack away at the loose skin around the blisters with my toe-nail scissors and to tidy-up the wounds. In a decisive moment I quickly drove the point of the scissors underneath the broken toe-nail and, with one swift movement, pulled the toe-nail out from the quick and dispensed with it. I used my remaining antibiotics, emptying the contents of the capsules on to the toe's open wound and the blisters. The tables were for the purpose of virus infection but I found it necessary to use them for my immediate need.

I chose a pair of lighter socks for another day of hot weather on the road again. The New Zealand-born possum and wool socks I had been wearing were ideal for the cool conditions in that land of the long white cloud, but not the best for the hot summers on The Camino in Spain. At least today was going to be easier and, noting as I exited the town that the sign-post indicated 15.4 km to Pamplona. I looked forward to taking it slow and steady on my sore feet and wounded, bound toes, and to arriving in the old city in the mid-afternoon. Sometimes I walked alone during this day and sometimes with other pilgrims en route, following the well-worn natural pathways. I often stopped for water, which was in plentiful supply in purpose-built fountains intended for use by passing pilgrims.

I walked for a while with a young Danish actor and his father, Henry, a psychologist who had retired from his practice and now spent his days as a budding artist, painting Picasso-like images of a working brain, with a touch of Ken Done colouring and Pro Hart flair. I gleaned this from the photos he showed me of his work, stored on his iPhone. We ate a meal together at an albergue café, where Henry explained his intention to walk the extra 100 km past Santiago to Finisterre, historically considered to be the end of the known world. The man of paintings of the inner workings of the head had a brain-wave method of releasing a burden of a mystical Viking who haunted him. My educated new friend was carrying a heavy iron cross in his backpack, a symbol of his demon Viking, and intended casting this cross into the ocean at Finisterre to rid himself of the burden of his demon. We sat for a long time after our meal and discussed the influence this ancient shadow had over his life and work as both artist and psychologist. I, too, was convinced that he should continue to Finisterre and rid himself of this evil.

Historically, millions of pilgrims have journeyed to Finisterre, completing the pagan ritual of burning their boots or clothing or casting something of a personal nature into the ocean at the end of the known world. This is usually done as the sun sets over the ocean, serving appropriately as the end of their journey of the past and, possibly, they're Camino. No doubt the pilgrim with a lesser burden would ponder what comes next, whilst revelling in the satisfaction of having completed The Camino; reflecting on what was gained and lost by the experience; perhaps giving thanks to the wonderful people met along The Way, grieving the end of a journey but welcoming the dawn of the next.

I thought for a moment about also walking the additional distance to the ocean and casting my symbolic Sword of Discernment, once acquired, into the ocean at Finisterre. My thoughts were interrupted by my Danish companion's parting words: "No matter what distracts you, return to and stay focused on the creative goal, whatever that may be, that attracts you." For the last couple of kilometres I walked with Willie a middle-aged Irishman from Dublin. I noted that he carried a very small day pack and he had resolved, on his Camino, to stay in the best hotels and have his luggage sent forward to the next location. Seeing the small day pack and the ease with which Willie from Dublin walked, I realised that this man obviously had brains, and that I had left mine somewhere back on the track, or perhaps in Paris where I had cracked my skull!

The decision was made then and there walking with Willie, I would jettison my tent and some of my gear at Pamplona. I figured out a way to reduce my backpack's weight by at least three kilos, to a more comfortable weight and not so awkward a burden to carry. Somehow the thought of reducing my heavy burden lifted my spirit and I felt light of heart – if not in reality. I stopped and wrote a note in my journal: a rule of thumb, never to carry more than 10% of my body weight in the future. The reality of this meant that I should not have been carrying more than 7 kg.

"A day spent learning a sonnet, chopping the trunk of a fir tree, catching two speckled trout and smoking a good Havana is worth more than a handful of hours spent in the air-con pressure-cooker of today's urban nightmare."

Consolations of the Forest (Sylvain Tesson)

After listening to Willie sell me on the joy of staying in five-star accommodation I decided, on entry to the city, to stay with Willie, and booked into the very same hotel for a night of luxury. It was a good thing that I stuck with Willie, as the city was very crowded with tourists all lined up at the tourist van in the middle of the main square, looking for directions to monuments, accommodation and restaurants and relaxing after witnessing the spectacle of the running of the bulls. I should have been aware that the city would be busy at this time of celebration. I had in fact stopped for provisions at the very same café Ernest Hemingway had mentioned in his best-selling novel, "The Sun Also Rises", in which he wrote about the running of the bulls, that very morning, but I didn't connect it with Pamplona and that this was time of the year for the bull celebration.

St. Fermin, one of the many venerated saints of Pamplona, is the co-patron of Navarre, the autonomous country bordering the Basque mountains that I had just traversed. Pamplona, the capital of Navarre, is where the Saint Fermin Feast is celebrated, and the home of the running of the bulls. St. Fermin had been converted to Christianity and baptized by Saturnius, the bishop of Toulouse, when Spain was under French rule. Saturnius and Fermin suffered martyrdom by being tied by the feet to a bull and dragged to their death. The three-day holiday celebration is an annual Pamplona event, but other towns and villages repeat the running of the bulls celebration long after Pamplona has returned to normality. I left the correo and swore under my breath at the running of the bulls and especially at Ernest Hemingway. I felt sure that most of the people who, in their drunken state, chanced their lives in the bull run in and around the Navarre region would not have a clue about the religious significance of the celebration. Pamplona has the largest population en route and the extra burden of tourists everywhere made finding landmarks difficult. I managed to get room at the hotel with Willie, convincing the hotelier to give me the remaining vacancy.

I had agreed to meet Willie in the foyer an hour later, to join him and some Irish friends for the evening meal. He seemed to find comfort in the environment of this strange city, with its narrow winding streets on the way to the hotel, and I had been pleased with his company. I settled for a shower and sleep, and woke an hour-and-a-half later but missed my pre-arranged foyer meeting with the Irishman. I decided to use my natural instinct to find my way around the city and, perhaps by chance, meet-up with him and his friends. Well, I did not ever see my Irish companion again but, as luck would have it, I walked to a café bar, and who should be seated there but the two Irish ladies I had left the night before in Zubiri. We had a wonderful night, swapping stories about families, friendships and drinking. It was a good thing I had given-up the booze some years ago, as these ladies really knew how to drink. I lost count of their copious wine-drinking after twelve glasses, each drink usually followed by a signal to the barman and a gentle Irish request for "one more, no more" every time they reordered.

After an enjoyable meal of a variety of tapas, in typical Spanish style, and far too many SIN (non-alcoholic) beers, I weaved my way with the ladies back towards the main square and said my farewells, promising that, on my next trip to the emerald island, I would visit them for a party and to meet the family. I took a photograph or two of the outside verandah of an apartment above a bar where Hemingway had stayed whilst writing "The Sun Also Rises". I was a little disappointed that I had only just missed this annual event, but saw no point in walking the course of the bulls after it was all over, as so many tourists lined-up on a guided tour were to do.

The city was still in full swing at 10:00 pm and it was still daylight as I made my way back to the hotel on a pre-determined route. I completed my washing, as was my daily custom, and hung all out to dry on my portable clothes-line. I made a note to visit the tourist van in the main square and find the main correo (post office) in the morning, to send my excess three kilo burden to Santiago. An early start again the next day, with a filling breakfast at the hotel, was followed by a walk through the streets visiting early-opening shops. The intention was to buy a charger adaptor for my now low phone battery, but I could not find one. Until I could purchase one, I would have to content myself with borrowing from an Australian or New Zealander along The Way.

The visit to the Correo (Post Office) to send my tent and excess gear to Santiago proved fruitless. It was the three-day anniversary holiday celebration for the Feast of St. Fermin, and all post offices were closed. The city was in a celebratory mood and tourists were still hanging about, despite the fact that the running of the bulls was over. It meant I still had to carry my unwanted extra weight in my backpack for at least another 80 km; allowing for walking an average of 20 km per day, I would have to wait four more days.

The whole region of Navarre had stopped, to celebrate the feast for the saint for days to come. In hindsight, I should have given all the extra weight items to a local charity, but my childhood conditioning over-ruled the logic. I was educated to believe that hard work had earned me these things, and not to let-go of them too easily. As it turned out, I later sent 5 kilos back to Australia so that I would not have to carry the weight on my return flight home. When it finally arrived back in Australia I placed most of the items, except for the tent, in a charity bin near my city residence. So my new-found motto in Spain, "Less is more on The Camino" failed me when it came to material possessions.

This advice proved correct and, as more yellow arrows appeared on buildings and doorways, I was soon back on the right path. I resolved from then on to ignore the scallop shells in the main and stick with the painted yellow arrows. The thought went through my mind that I should buy a map, but so far so good, so I just let the idea go again for the time being. The yellow arrows were a vision of Don Elias (1929-1989), parish priest of O'Cerbreiro, a place known as the scene many miracles and strange happenings. The good Don had studied, in great depth, the history of St. James' pilgrimage to his final resting place in Santiago. He wrote many articles, documented evidence and even wrote a thesis on The Camino for the University of Salamanca. After years of studying the St. James' Way, he was convinced of the importance of this ancient trail and set himself the challenge of reviving the route we now call the French Way. In 1984 he put into motion his mission of rescue, cleaning and marking the trails along The Camino, starting at Roncesvalles in the Pyrenees.

The Godly priest also started painting the iconic yellow arrows to indicate the right direction, at various tricky crossroads along the trail. Legend has it that Don Elias drove across the whole of northern Spain, his Citroen GS packed with yellow paint, painting yellow arrows indicating the route to Santiago. He started an association and created groups to maintain his arrowed route and revived the various stretches that comprise the Medieval pilgrimage route. He travelled to other European universities and conferences to explain the importance of The Camino de Santiago as a place of communication and understanding for people of many nations. We probably owe him for the fact that The Camino still exists at all.

On the outskirts of Pamplona, I stopped at a café to rest my feet and enjoy a second cup of coffee. Whilst waiting for the barista to make it, I phoned my friend, Ron, back in Australia, to update him on my progress on The Camino. He informed me of the tragic train crash in Santiago, news of which was plastered all over the newspapers and television in Australia. I managed to sight a Spanish newspaper headline which had a small late editorial about and photo of the accident.

CHAPTER 4

LESSONS FROM THE DEAD.

It was still early morning and the news had not hit the mainstream newspapers. People were not yet about on the streets; television viewing would come later in the morning. All thirteen carriages of the train had derailed; the train had been travelling at twice the posted speed. Four carriages had overturned, killing seventy-nine people, and a large number of pilgrims had been injured. The train driver was charged with multiple homicides, and with causing grievous injury. Many of the two-hundred-and-eighteen passengers were pilgrims converging on the city of Santiago for a Christian celebration. I left the café after viewing the news and thought how about short our season in the sun really is. It does not matter what status, intellect or financial position one is experiencing on this planet, in the end, death is the great leveller. I thought a death song from Harry Manx, a Canadian song writer that had a timely chorus as a timely reminder "Oh, oh death pass me over for another year, another year."

As Pamplona fades into the background, the pilgrim begins the long ascent to the "hill of forgiveness", where the pilgrim statue at the "alto" is a timely reminder of the thousands who have walked this path for centuries. The 360-degree panoramic views of Pamplona and the valley ahead are sights to behold. The descent to Puenta la Reina (Queen's Bridge) and the Medieval alleys and the impressive 11th century bridge over the River Arga are other wonders for the pilgrim. The Camino continues to the monuments of the Estella and the free wine-fountain at the museum of Bodegas Irache. Most of the walking passes vineyards, olive trees and cereal crops to Los Arcos. Here The Camino changes to the rolling countryside, where the pilgrim leaves Navarre and enters the La Rioja region, famous for its red wines, passing from the dramatic ruins of Clavijo castle to the region's capital city of Logrono, known for the best of tapas and Rioja-style food specialties, a reward for the spirited pilgrim, and rest and recuperation after such a long but beautiful part of the Way.

The final exit from the city was by way of the Citadel park, with views of the approaching climb to the small town of Cizur Memor. I stopped a while, once again to rest my feet and treat my blister with new band-aids. I had reached a small café after a relatively steep climb in the heat of the mid-morning, thankful for a break under a shaded awning. The place was crowded with many pilgrims, and I spoke to a young man from India who was attracted to the meditative movement of his Camino Way. Another young man, an American, waved his hand to me and made room on a bench seat opposite two Canadian girls. The two young women appeared to be in their late twenties or early thirties. We swapped stories of our homelands and the joys of meeting people along The Way with the ever-familiar "Buen Camino" greeting, a wave or two, and always with a smile. I quenched my thirst with a Spanish SIN beer and ate a pizza before returning to the track. I left the little oasis in the sun and waved goodbye to my new-found young pilgrim traveller friends.

The climb up the steep slope to the wind-whipped Alto de Pardon was tough, but worth the effort. There I proceeded to take photos of the wonderful picturesque views of far-off mountain ranges and the closer, colourful valleys. The last of my remaining iPhone battery life faded-out and I contented myself with writing in my journal about the sights I could no longer record on my phone's camera. The day seemed to be getting hotter and I reckoned that the temperature had reached forty degrees. I had aimed to walk to Puente la Reina, a distance of 23.8 km from Pamplona, but I had already covered some 18 km in the oppressive heat and felt that was far enough for the day.

So, I decided to stay at an Albergue in the next village. The weight of my backpack was taking its toll on me in the blistering heat and the blisters on my feet were becoming a lot worse. I stayed the night at Camino de Pardon, which had a lovely restaurant and typical four-course meal, free wine for the drinkers, and ample bread, all for a total cost of only four Euro! There was no way that you would get even an entrée for that kind of money back home in Australia.

Nothing remained of the Medieval town of Alto de Pardon; it consisted mainly of the albergue. I had taken as my sleeping quarters this quaint abode and had an enjoyable meal in an up-market restaurant for such an isolated location. This little town had once housed a basilica with a pilgrims' hospice and a hermitage. Now the only landmark was a row of some forty windmills standing on a nearby hilltop, providing electricity for the region. The energy company had erected a sign with an inscription: "Donte se cruz a el camino del viento con el de las estrellas." (Where the way of the wind meets the way of the stars.)

After a shower and further treatment of my blistered feet, I settled into bed for an early night with a final prayer before falling asleep: that a correo would be open along the pathway, defying the saintly celebrations. I passed through Uterga before daybreak the next morning and heard the church bells ringing in the small nearby village of Obanos. The sight of the famous six-arched Romanesque bridge over the Rio Argo at Puenta la Reina came into view after a slow trudge by wheat fields and vineyards. The crops looked brown and parched from the dry Spanish summer. Crossing the bridge, I remembered reading of how the town had grown around the bridge, which was built on the Santiago route so that pilgrims could avoid the ferrymen's expensive tariff, and also to save them a treacherous boat ride. To my disappointment, everything in this town was closed for the anniversary celebrations.

The main street was busy with young people falling out of doorways, drunk from a night of wild dancing and red wine; all dressed in the same red shirts, black pants and red rags on their hips, mimicking the matadors of the historic arenas that once drew crowds to watch the matador kill the bull - or vice versa. I climbed a fence to watch half-drunk young men attempting to fight a young bull in an enclosure in the square in the middle of the town. The small balconies that hung over the main square were filled with faces of old folk watching the antics of the alcohol-fuelled, budding matadors. I was thankful to leave the street, where the bulls would soon be released for the mad street dash in their running of the bulls celebration. Not as big a deal as the Pamplona celebrations, but still very dangerous all the same. Apart from my view of the stupidity of the young men in a drunken haze, I did not relish the thought of outrunning and fighting a bull with a red handkerchief. I was quickly out of the street and back on The Camino Way.

I had sprained my right ankle the day before and, on the outskirts of Puente la Reina had stopped to treat my blisters again, cooled my feet in a nearby water hole and attached an ankle guard over my sprain. I was of the old school of thought, believing that continuing movement was the best medicine for a sprain, but it did not work so well with blisters. As for my heavy back pack, I had not reckoned on the public holiday ending on a weekend, so I would have to wait until the following Monday morning before I could find an open correo to send my heavy burden on to Santiago. The thought of my mantra, "Less is more on The Camino", played in my head as I left Estella in darkness, determined to make the 22 km to the Los Argos by nightfall. The locals in Estella advised me that there would be no water for the next 12 km, so I wanted to get this part of the journey over before the temperature rose too high and yet another forty-degree day would have to be endured. It was a wise move, as without water and shade, of which there were none, dehydration could result in a health crisis.

The rough yellow signs pointed the way, and I was thankful to Don Elias once more, despite the Camino shell-signs that had been displayed incorrectly. I no longer had any battery charge in my phone camera, so I had no photographic record of the journey now. I contented myself with recording details of what I viewed and experienced in my journal in lieu of in the phone. I had asked a number of pilgrims to take photos for me and send them to my email address later; some did remember to do just that, so to those pilgrims I prayed a "thank you". I committed to memory the image of the rolling hills and vineyards at the half-way mark of Villamayor de Monjardin. The relief elicited a sigh from me when I sighted an imposing hilltop castle and entered the village square, seeing a free wine-fountain in operation. My mind wandered to the letting-go of painful experiences. The divorce and the inevitable court battle that ensued; my son Peter's suicide; the sense of abandonment from my family; and the loss of material possessions had all taken a heavy toll on me, the stress resulting in my decline into depression – and in the midst of all that, my mother's health failed, one friend suicided and another died.. I had thought my life was over. Thankfully, all this was now behind me, including the horror of being in a pit of hell whilst in the mindset of depression.

My mind returned to the road and the mental-healing of The Camino de Santiago, my quest for a symbolic sword and the motto, "Be as gentle as dove and as vigilant as a female serpent" all made me realise that life had the rough with the smooth. Another mate, Noel, came to mind, as he too had been to hell and back. I often heard Noel start his conversations with the words of a song, "Some days are diamonds, some days are stone", and suddenly I found myself laughing at myself as I trudged my happy path of destiny.

I met-up with a group of young Dutch students on their university break, doing a section of The Camino over the next two weeks. We sang and danced our way along he track, singing songs of the seventies and eighties, and it was fun to be a kid again. The Dutch kids moved on up the track and I waited for two Belgian girls who had been with us all as we climbed a mountain path. Now they were well behind, so I had said goodbye to the Dutch and turned back down the hill to check that the young women were safe and well. Pretty soon they came up towards me and we all continued our journey. One of the girls wore a shirt with a visionary sign: "No sureness tu Vida, Vive tu steno" (Don't dream your life, live the dream).

The girls introduced themselves as Marianne and Nadine, and I was pleased with their company as we climbed the mountainous dirt road. We discussed the consequences of divorce, as both girls had recently been through the same experience and were on a healing Camino break, even if it was to be for only a couple of weeks. We walked on, singing rock 'n' roll songs and sharing some music via Nadine's iPhone. They also drew my attention to some very dark but emotionally-moving Belgian songs. We began to increase the pace of our walking and rejoined the Dutch students and all enjoyed a happy sing-along of songs from the eighties. The Belgian girls slowly fell behind again when we reached to top of the next incline, so I made sure that I could see they were safe before deciding to walk on alone this time. The Camino has a strange effect on one's sense of compassion. More than once, I found myself concerned for the welfare of others rather than for my own; equally, other pilgrims showed concern for my wellbeing. The exchange of food, water or some medication to help a fellow pilgrim was a natural occurrence along The Way.

As I ambled along, I met a guy who was suffering joint pain from walking. I offered him some anti-inflammatory tablets which I found helpful in reducing the pain in my often swollen feet and now swollen ankle. He refused, saying he was OK. Later, I was appreciative of the fact that I had some left to ease my own pain further along The Camino Way. As I walked I fell into step with a young attractive girl who doing her own Camino of pain, recovering from a recent relationship break-up with her gay lover. She wasn't the first gay woman I encountered on The Camino, and never can understand the sexual attraction one woman would have for another.

Stephanie was twenty-three when she married, and had been the youngest gay woman in Canada to tie the knot under that nation's then new gay laws. She had divorced some ten years earlier and, while doing a teaching degree at university, fell in love again. Her partner of the past decade proved to be very controlling, and my new-found pilgrim traveller-companion had escaped to Spain to do a Camino. Stephanie had called off the relationship before leaving Canada, but her ex-partner was harassing her and continued to make frequent phone calls, filling Stephanie's head with negative thoughts.

We reached Los Argos and booked into an albergue for the night. I felt sorry for her being in so much emotional pain and sat on her bed until after midnight, listening to her tale of woe and the difficulties she was having with her now ex-partner. I encouraged her to phone her father, and, after having a good cry she did seem a lot better for having done so. There was only one other person in the albergue, another woman who ventured into the dormitory-like room after midnight. This person provided the break I needed, to suggest to Stephanie that it was time to get some sleep.

The old lady who ran the albergue took a liking to me and insisted on treating my feet, making her way to a medical kit behind the reception desk when I went to pay for my accommodation early the next morning. The old girl was like a concerned mother, and cleaned my wounded toe from which I had removed the toe nail some days earlier. She cut away hanging skin, dressed the blisters and toe with iodine and finished the task by sealing the wounds with band-aids. All the while, Stephanie looked on, attempting to tease me and the old woman. Stephanie, who spoke fluent Spanish, told me that the old Spanish woman had indicated to her that she wanted to be my wife. I now knew why the old dear was giving me so much individual care. I laughed at the prospect of being the husband of such an old lady and, apart from that, I did not relish being her slave, washing sheets and making beds for pilgrims for the rest of my days. I said my "Buen Camino" to Stephanie, wished her well for the remainder of her Camino, and thanked the old lady before she tied me to a chair or did something even more sinister. After eating breakfast in town, I returned to the track which now wandered through endless vineyards and fields of golden wheat. I reached the Medieval hill-top towns of Sansol and Torres del Rio, stopping occasionally to make a journal entry or refill my water flasks.

The Camino is an inward journey, as well as an outward one. Whilst you meet many pilgrims along the road to Santiago, The Way is not so much a social experience, but more an experience of endurance, strength of character and soul-searching independence. As a pilgrim you get to know that the real task of your Camino is getting to know your physical endurance, and learning how to let-go internally. I originally thought that my Camino was to be a spiritual pilgrimage, but soon realised that I was experiencing a journey of the spirit…my own!

After staying the night in Los Argos, I journeyed-on a further 22 km that day, and a similar distance the next. The following day was not to be without incident. About nine kilometres from Logrono I noticed a make-shift sign with an arrow pointing to the left; the sign read, "Bar 1,000 metres". It was an extremely hot day and the thought of an ice-cold drink enticed me to turn from the beaten Camino way and take a side dirt track to a small village upon a hill top. The bar was at the top of a steep stairway which entered the main street of the village, where I was surprised to see that I had to cross a busy two-lane highway to get to the bar. After quenching my thirst, I enquired as to another route back to The Camino Way, to save me back-tracking the 1,000 metre path I had just walked. The Spanish guide directed me to another road, and when I came to a fork in the road I took the left turn as instructed. After walking some 500 metres the track widened, and I was forced to the edge of the path to allow a large Caterpillar tractor to pass by. At last I came to a now familiar arrow painted on a large rock at the side of the track.

The arrow on the rock pointed to a pathway at the edge of a vineyard and I began to walk along what I thought was the correct route again, but had not reckoned on the large arrow-marked rock having been moved in the wrong direction. On reflection, I later remembered that there had been a huge rubber tire mark across one side of the rock and a similar tread-marking embedded in the ground. The large tractor that had passed me had obviously run over the edge of the rock, turning the arrow from its intended direction. After walking through the vineyards for a long time, I was realised I was lost. I climbed to a high rocky ledge but could see no sign of life or a road, so I ventured on, not wanting to retrace my steps. After walking through a grassy field and a paddock full of burrs, I found a landmark; the meaning of the warning sign in Spanish was obvious despite the language barrier. The sign was typical of signs on properties back home: "Warning. Private property. Keep out." I had come across the occasional properties in Australia with the added words: "Trespassers will be shot." The heat of the day bothered me more than the signage, so I climbed the chained fence and moved into the shade of a large boulder, the only structure with shade as far as the eye could see. I sat down beside the rock and picked the burrs from my socks for a long time, in a semi-meditative state. After a time, I followed the high fence, once again climbed over it, and came to a four-lane highway which I followed until I found a sign indicating 5 km to Logrono. I had in fact walked some 5 km off the beaten track but, by the grace of God, in the right direction. I left Logrono after my usual breakfast ritual of orange juice, coffee and croissants. The French had certainly left a delicious legacy behind, in introducing fine bread and croissants to this region of Spain.

The track from Logrono to Najera, 29.6 km, followed natural walking paths and side tracks close to main roads, passing near a man-made nature reserve and a reservoir lake. Somewhere near Navarrete, I fell into step with four Frenchmen. We exchanged the usual "Buen Camino" greetings and had wonderful conversations, ranging from education to current world economies, politics, taxes and leadership. Allene, a French-born English teacher who lived in Australia, translated the French to English for me, so it made our "inky-dinky parlez vous" quite enjoyable. It certainly made the near-highway walking and the decidedly industrial stretch of the track between Navarrete and Ventosa fade into oblivion. My left ankle sprain, despite being heavily bandaged, was causing me difficulty in walking and my blistered feet gave me no mercy either. I slowly drifted behind the Frenchmen on the remaining 10 km to Najera. Now, for some strange reason, my mind drifted to the past and the people who had influenced my decision to journey to Santiago; my obsession with the outward expression of a Sword of Discernment being also of paramount concern.

CHAPTER 5

LIKE SHIPS IN THE NIGHT.

I was reflecting now on how some people come into our lives to teach another lesson on our spiritual journey. I remembered reading, from an unknown author, that sometimes lessons are not realised until the teacher has passed to a new way of living, or has in fact died. You know at the time that they are meant to be there, to serve you, to teach you a lesson or to help you figure out who you are or what you want to be. All too often you never know who these people might be; they may be a friend, a neighbour, a lover, or a complete stranger. Your intuition knows, from the moment you lock eyes with them, that they will have an effect on your life in some profound way. Sometimes events occur that may at first seem horrible, painful and unfair, but on reflection you find that without overcoming these obstacles you would never have realised your full potential strength, will power or heart.

Everything happens for a reason. Nothing happens by chance or by means of good or bad luck. Illness, injury, love, loss, moments of greatness or sheer stupidity – all occur to test the limits of our soul. Without these tests, whatever they may be, life would be a smooth, paved, flat road to nowhere. It would be safe and comfortable, but dull and utterly pointless. The people we meet who affect our life and the success and downfalls we experience help us to create who we are and who we will become. Every bad experience can be learnt from; in fact, they are probably the most poignant and important ones. If someone hurts, betrays us or breaks our heart…forgive. It is the way we learn about trust and being cautious about whom we open our heart to. If someone loves you, love them back unconditionally, because they are teaching us how to open our heart and eyes too things.

There, on The Camino Way, I resolved to make every day count, to appreciate every moment and to take from those moments everything that I possibly could. I knew that I may not experience it all again.

So, talking to people I would possibly never see again, and taking the time to listen, has been an education. I could see now that I could make of life anything I wished, I had only to act and to believe. I had created the life I had led until now, and I would create my own life in the future – but it would be a far different life than the one I had been living. I would have no regrets; now, if I loved someone, I would tell them and if I didn't like someone, I would tell them why, for communication may teach me a new way of looking at that person. I resolved to learn a new lesson in life every day. For some strange reason, at this stage of my journey my mind kept returning to thoughts of my father and others who had died - those who had an influence on my life - and the lessons I had learnt by having been a part of their life on earth.

"Life is mostly froth and bubble,
two things stand like stone,
kindness in another's trouble
courage in your own."

Adam Lindsay Gordon
           Poet and author.

One time hero.

My father was a brilliant mathematician, engineer, musician and creative mastermind. When it came to creating pieces of art from wood or cast iron he had no equal. Whether working on a diesel motor, turning wood to make furniture or bending cast iron to make something decorative, he was pure genius. The same applied to his musical ability; his main form of relaxation was playing the piano at home. He had worked hard as a boy during the depression years, and we still had that instrument for many years after he had passed.

 Dad had been dux of his class in his final year at school, studied engineering, and was a competitive swimmer when young. His most burning desire was to own his own business, and as he always held a fascination for engines it was a natural progression for him to eventually buy-out his boss' business and run a well-established engineering operation. He was always meticulous in tuning a car's engine and ensuring that all was left clean and tidy after a service. However, his greatest passion was working on large trucks. Dad was only a very small man, of Irish stock, but was always cool under pressure. He had an added advantage when working with trucks, in that he could sit under the bonnet, right with the engine where, with his small hands, could reach areas in the motor that most mechanical engineers could not. The usual method of working on a truck's motor is to hoist it out on a chain and secure it on a bench for repair or maintenance. In most instances, my father didn't need to do that. He actually taught engineers in his employ the techniques of working without removing the engine from the truck. He also designed commercial trailers for road transport and involved his staff in the process. He had a small metal plate secured to the rear of the newest creation: "Built by Cramatic Constructions" – Cramatic being the first letters of the Christian names of those employees involved in the building process: **C**olin, **R**obert and **M**ax, **A**thol, **T**om, including Charlie!

It was not too many years down the track that he expanded the business to be the biggest motor dealer and truck-service business between Newcastle and the Queensland border. No man I ever knew worked the hours my father did. It was not unusual for him to work through from 7:30 am until 2:00 am the next morning on some engineering marvel, or to arrive home for a couple of hours' sleep at 11:00 pm and then go back to fix a transport truck which had broken-down on the main highway north, working until dawn to rectify the problem. Dad's always dependable mechanical skills in quickly getting a truck road-worthy were well-known on the north coast of New South Wales. He always ate a full breakfast that my ever-dutiful mother prepared, and then sat in his car long enough to smoke a cigarette while the engine warmed-up, before taking off. Long days and nights at work were his daily routine for the best part of the first twenty years of my life.

It was not uncommon, either, for him to catch the night train south to collect the latest model British car from the Sydney docks and, quite often as a small boy I was allowed to travel with him. There were no shipping containers in those days of the nineteen-fifties; cars transported on ships from Europe and the U.S.A. were covered in tar, the black rubber-like substance plastered all over the cars protecting them from the ocean waves and the prospect of rust. All vehicles and machinery were chained or tied-down with ropes on the deck or in the hull, but were still susceptible to sea-water damage from the wild seas. The task of cleaning the tar off the cars, using a cutting compound before being hand-polished to show-room condition, was the dealer's job. Trucks did not pose such a problem as Dad's dealership was with the American company, International Harvester, which arranged the transport. All Dad had to do was collect the shining new trucks from their Sydney warehouse. International Harvester's tractors and machinery always arrived by train, so there was no need to venture past the local railway platform to collect them.

The dealership also sold a lot of farm equipment. The Mid-North Coast in those days was thriving on the back of the timber industry, dairy, banana plantations, fishing, and meat and vegetable production. The cars were the problem-child for the dealership, as all his car supplies were imports direct from Britain. Dad had Standard, Triumph and Rover agencies, and another that escapes my mind after so many years. Driving the vehicles north involved a 400 km journey that took at least twenty-four hours – if it was a good run. Dad navigated dirt roads, river-crossings and pubs en route. The trips were broken by Dad's tales of his youth, singing Irish songs along the way and the inevitable pub-crawls.

My father was a pragmatic businessman, a keen community-minded citizen and a philanthropist well before it became fashionable to be one. He was on the steering committee to build a new Catholic church for the district, but did not attend church. He gave personal monies equally to the Salvation Army and the Anglicans. As a patron of the golf club, he took great delight in providing money for the sport, yet never played a game. He was also a patron of the he local surf club despite the fact that he never went swimming. Considering his athletic ability for the sport in his youth, he helped raise funds for, donated money to, and helped build a local swimming pool for the town, and an iron lung for the hospital.Politically, he held allegiance to the left of politics, both personally and as a businessman. Whilst employing a small number of employees, he was always on the side of the worker more than for his own needs. He studied the rise of Bob Hawke in his ACTU days before his entry into parliament and ultimate rise to Prime Minister, and was a regular attendee at local Labor Party meetings. Dad was also on speaking terms with the then Liberal Prime Minister, Sir Robert Menses, and was instrumental in sowing the seeds for a Labour Day holiday long before it became established.

Fond memories float back to me now of his open invitation to our home for any musician visiting our town. Our home always had a party in progress whenever Dad was in a musical mood. I don't know when he lost his way. Maybe it was when I was at boarding school that his life went into decline; the drink and prescription drugs soon got the better of him. As well as watching his business slide into oblivion, I watched him slide into alcoholism and ultimate death. I loved him so much, but he was always an enigma to me and, I guess, to my mother as well.

Dad and Days Gone

I saw you stumble,
I felt your fall
from some great height
on your…majestic wall.

The mind's eyes weeping,
what a ghastly tale,
as you went struggling
……down the trail.

Well I watched you rise
to a world of fame
in some midnight madness
on a lonely plain.

Like you, the light blazed
a bright road for me,
it only led to…misery.

Though you could not see
the rot set in,
'twas when I followed
drinking drink again.

Yeah! I followed your footsteps
down the dark-lit path,
on my way out,
it could not last.

You were my hero
dear love, good old Dad,
a drinking companion,
some good times we had;
but mostly sadness
for the things left undone.

No more cymbals, no more chimes,
no more beat of the drum.

Like you in the power
once bitten by wine,
gripped by the grape,
stumbling blind.

I found my way out
through a tormented mind,
a power that answers
much greater than mine.

So where is the oil rag?
Where is the grime?
Lost in the rhythm
that rambles to rhyme,

passed by the footsteps
in shades of time,
the engineer drowned
……in a fog of wine.

Well I watched you rise
to a world of fame
in some midnight madness
on a lonely plain.

And I am here now,
biding my time.
Yes, I am here now
biding my time.

You were my hero
dear love, good old Dad,
a drinking companion,
some good times we had;
but mostly sadness
for the things left undone.

No more cymbals, no more chimes,
no more beat of the drum.

Sarah Catherine

Climbing the "hill of forgiveness" and the timely reminder of the thousands who had walked this Way before me, letting-go of the many burdens of their lifetime, opened in my mind and heart another wound that I had buried deep in my subconscious. Another loss, another tragedy over which I'd had no control at the time, and of which I needed to now let-go on this Camino.
  When you have an experience of the birth of a still-born child, it's a shattering event for mother and partner. Whilst my ex-wife and I had two sons, aged three and five at the time of Sarah's birth, it was nevertheless a very emotional time, and a sense of great loss for us. I had been at my then wife's side for the beautiful experiences of the births of my lovely boys. This was to be repeated twice more during our married life, with the births of our third beautiful son a couple of years after Sarah's non-chance

at life, and our last child who was, by what seemed a miracle, a baby girl. Witnessing the birth of living children is a joy for any father, who has little to do but be at his partner's side offering encouragement and, maybe, administer the nitrous oxide to help relieve the pain of labour. Of course, being an addictive personality, I did partake of the odd hit or two of the laughing-gas myself during those painful hours of my then partner. I've often wondered if nitrous oxide is nothing more than a placebo for pain relief during childbirth, as it had little effect on me. The outcome of witnessing the birth of one's own child is a joyous state of mind that is like no other in a lifetime of living; seeing the child for the first time is heavenly. At the time of Sarah Catherine's still-born birth in a country hospital, there were four other tragic births, each living child born with a deformity. Although it is many decades since that night of pain and tragedies, I do recall that one child was born blind and another had a cleft palate. My own state of mind was caught-up in my own family's pain and shock to pay too much attention to the other sad events.

Sarah Catherine's autopsy revealed that the flaps to her heart had not formed properly so, had she lived, her long-term chance of survival back then was poor and her quality of life, whatever that may have entailed, would have been limited. I did take note at the time that an extract of "Agent Orange" was being used as a pesticide in the district. I guess it was a cheap form of crop-dusting as supplies were plentiful, being left over from the war in Vietnam. I suspected, but never did prove, that the pesticide had entered the town's water supply, and I had also come into contact with yellow cake uranium in the cotton belt where I did some work during my then wife's pregnancy. I had nothing to verify either of these possibilities, although the evidence of the number of deformed babies and Sara's still-birth seemed to me to be more than a coincidence. However, I never suffered any ill-effects myself, nor did my ex-wife, so it is pure conjecture on my part. Perhaps it was my way of blaming something else for the tragedy rather than seeing it as, perhaps, an act of God.

As Sarah Catherine was being removed from the womb, both my wife and I had a strange experience. It was as if a curtain of light from above surrounded us; we were in a cocoon of silence, and a deep sense of peace came over me. I could see the doctor carry our still-born baby and hand her to a nurse who took her out of our sight. They were outside the cocoon of light, but I caught a glimpse of a perfectly-formed little dark-haired girl. I have never been able to explain this paranormal happening, except to say that it seemed real at the time. The legality of registering a birth certificate in order to bury her was harrowing. The recall of this strange happening, and it still having some unexplained meaning, came to me again as I walked my Camino.

OH! SARAH, SARAH

Oh! Sarah, Sarah, where are you now,
in the spirit world beyond?
The first light of father's daughter love,
as the star-filled rays did come.

Oh! Sarah, Sarah, the light of peace,
cast down on daughter and son.
Your birth was death,
death brought light
as star-filled rays did come.

Oh! Sarah, Sarah, celestial love
took away the pain
of a mother and father
who trust in peace,
we may see your face again.

Peter

It was a small gathering at the grave-side for Sarah Catherine's funeral service, only immediate family and a couple of friends. On the way back from the burial, my then three-year-old son, Peter, asked me where she had gone to. He was seated in the back seat of the car and kept leaning forward restlessly, determined, with his enquiring mind, to have an answer. I explained that she was with God, but he continued to probe with questions, wanting a more definitive answer. I tried to explain, in my heart-felt pain, that she was in heaven. He wanted to know where heaven was, and I pointed to the sky and said, "Up there." Peter remained silent for the remainder of the journey home, until I parked the car. I let him out through the back door of the car and he ran from the garage to the driveway. While looking up at the sky, he began jumping up and down. He continued jumping for some time, all the while looking up and calling out, "Take me up, take me up."

Peter was always an inquisitive child, so full of energy and enthusiasm for life. It seemed that all his batteries of energy were overcharged and he could not get enough of life to release what was bubbling-up inside him. One of my more memorable experiences of Peter was him getting drunk at breakfast time when he was still a small boy. He managed to make his way to the refrigerator and fill his bowl of Corn Flakes with white wine; we always kept a wine cask refrigerated for a quick "fix" in those days. He did not settle for one refill but repeated the routine until we noticed him rocking from side to side at the table. I put him to bed before I went to work and he was still asleep when I returned home in the evening.

If anyone was going to do something out of the ordinary, it was Peter in those days. If it wasn't getting his head stuck between the slats in the staircase, requiring a call to the builder to dismantle a step to get him out, it was his mischievous trickster mind causing havoc.

I recall a camping holiday at the beach, when he was still at pre-school age. Two family friends were camping near us in their tent, brothers-in-law who met every year at the camp site for Christmas. both were amputees. One had lost a leg as the consequence of a blood-clot and the other had lost both legs due to an accident. Peter was intrigued with their artificial limbs and ventured into their tent to investigate. He quickly made himself known to the men as they moved from the front of the tent to the inner shade, away from the heat of the morning sun. Peter first tapped the leg of one amputee, then the other, before enquiring how they walked on them. He then asked one of them to remove his leg, then promptly walked to the front of the tent with it. After propping it against the tent pole, he returned to the second man and had him remove both legs. He repeated the process, taking both legs to the front of the tent.

Both the amputees were amused and fascinated by Peter's mission, and watched as he struggled with the legs to the front of the tent. Apparently he then stood looking at the two gentlemen before looking back at the legs. After a time, he looked at the men squarely in the eyes and said, "Now you can't walk.", and returned to our adjoining tent. The two amputees later retold this event and we all laughed with amusement at Peter's activity, although we never really knew whether or not Peter saw the funny side of his actions.

In late primary school his skeptical mind questioned the God theory on more than one occasion. The religion teacher reported that, in junior primary school, she was explaining that whenever she baked a cake, she always had a statue of the Virgin Mary nearby in the kitchen and prayed to her, and her cakes always cooked to perfection. Apparently Peter quickly shot up his hand at the end of her statement and remarked, "Excuse me, Miss, isn't that idolatry?" We never did get to the bottom of his unusual attitude to religious belief, nor his appetite for entrepreneurial activity. While he was still a young lad, I taught him how to use and respect firearms. I had inherited a firearm-dealer's licence, and sold guns, reloading equipment and explosives for a time during my former business life in the country.

The three boys learned to respect guns, but it was Peter I was the least worried about when it came to shooting. Peter enjoyed the idea of shooting, did have a healthy attitude towards firearms and understood the need for safety. However, he did not relish the idea of killing anything that had life of any kind. This was proven to me one day when he accidentally shot a rabbit. He exclaimed, "I got it" with tears streaming down his cheeks.

I purchased motor bikes for the boys when they were all in high school, and they had great delight in mastering the machines. Like me, they grew up in the bush and the outdoor way of life was right up their alley. Peter didn't just settle for the fun of country life, though. He always went the extra mile; if it wasn't helping the local vet deliver a calf or helping round-up cattle or sheep on his motor bike, it was asking the local timber-mill owner about the running of his business. He also enjoyed working in my retail business, his efforts at the time far outweighing those of many adult employees. Peter and his elder brother, Scott, were as different and chalk and cheese as children when it came to work involvement. Peter would be in the thick of things with work, whilst Scott delighted in supervising the activity, all the while sitting on his bum reading a comic or merely daydreaming while Peter did the hard yards. Later, in his teens, Scott became interested in photography and thought it more important to take photos of men at work than to actually engage in the physical activity. To his credit, he took on job roles as a young man that did involve a lot of physical work, but later honed his skills in sales and management, and follows the same successful career path to this day. Perhaps he had it right all along, as the lifestyle of work has changed dramatically in recent years. My youngest son, Sam, has always shown a flair for media and art, and has followed his career path for a decade now, completing many diplomas and marketing courses as well as furthering his university studies in law. He was too young to be mindful of the exploits of Peter and Scott.

The family's move to the city was not initially appreciated by Peter, but he quickly settled into the different way of life. Scott was attending boarding school at the time, so Peter was the senior member of the family in his eyes from then on. I think some of the fights that later ensued between Peter and Scott were more entered on sibling rivalry, and usually ended with them shaking hands.

Our first residence in Sydney was near a golf course, so it became routine for Peter to walk around the course after school looking for lost golf balls. When he had collected a bucket full, he would come home, do his homework, eat dinner, shower and go to bed. His weekend routine was to stand outside the golf course's club house and, under the nose of the pro in the golf shop, sell his inventory of golf balls to the weekend players. Later, when we moved to live near a busy road in Chatswood, many road accidents occurred in the intersection outside our home. Peter set-up shop at our front gate, selling hub caps from the wrecked cars, and this inevitably ended with a stockpile of spares in my carport. We always had regular visits from tow-truck drivers with a ten-dollar commission for Peter, who became a good spotter for them when accidents happened locally. He would see the accident in our intersection, inform them and later collect his fee. I had to set some ground rules for this activity, so I explained to Peter that if somebody was hurt in an accident to forget about his tow-truck fee and first telephone the ambulance, then the police, and then the tow-truck driver. As far as I know, he always honoured this agreement. Peter was an extremely honest and generous person, always showing exceptional character and charity to those less fortunate than himself. He would give you the shirt off his back and all of his money if you need it, with no questions asked. However, when it came to business deals he had no equal. It was at primary school that he learnt how to do tough deals, so he had business savvy at an early age.

When he went off the boarding school to join his brother, he was a handful for his teachers. They had a difficult time getting him to toe the line and accept the boarding school routine instead of his own agenda. Peter hated the school at first, because he was a home boy and family meant everything to him. He eventually did settle into the school, but not before running away one night. We were informed in the middle of the night that he was missing from his bed. I thanked the night security for informing us, and woke my wife to tell her. We were both back asleep ten minutes later; it was Peter, and we knew we had little to worry about as he would work it out, as he did with just about everything he did in life. True to form, he phoned at 7:00 am to tell us that he had slept under a bridge in an outer suburb with some mates, and was returning to the school. On his final day and graduation he returned home and insisted on wearing his school uniform for the rest of that day. He really did love that school and remained close to his school friends until his dying day.

Peter's early business interest put him in good stead for running his own business in his early adult years. He tried his hand at landscape-gardening and completed a horticultural course. He worked for a guy he knew for a time, but left the job because he was frustrated with his boss' shoddy workmanship. He worked with me for a year or two, running the paper-merchant arm of my wholesale business, and did a great job. Later, well before its time in the commercial world, he built a direct internet business with a friend, under the umbrella of my business. While still working for me, he studied for a business diploma, but in the first year he challenged the key lecturer on his business knowledge. He disagreed with the lecturer's teaching methods and, in front of the class told the lecturer that if he was any good he would be running his own business and not lecturing students. Peter left the course because of that.

This was typical of Peter, who was never backward in coming forward, always, to his way of thinking, telling it like it is. When it came to decision-making, it was either Peter's way or the highway. He was later offered a cadetship with a major international company and, according to the CEO, did a great job for them. However, he gave this job away after about a year when he realised that the CEO took Wednesday off to play golf. Peter told me that he was not there to line the owner's pockets by his skills while his boss was on the golf course! The CEO of that company told me at Peter's funeral that Peter was always his own man, even when working for him. Peter once approached a board member of a major cigarette company, in a public arena, asking him how he felt about stuffing-up people's lungs with cigarettes. There were many similar instalments in Peter's life that rang true in the same vein, and I wondered, after his death, whether his strong will and decision-making was an Achilles' heel, resulting in his ultimate decision-making when he suicided.

It was our routine together, when we had a paper-merchant business, to start at 5:30 am. The premises where we stored our inventory and assembled customers' orders were housed within the boundary of a trucking depot, so our daily ritual took us past a host of trucks on our way to the warehouse. Peter, as always, was dressed in his Sunday-best gear. On this particular morning he was wearing a pink polo shirt and one of the truck drivers stuck his head through his window and called out, "I see you've got your sister's shirt on, mate." Peter, without hesitation, replied, "No, mate. You're mother's". That was our Peter, always as sharp as a tack, but always right in his own mind when it came to decision-making. The crack in his armour was the manic depression and the unfortunate false diagnosis of an illness he did not have. The thought of dying in long-term agony, coupled with his mania, was the catalyst that killed him.

Peter

We had a son, his name was Peter,
was the pride of the family,
somehow he became the rock,
the knead that held our clay.

Every kingdom needs a jester,
it was our 'twas plain to see.
he was always up to mischief,
playing games on all he'd see.

True at heart he was a bush boy,
shooting slugs to kill a rat,
riding motor bikes in round-up,
climbing trees and all of that!

Loved his model train when raining,
liked to watch an eagle fly;
heard the sound of pine trees falling
with a gleeful smiling eye.

Loved to ride his Yamaha
with its big black exhaust;
got his kicks with pro-linked suspension

and low handlebars of course!

He'd speak of chicken cooking
and the smell of country air,
of the laughter of some people
and the roses he smelled there!

Loved to feed small pigs when snorting,
and hear the thump of rabbit's foot,
watched for hours small birds flying,
climbing trees and cutting wood!

When he moved into the city
loved to play his rugby game;
didn't like the thought of losing,
took great relish in the fame!

As he grew he was a dresser,
wearing his Tag Heuer watch,
always dressed in Ralph Lauren,
Nike Airs his brand of course.

He found his joy in Christmas paper
and the lights of the Christmas tree,
loved to give, and watched the smiles
in gift-giving family.

Just a boy who loved the world,
all that gathered there within,
through the light of his great spirit
a darkness was creeping in.

So he drove himself in work life
and he climbed the corporate tree,
but not before he set up business
with me and my family.

When the darkness in his mindset
began to take a hold,
took a job in west New Guinea
where he found a pot of gold!

He was jilted by a lover,
falsely diagnosed as ill;
began to doubt the life he lived,
stopped taking depression pills.

It was then the rot set in
he decided to let go,
so with noted pen on paper
he said goodbye and he just packed it in.

When the sun sets on Santorini
and the Greeks just take it in,
I remember what he said,
it wasn't the happiest he'd been.

Sometimes when I see a bird fly by
I can't help but think of him,
walking hand-in-hand together;
we were both little boys back then!

Yes, he cut his fair share of life
and he roared like a meteor
across the skies of his perception,
but he burned out in the end.

Now I miss his smiling face
and his devotion to family,
feel the sadness that I know
of the pains without relief.

Oh! We his blood
are so grief-stricken;
God in heaven
give us peace!

There's a cockatoo that's flying
in the shadow land of heart,
across the great Australian landscape
on the other side of dark.

Yes, its flight is toward the dawning
where it will cry to morning sun,
telling all of nature's glory,
of a suicidal son.

It's time to let him go now,
may your boy's soul rest in peace
whilst those of us still living
do our best to find release.

We shall overcome.
We shall overcome.
We shall overcome
Someday.

Deep in my heart,
I do believe.

In the early hours of the 18th August, 2003 he hung himself in the meat room of the shopping complex he had helped build. Peter left a suicide note, saying goodbye to his family, as if he were going away for a holiday. He merely repeated that he could not take it, was sorry, and that he would miss us all. I was the only one to whom he gave a personal mention.

The local church in Port Moresby held two services for Peter, and both times was packed with natives. Peter's favourite boots and tagged shirt were placed on the altar as a tribute to him. One of his mates, whom Peter had saved from committing suicide himself just one year earlier, went over to New Guinea and returned with the coffin containing Peter's body. The final memorial service was at his old school, where the chapel was packed to capacity with people who loved him. As his father, he is with me every day, and walking my Camino was helping me come to terms with his death. He is with me every step of the way on the journey of my soul. I would sometimes cry in the presence of strangers along The Way of my Camino as I retold the life and death of Peter. My final letting-go was to be at the Cruz Ferro, just past Foncebadon, where I would climb the high point of the Irago Mountains in the days ahead. Deep in my heart, though, I knew his spirit would never leave my soul whilst ever I had breath within me.

My mother had died just a year before I left for my Camino, and the fact that I seem to have lost many family members along the way now came back to haunt me. I decided to file away any thoughts of my mother for another day, and considered what lessons I had learnt from my journey on this Camino Way thus far.

While jotting notes in my old journal I found a page half-way through the notebook on which I had written about a friend of the street whom I had known in my youth. I remembered writing thoughts down, and pondered our short time together. Yeah! Morris was certainly a man of substance who lacked the social graces but, nevertheless was a man for all seasons as far as I recall. Morris of the Street. Most of what I remember of him does not come easily. Morris was a man of the street, existing on the edge, drifting in and out of familiarity and loneliness; the occasional dollar earned, but all too often hungry. He held a wisdom that was much greater than merely being street-wise. To me, he was a charismatic pragmatist of intellectual isolation. We met occasionally for a steak or a beer, engaged in deep conversations about life, love, regrets and the things that mattered to humanity and to ourselves.

I suppose I resonated with his deep thinking and good conversational ability. He would initially enlighten me with his view-points but sometimes he just retreated into isolation. Morris wrote the occasional article for The Bulletin magazine; usually, his view on Christ-like stuff, sticking it into the Catholic Church for its institutional outlook on the world and its population; exactly the kind of anti-establishment view The Bulletin relished as headline news to increase its circulation. Morris' opinions were only some of the many that The Bulletin used as headline news during economic down-times for newspapers and magazines. He wrote the kind of news pieces that grabbed the attention of the masses and so-called intellectuals who liked to quote The Bulletin's articles in conversation. Morris' views were always radical, but they spoke from the heart, endorsing the nature of man. We made a film together; it was Morris' idea, but developed the script in unison. I did the filming, he did the directing. It was a rather depressing insight into the people of the street. We delved into their living spaces in the back alleys and dark corners of our city; filmed them while they lined-up at soup kitchens for a feed, and generally made a nuisance of ourselves to fulfil our cinematic reality. I guess, deep down, we were trying to make a difference and convey to the masses that many people lived lives of quiet desperation.

We completed the film, and although it was considered to be a reasonably good documentary, did not see the light of day. Censorship rules. After all, it was the seventies. I lost track of Morris back in the late seventies when I went bush for a number of years. A mutual friend told me that Morris had died in the street a year before I returned to live in the city again.

CHAPTER 6.

FROM DARKNESS TO LIGHT

Whilst much of the day was spent in contemplation of some of the people who had passed and who had a profound influence on my life, a lot of the day was lost to me. At one point I drifted off the beaten path again and came to a crossroads; by trial and error I found my way back on course and I resolved to buy an English translation guide book of The Camino as soon as I reached a larger town. At least I had recharged my phone, with the assistance of a Frenchman who had resided in Australia for many years. Allene lent me his compatible adaptor at a seventy-bed albergue where we had stayed the day before. It consisted of one long narrow room with small bunks, two high, side by side and end to end. All the bunks touched each other so that when someone even three beds away moved you felt the vibration; another one of life's sleepless night's experience, not to be repeated.

My day began in the semi-darkness of dawn, and I made it to the next village a few kilometres down the track for my daily ritual on my journey to Santiago - freshly-squeezed orange juice, coffee and croissants. I tramped the wide farm tracks through fields of green and grapes for the 21 km from Najera to Santa Domingo. It was another hot day, with little shade, and the water stops at Azofra (5.8 km) and Ciruena (9.3 km) along the way were like oases in the desert, allowing me to refill my water bottles in the town squares' fountains. These monuments and fountains were always to be found in towns on the direct route of The Camino. The last leg of my days' journey, some 6.8 km, was broken by the roar of passing trucks on a nearby busy highway.

Santa Domingo's claim to fame is the historical tale of live chickens, whose ancestors still live in the cathedral. The story goes that the German Hugonell family, father, mother and son, stayed with a farming family during their Medieval pilgrimage to Santiago. The farmer's daughter tried to seduce the boy, but after he refused her she went to the authorities and accused him of theft. Upon finding silver-wear items in his backpack, which had in fact been placed there by the farm girl, he was found guilty and was hanged. The grief-stricken parents went on to complete their pilgrimage and, on their return journey, went to visit their son's hanging body. To the parents' and the authorities' surprise, the boy was still alive. The parents hurried to the magistrate and begged for their son to be cut down and forgiven. The magistrate had only just sat down to a hearty meal of fresh chicken. He replied, "He is no more alive than this roasted chicken I am about to eat". At this, the chicken stood up and miraculously came back to life, feathers and all. In remembrance of this story, live chickens, said to be descendants of the story's resurrected fowl, are kept at the cathedral. The other miracle reported was that of Saint Domingo, who cleared the road to Santiago and built bridges in the area. Legend has it that he fell asleep whilst clearing a forest, and angels picked up his scythe and continued clearing the undergrowth. I enjoyed my stay in Santa Domingo; it had quaint, neat streets with interesting shops and great food and accommodation.

Another strange thing I noticed on The Camino was that when I handed over to a power within, which I did not attempt to define, and just let everything unfold of its own accord, wonderful things occurred. One of these happening miracles was when I looked for an English translation guide book. I just began walking the streets in the hope of finding an information centre and happened upon a book shop with a window full of books in Spanish.

At the front of the shop's window, on display, sat the only English-language guide book in the whole shop. It proved to be a real treasure for me on my journey to Santiago, as I was able to check out the topographic route, likely stop-off points and possible accommodation locations along the way.

I started the next morning searching for an ATM with an English menu, but had no luck, so I settled for breakfast at a sidewalk café. As I had very little cash left, I elicited the help of the café's young waitress, who led me to a nearby ATM and used my travel card to withdraw money for me. I paid the breakfast bill and was soon on the next leg of my journey, to Belardo. At a small roadside stall in Granan I purchased some fruit for the remainder of the day's walk. I also replenished my water supply from a nearby fountain, and was advised by the stall-holder that although it was still early in the day, the temperature had already reached 36 degrees and there was no sign in the clear blue sky of relief from rain; not good news, as more of the journey that day consisted of paths next to a busy highway. The continual pounding of my feet on the path and road surface played havoc with my blistered feet.

My mind drifted to Shirley MacLaines's book and her Camino journey and, as I entered Vilonia de Rioja, I thought of her fear of dogs and stories of vicious dogs on The Camino. The story goes that they attack in packs, like wolves or dingoes. The mountain village of Foncebadon had been known as the place to have a real fear of dogs, as they had been known to have attacked in packs in the area. Foncebadon was a couple of weeks away, so I was not concerned at this point in my journey. Also, I had no fear of dogs in general, and had experienced dingoes coming into a campsite where I had stayed with my uncle when I was a small boy. The wild dingoes had come howling just outside the glow of our campfire, and we could see the fire's reflection in their eyes. Even then I was not scared, as I knew my uncle would protect me, He fired a rifle in the air and they scattered all through the surrounding bush. I did lay awake in the tent for some time that night, listening to their howling in the nearby hills, before drifting-off to sleep.

The dogs I had encountered on The Camino barked a little, but mainly just lay about looking sad and half-dead in the heat of a Spanish drought. Now cats are another thing for me. I am just not a cat person, but there is never a time that cats are not attracted to me. If a room is full of people and there are one or two cats, they always end up coming to me, and my travels on The Camino were no exception. These days I just accept the fact, stroke their fur and listen to them purr, but I would much prefer to stay clear of them.

As I entered the village of Vilonia de Rioja I made my way to the fountain in the square and filled my water flasks for the next leg of my journey. I sat on a nearby bench, under the shade of tree, to enjoy some bread and the remainder of the fruit and nuts from my backpack's supply. I knew, from my recently-acquired guide book, that there was more than another 8 kilometres to Belorado in the extreme heat, before crossing into the region of Costilla y Leon. I was beginning to enjoy my peaceful bench seat and the shade, with the food spread before me. Suddenly, I was invaded by a large number of feral cats. They seemed to appear from every door, nook and cranny in the village square. I looked along the street, to see even more emerging from doorways and all heading towards me. I wondered if my thought of Shirley MacLaine and her fear of dogs, and of other strange happenings on The Camino, or my own disdain for these feline creatures was a lesson from the universe for me.

As a rather large cat jumped onto the bench beside me, I quickly packed-up my food and belongings and exited stage right. The big cat meowed, screeched and jumped at the tree, barely making it and, sinking its claws into the bark for security, climbed quickly and sat on a branch. Meanwhile, an old man had appeared, surrounded by yet more cats, carrying a skinny, sick-looking kitten. He went to the bench where I had been seated and all the cats surrounded him. I guessed this was a daily ritual in the town at this time of day, and it was not the place to be for someone like myself who felt they had a fur-ball in the throat. I made the way along the road and found another location to finish eating my lunch.

However, still more cats appeared from doorways which the house owners were opening to allow the cats out for a while. I decided to leave that village without finishing my lunch, resigned to the fact that I had no other choice if I wished to escape the cats. I cast my mind back to Shirley MacLaine and her encounter with the vicious dogs. Shirley had walked her Camino in the summer of her sixty-ninth year, my age now, a decade before me and my encounter with the cats. I would have preferred to have had Shirley's experience with the dogs, but I had not yet reached Foncebadon. I vowed to not think about cats or vicious dogs, but to focus on my Camino, in case I manifested something I would later be sorry for. As it eventuated, Foncebadon produced another experience for me, the discomfort of which I would carry long after completing The Camino. I distracted myself by thinking about the lessons I had learnt from the living during my journey of discovery and ill-health after the pain of loss of those most dear to me in the past decade.

****

Leaving Logrono by the ancient pilgrim's gate, Puerto del Camino, it is then back to the vineyards of La Rioja and on to the 12th century town of Navarette, built by the Knights of the Sepulchre, and a pause in the Medieval town of Najera, with its panoramic views of the entire region. Quiet country road follow, with the La Demanda Mountains to the south.

Through the small villages of La Rioja dedicated to the region's patron, La Virgen de Valvanera, and on to the starting-point of The Monasteries Route to the Yusa and Suso monasteries of San Milan de la Cogolla, considered to be the birth-place of the Spanish language. Then, on to the beautiful city of San Domingo with its close history to The Camino de Santiago.

The trail from San Domingo starts on uneven terrain through woodlands and crop fields. Near Belorando the Oca Mountains is the last range to be seen before entry into the Meseta, the central Spanish plateau. On the way to the pleasant hamlet of San Juan de Ortega, the trail reaches the mountains of Villafranca de Oca then weaves through gorgeous woodlands of oak and pine before reaching the town.

The Way then continues across the mountainous terrain of the Sierra de Atapuerca, with views to the Burgos region as the pilgrim descends to the flat river valley and then to the suburbs of Burgos, the home of the beautiful cathedral and the history of El Cid.

CHAPTER 7

LESSONS FROM THE LIVING.

Deep in thought as I tramped along, I was remembering the impact Sandy MacGregor had on my life in past happy times and in the tragic ones. My first encounter with Sandy MacGregor was in a former national employment role I had with an insurance company, back in the early 1980s. Although my role involved the training of managers, I also wore another hat when called upon to do so – the evaluation of guest speakers, and marketing material for training purposes and for our managers to use in their roles.

It was here that I heard Sandy's story, but did not then realise that our lives would cross many more times during the following two decades. Sandy would become a confidant and good friend in the times of my darkest hours. He was marketing his method of meditation at the time, teaching a mind-mapping technique of mental persuasion over body and mind to reduce stress for executives whose habits, like mine at the time, were using booze and too many cigarettes as a way of relieving stress – certainly not a healthy alternative. Sandy had come across these relaxation methods by accident, and has devoted a major part of his life helping others with his unique techniques, putting his methodology into daily life through practice. Something had happened in the early 1980s, when his son, Andrew, who had suffered from asthma for the majority of his seventeen years, became very ill and was hospitalised and treated with cortisone. A former military man, Sandy took Andrew to another doctor who taught him a method of relaxation and stress-release during the asthma attacks. Andrew learnt to master his breathing difficulties by using the doctor's techniques, and recovered. Andrew was later in a major motor bike accident and his leg was broken so badly that the doctors wanted to amputate it. Determined to save his son's leg, Sandy again contacted the doctor who had taught Andrew his asthma relaxation and breathing techniques. Over time, and with much patience, Andrew beat the pain with the meditation methods and, like the asthma, his leg healed and he fully recovered.

Sandy was a graduate of Duntroon, the Royal Military College in Canberra, and is a Sydney University graduate in Civil Engineering. In the army, he built roads and bridges, and was a natural choice as Commanding Officer for engineers during the war in Vietnam. He was awarded the Military Cross for bravery in tunnel conflict, and also received a bravery award from the American military. In his own words, he was an analytical, logical, prove-it-to-me person who meticulously planned and carefully analysed facts rather than dreaming or acting on emotion or intuition.

However, the events that changed Andrew's life convinced Sandy to set about learning the doctor's meditation techniques. Over the next six months, he lost 22 kilograms of weight and amazed his doctor by reducing his blood pressure by 20 points. He now had proof of the power of the subconscious mind, devoured every book he could find on the subject and found himself on a new journey in life. It would prove to be the catalyst for saving his life, and the lives of many of us who are grateful to Sandy and his mind-mapping methods and the use of meditation in our daily lives.

Sandy's journey took a major turn on 23rd January, 1987, when three of his daughters and one of their friends were shotgun-murdered in the safety of their own home, where they lived with their mother. Sandy had remarried and had two children with his second wife. Despite his experience in leading men during the Vietnam War, he was totally unprepared for this event, in total shock and disbelief. An old friend from their military college days encouraged him to participate in some seminars to relieve his grief by talking about the event and his girls. He did not get the chance to bottle-up his emotions - which was the major cause of my own anxiety and depression after my son Peter's suicide in 2003.

Sandy returned to meditation to release the anger that raged within him towards the person who had killed his daughters. He questioned himself on his role as a father, and about the events that had changed his life. The negative questions of "Why me?" and "What have I done to deserve this?" were typical questions resulting in wrong answers which caused guilt. He eventually settled on positive thoughts such as, "I did the best that I could at the time" or "I accept what I have done and now I know I'll be better next time". He disciplined himself to meditate every day, initially for short sessions, building up to longer periods of thirty minutes and then an hour, sitting quietly in a room sifting through all sorts of questions and answers, dealing the with issues of anger, hate and revenge. He went on to write many books on the subject, spoke on radio and television and conducted many seminars on helping others use their inner strength.

I learnt Sandy's meditation techniques, attended live seminars on a couple of occasions and used his positive mind-mapping and goal-setting techniques after the suicide of my son. During live-in seminars, Sandy helped me deal with grief in a positive way. I will always be grateful to Sandy for being there for me in my darkest hours, and for just being my friend during uncertain times.

Sandy went on to forgive his daughters' murderer, and actually went to the gaol, confronting the young man responsible for the killings. He told me that he advised the murderer that he was forgiving the killer for himself and his own compassion – not what the killer may have expected. Such is the calibre of the man; in a true spiritual understanding of his own, he forgave the killer. The story of Sandy's life and his forgiveness was the subject of an Australian television programme a couple of years ago. These days, Sandy still runs annual live-in seminars to help those in need of setting new pathways for their lives. He also arranges and leads tours to Vietnam. Committed to the people of that country where he was instrumental in turning the Vietnam War to a peaceful solution, and in which he was decorated as a war hero for his engineering work and tunnel warfare."Go to your peaceful place." was the mantra Sandy MacGregor taught me.

As I trudged my weary path of destiny along The Camino Way I was reminded of words Christine had brought to my attention all those years ago; a devotion that we performed together on a daily basis. It was to read the thought for the day from a little book called "God Calling."

The readings in that little book were inspirations of two anonymous women living in England during some distant past, who claimed that their message was given to them by the Living Christ Himself. "And his gentle voice we hear, soft as the breath of evening, that checks each fault, that calms each fear, and speaks of heaven."

My skeptical mind does not now believe that the majority of these meditations were Christ-inspired, but I am confident that, in the spirit of those women, therein He dwelt. Recalling those daily reflections, the Christ of their guidance opened their eyes to many things which they and this generation very much still need to know. It was a habit that Christine and I in our then state of being needed and tried to live by. It was also Christine's habit to leave little notes around the flat that we shared, taken from "God Calling" and her own inspirations. I sometimes later wondered whether she herself may have been a living channel for me, from the Christ and those women who channeled the little book. The day was hot and my body was overheated and somewhat dehydrated as I took one more painful step towards my destination and the mythical symbol, the Sword of Discernment of my inner longing. The voices of Christ, of Christine, of the two women - all as one spirit uplifting - came to me in my intransigent state, as they had done in the past during my darkest hours. "I am fighting back now, because when I'm (Christ-) strong

(Doug) I save!" And then, "The ache of love…Seek My wonderful truths and you shall find…I command you to remember I have spoken…I have no rival claimants, and if men seek the babble of the world, then I withdraw." "Life has hurt you…only scarred lives can really save". The Way was becoming more difficult, but with painful persistence, I took another weary step forward towards my symbolic sword.

I had met Christine at one of Sandy MacGregor's meditation sessions and it was not long after that we embraced and moved-in to live together. It was fortuitous, really, as we both had great need for love and understanding of our buried pains and were drawn together like passing ships in the night. Christine became my trusted confidant, as she struggled with depression following a divorce and the recent loss of a grandchild in a tragic accident. I was unaware, at that time, of the approaching storm that was to invade and devastate every fibre of my existence. I was, I thought, strong in mind, body and spirit and could overcome any difficulties. Despite still fighting a divorce settlement, having lost a son and a good friend through suicides, struggling to keep my business interests afloat and placing my mother into full-time care, I believed I was invincible. Christine proved to be the catalyst for a turning-point in my life. I was unaware of her depression for some time and our feelings for each other seemed to quell any negative emotions that persisted under the surface for me.

Christine seemed to be the answer to my prayers, as did my continual daily drinking to excess. As fate would have it, Christine recovered from her depression as I slipped into mine. It happened during a night out, when I became too drunk to drive home. As a passenger, while Christine drove, a mental flash of lightning-like stress-filled emotion exploded in my brain and I started screaming. All of the buried pain that had occurred over the years came bubbling to the surface in one devilish cauldron. After a time, I calmed down and Christine tucked me into bed, but not before I phoned a police chief I knew, who believed in the power of prayer, and we prayed together. When I awoke the next morning, Christine nursed and cared for me, and did so for the next six months, with love and words of comfort. She finally encouraged me to seek professional help, and I was treated with a course of anti-depressants. I met with so many well-meaning medical people, but nothing seemed to relieve the depression and deep-seated pain I was experiencing.

A note from Christine came to mind: "Doug, you need a grief counsellor to help with your suicidal thoughts, loss of control, anger and despair, to deal with the many losses through life, including (that of) your son Peter. You will help your family best by helping yourself. Don't dump on other people, but do write a daily journal, meditate, pray and exercise. Retire for now and take the weights of yourself financially. Don't let people dump on you. I can help you with these thoughts because I have been there to some extent but I can't help you to recover, you MUST SEEK professional help. You MUST go through the process of grief and recovery. Then you will be as strong as never before." And then, "Christ is there. All the angels are waiting to help you through this crisis. Call on them to help you through this crisis. Call on them for aid; demand their assistance through your dark night of the soul". When I was well enough, Christine encouraged me to clear myself of all excess material possessions, pack-up house and move to the country; doing so also provided an opportunity to be close to my mother during her failing health, who did not have too long to live.

We said our goodbye over coffee in a local café and I moved up north to a beach village to nurse myself back to health and spend some time with my mother. She was now requiring full-time nursing so I became a volunteer, working in the nursing home one day a week. During my days outside of this one-day devotion to others, I walked the beach, wrote my feelings down in poetic form and completed a book of poems. To ease my isolation I joined a group of men who met one night each week to express their inner feelings of conflict and to learn how to manage their anger. I also joined a bush-walking group and relished my Sunday walks with them. Other than these activities, I isolated, meditated, ate healthy food and gave-up drinking the hard stuff.

As I walked The Camino Way, contemplating my time with Christine, I came across a large rock in a peaceful place, near the top of a mountain range. Someone had painted, in white paint, "Chris". The road to Santiago is always full of mystery and coincidences, and I heard a voice within once again, a message from Christine: "You are building up an unshakable faith. Be furnishing the quiet places of your soul now. Fill it all with all that is harmonious and good, beautiful and enduring. Home builds in the spirit now and the waiting will be well spent". Christine was, for me, a guide and a guardian angel in my greatest hour of need. She showed me so much love and understanding as I slowly found myself letting-go of my ego. There was a long road ahead for me – and still a long road to Santiago. I was slowly losing the delusion of a Sword of Discernment, but felt I should follow my imagination and trust in the slow work of God as I walked the now painful route to Santiago. Christine had been my spiritual guide of belief in the past, and now it was an ancient pathway that I was drawn too, and more words from her pen came to mind. She had written so many inspiring notes to me on lesson to be learnt in my them suffering. I reached into my back pack and found the old note book were I had jotted down the ones that resonated most to me at the time.

"Pay attention to the thought and ideas that come to you. These thoughts are answers to your prayers for guidance. be mindful of the doors that are opening and shutting, walk through the doors that open and learn from the doors that shut, your prayers are being answered… ."

"Don't try to force open the doors that appear closed to you. Instead, ask for guidance, and see if the doors are closed because of negative expectations, or it's simply a sign of timing."

"Take care of your physical body, eat healthy foods, exercise regularly and avoid toxins. Your body will emanate harmony and if you follow the guidance you will feel terrific…increased energy and happiness is your reward."

"…Take steps right now to create time for relaxation. Don't allow yourself to be swayed on important issues."

"When you are ready, new blessings will come to you in life."

"It's important to express your feelings, the more you release, the more free you will feel."

"Be careful of self-destructive tendencies, which come as misguided guilt. Help is there whenever you need it. Your desired outcome will come in the near future. Yes, you will receive your wish. Patience and positive thinking is what you need."

It was inevitable that the events surrounding me and my life would result in my falling into a hell which - to a great degree – was of my own making. The tragic events that engulfed me had come to a head with the ensuing depression and Christine's nursing and my subsequent return to nature. Once I thought I had recovered, I returned to drinking again. Whilst I did not drink during my month's excursion to the country to recover from the depression, I soon enough returned to alcohol when I felt I had fully recovered from the dark night of the soul. Alcohol had become my best friend in the past and, for a time I had believed that without it, and the numbing of my feelings it provided, I would not have survived. The daily drinking, and the artificial stimulation it brought, had reached a crisis point when I crossed the thin red line with my screaming episode. Fear of following in my father's footsteps had kept me sober for six months while I was depressed, but the disease of alcoholism is both cunning and baffling, and I returned to the drink. I had run short of money, and on my return to Sydney managed to find contract work in my old field, Business Development. My apparent return to a well-worn cyclical path of work, drink and play was once again in motion. Once more I began to binge-drink and once more descended into the well of depression. So, in my newly depressed state, I booked myself into rehabilitation, as I was quite exhausted and needed time-out to focus on my recovery. As fate would have it, I was placed in a room next to a retired psychiatrist and our daily conversations resulted in me taking notes of his pearls of wisdom. He, too, was an alcoholic and, although I did not know at the time, he was quoting wisdom from the alcoholic's bible, The Big Book. After a month, I had recovered sufficiently to return to work. Before I left the rehabilitation centre I visited with my new-found doctor friend to wish him well in his recovery. The good doctor suggested that I attend AA and let what happened there wash over me. Up until this time, I did not believe I was an alcoholic but, having nothing better to do, I decided to attend an ID meeting, commonly known as a drunk-along. It was during this meeting that I met a man who would have a profound influence on my sobriety. The intention is that when a person is invited to speak, he or she will relate what it was like when they drank, what changed and what it was like now. The alcoholic invited to speak that night was Norm. I do not remember much of what he said that night, but having heard him many times since, I believe it was probably his usual opening remarks: "Hullo. I'm Norm and I am an alcoholic. I had my last drink on the 18th of November, 1982. I phoned AA in desperation, seeking help, and the person on the other end of the line said, 'Do you have a drinking problem, son?' and I answered, 'I might have.'" Something he said that night, in his usual insightful way, triggered my realization that I was indeed an alcoholic. Although I remember little of what was said that night by Norm or by any other speaker, I only know that during Norm's "share" I had a clear vision in my mind of a pattern of drinking over a lifetime that had caused much trouble and strife in my life and the lives of my family members. The enlightenment didn't end there, as I also recognised the same pattern in my father, his twin brother and almost all of his male siblings. Alcoholism killed my Dad, and likewise killed his relationship with my mother. I resolved to stop drinking from that time onward, and have managed to do so for the past seven years. This of course has not been without the support of Norm and others of my AA family. Norm, in particular, has chastised me, encouraged me to deflate my ego, instructed me in the ways of AA, and has always been there during my early bouts of depressive darkness.

Sometimes, in desperation, I would phone him in the middle of the night, interrupting his space with what must have been inopportune timing. I have always gained something positive from his sharing at AA meetings, especially during topic meetings, which are more to my liking now that I have been sober for some time. He has a distinct ability to produce one-liners that resonate with my heart and head. For example, when talking on the subject of God and a power greater than one's self, Norm refers to God as "Not Norm", or "GOD", an acronym of "good orderly direction". The classics from him that I like are: "I used to be annoyed because God got the job before me," and, when talking about the disease of alcoholism, "When I was born, they should have stamped my bottom 'Warning. Do not feed alcohol'".

Norm enticed me with many books, CD recordings about AA, DVDs and music. He seemed to know when I needed to hear the words of a particular song, view a film or read a book beneficial to my sobriety. I suspect he went out of his way to buy or record ideas just to improve my education about AA's twelve-step program. It is still a constant habit of mine to meet with Norm on a weekly basis for coffee and a chat, as he has a vast knowledge of the ways of the world and, in particular, the history of AA, tips for sobriety and the handing-over to whomever or whatever is running this thing we call life. The proof of any information one receives in truth is a gift. These days I like to know the facts, but still enjoy the fiction of using my imagination. However, when it comes to the matter of my sobriety and what I need to do, a day at a time, to remain sober, I still draw on Norm's wisdom. After all, he has been sober since 1982, and that fact alone is sufficient reason to follow his sound advice about the AA's twelve steps.

****

The Way from Santo Domingo to Belorado to San Juan de Ortega.

The moments turned into hours and the hours into days, my body's and mindset's determination to reach Santiago and find an outward symbol of the Sword of Discernment which I carried within keeping me focused every step of The Way. I had walked mainly alone for the past four days, but on the journey there was always a friendly face, a smile and a friendly greeting. These encounters with fellow pilgrims in the many villages between Santo Domingo and Belorado and beyond, towards my next goal, Ages, made the journey a little less of a task. On reaching Ages, there would still be 518 kilometres to Santiago.

My melancholy mood and thoughts of the dead were now replaced by a new focus, that of the living. I thought of Felix, the young American with whom I had sat and exchanged some softly-spoken kind words. To all appearance and purpose, he was a scary mother, with two rings in his nostrils, a number in his lips and ears and who knows how many tattoos on his head, arms and body. It is said that you should never judge a book by its cover, and this was certainly true of Felix. He had escaped from New York City for a break from the street kids whom, as a psychologist of the street, he did his best to help. As I left Felix sitting under a sidewalk awning escaping the heat of the sun, other memories floated back to me. My thoughts went to the Dutch kids with whom I'd had a sing-along on the track some hours previously; Martin, Elizabeth and Marie, each with their own story of why they were doing The Camino. I reconsidered my time with the Canadian school teachers, Julie and Nicole, who encouraged me to return to an evening Mass celebration with them. Mass was something I had not celebrated for more than two decades.

I was still having phone-charge problems, and borrowed a charger plug from Cynthia, a mid-thirties New Zealand woman, who preferred to sleep out alone on the tracks in preference to staying in albergues. I guess she needed the time to herself, rather than being in the often crowded albergues. Cynthia did not carry a tent or protective clothing and, except for her sleeping-bag and a small amount of clothing, lived lightly on the lam. She reminded me of the flower people, the Hippies of some long and distant past. Her partner, aged thirty-three, had died of a heroin overdose, and she told me that she, too, had been hooked for a long time but had quit five years earlier – possibly around the time of her partner's death, I assumed, although I did not question her any further about her past. She was now a spiritualist, and showed me some of her iPhone shots of her spiritual drawings, evidence that she did have considerable artistic talent. I could see a great artistic brilliance, but that could not compare with the illumination of her gentle nature. I promised to return her phone-charger plug somewhere along the track, but we did not set a time or place to meet. This was typical of The Camino; the trust between people I met and the kindness we're extraordinary along The Way.

The day's journey from Belorado to the monastery of San Juan de Ortega was some 25 km. I was aiming to reach Ages, a mere 3 km further along the track, but my blistered feet felt as if someone was driving nails through them, and my swollen ankles made it difficult to walk at a fast pace. So, I just took it all a little slower and lessened my focus on Ages as the day's goal. It was a lovely day for walking, mostly over earthen paths passing through frequent villages. The trail crossed the remote Oca hills, infamous as a dangerous route since Medieval times because thieves and rogues had been everywhere - a vast contrast to my experience to that point on The Way, especially on this part of the route to Santiago.

Legend credits San Juan de Ortega, the disciple of San Domingo, with clearing the pathway through the dense undergrowth in the thick oak and pine forests. I often took breaks and rested under a tree out of the heat, thankful to San Juan for his efforts, and for the company of Raimon, the funny man who frequently stopped to smell flowers. He smelled flowers, picked leaves from trees or studied the undergrowth. No matter how far I fell behind him, I always managed to catch-up, even despite my slow pace on this day. He stayed a little longer to study the flowers at our last rest stop before San Juan de Ortega. I left him on the track, where he was excited about the fact that he had actually found a four-leaf clover. We did catch-up a day or two later, in Burgos, and enjoyed a cool drink together. On a side road, I walked past a monument to the thirty-three men who had been taken to this location and shot, as traitors, by General Franco during the Spanish revolution. The walk to this spot was arduous, as it was long and dusty and in the open, although close to a forest on both sides of the track. I escaped the heat, to a spot under a tree and, seated not far from the monument, contemplated the words on the stone which, roughly translated, read, "It is not for what they died, but how they died."

The track from the monument to San Juan de Ortega was 8.6 km of pain for me, eased somewhat about 1 km from the village by a small stream flowing under a walkway where I soaked my feet and bathed and treated my blistered feet for a time. This was life-saving water, and the treatment became a ritual for me, all along The Way to Santiago. I even took the liberty of soaking my feet in water draining from paddocks, or in storm-water canals. This later proved to be a grave error, as I developed a skin condition on my feet and legs which took some time to cure on my return to Australia. However, on my Camino, it was a God-sent relief from the heat of the Spanish summer.

CHAPTER 8.

PILGRIM'S TRAMP

The sight of the San Juan de Ortega monastery was a welcome one. The whole area consisted of a monastery which doubled as an albergue, attached to an L-shaped chapel where the body of San Domingo's disciple, San Juan, lay in an exposed tomb. Nearby stood the only other building, a café, also an extension of the monastery. I quickly showered and changed into fresh clothing and put sandals on my poor wounded feet. I enjoyed a meal with some Italian bike riders then adjourned to a stretch of grass opposite the monastery, where I was surprised to find Cynthia getting ready to camp for the night. We spoke very briefly while she prepared her evening meal. I left her, promising to return to give her the charger pug she had lent me. Once again I was surprised by the presence of the two Canadian school teachers in the dormitory. They invited me to join them at the Mass which was about to start in the monastery. Although the Mass was in Spanish, I understood the sacred ceremony, having been educated in the Latin Mass as a child, and the Spanish didn't seem to differ much from the Latin I remembered from so many years before. After the Mass we adjourned to a side altar where the body of the Saint is interred, and the priest read the Pilgrim's Blessing and the Pilgrim's Prayer to St. James. It was all very moving, and a timely reminder of the purpose of my journey on The Camino I went back to the dormitory and recharged my phone before returning the charger plug to Cynthia at about 10:00 pm. I said a goodnight and "Buen Camino" to the young woman who seemed to be lost in another world. It was to be the last time I would encounter her on my Camino. She was still seeking answers in a logical way and I hoped and trusted she continued with her Camino to Santiago.

Monastery of Saint Juan de Ortega -Pilgrim's Blessing (English translation)

"Oh God, you gifted your servant Abraham of the city of Ur of the Chaldeans, safety in all his pilgrimages, and you were the guide of the Jewish people through the desert. Please, through the intercession of San Juan de Ortega, with whose tomb we are, to save the children of yours who, for the love of your name make The Camino de Santiago! I ask for them on the road companionship, guide at the crossroads, breath in fatigue, defence in danger, shelter along the way, gentle breeze in heat, protection before the cold light in the darkness, consolation in disappointment and firmness in purpose, so that with your guidance they arrive unharmed at the end of their pilgrimage, and enriched thanksgiving and virtues, return them safely to their homes full or perennial joy. We ask this through Christ the Lord. AMEN."

"May the Lord, through San Juan de Ortega, direct your steps and be favourable in inseparable companionship along the way. AMEN."

"May the Holy Virgin Mary dispense her maternal protection, defend the dangers of soul and body, and under the mantle of Mother may you deserve to arrive safely at the end of your pilgrimage. AMEN"

"May San Juan de Ortega accompany you along the way and spare you from opposition and danger….and may the blessings of Almighty God,

Father, Son and Holy Spirit descend upon you. AMEN" "While walking your life's path you're never alone for long on the path Santa Maria goes. Come with us to walk, Santa Maria come. Come with us to walk. Santa Maria come."

"IN THE NAME OF JESUS, WHO IS THE WAY, THE TRUTH AND THE LIFE, GO IN PEACE AND SAN JUAN DE ORTEGA GOES WITH YOU.

Pilgrim's Blessing

When the Son of Man comes in His glory with all of His angels, He will sit on His royal throne. The people of all nations will be brought before Him, and He will separate them, as shepherds separate their sheep from their goats. He will place the sheep on His right and the goats on His left.

Then the King will say to those on His right, "My father has blessed you! Come and receive the kingdom that was prepared for you before the world was created. Because when I was hungry, you gave me something to eat, and when I was thirsty, you gave me something to drink. When I was a pilgrim, you welcomed me, and when I was naked, you gave me clothes to wear. When I was sick, you took care of me, and when I was in jail, you visited me."

Then the ones who blessed the Lord will ask, "When did we give you something to eat or drink? When did we welcome you as a pilgrim or give you clothes to wear or visit you while you were sick or in jail?" The King will answer, "Whenever you did it for any of my smaller brothers, you did it for Me."

And these will have eternal life.

Brother John Of The Order Of Mother Theresa

One of my daily rituals at my days' end destination was to visit the local church for a short rest before venturing into the village to find an albergue for the night. The churches I visited were usually very small, seating between fifty and one hundred people and most of them venerated a local saint or the Virgin Mary. The exception to the rule was when I arrived at the monastery of San Juan de Ortega, when I first showered then made my way to a café before attending a Mass for pilgrims and the Pilgrim's Blessing. I found these visits to churches, monasteries, cloisters and chapels to be welcome oases at the end of each daily journey along The Way, and a good means of escaping the heat. They were always pleasantly cool inside because of the high exposed-beam ceilings and plastered walls that were the order of the day in every holy place I ventured into. The influence of the Medieval kingdom of Narvella in The Pyrenees; The Romanesque architectural styles of the Iberian Peninsula; the Moors, who destroyed and rebuilt; the Spanish themselves in their devotion to Saint James – all were in evidence in every historic building in northern Spain. For me, in the little chapels and churches along The Camino, all these influences were evident.

Exploring the fine and simple architecture of these places of worship, while following my habit of removing my boots when seated in a meditative state on a pew, always fascinated me. I was the only pilgrim in most of these places, except for a monk who seemed always to be in the same place ahead of me on the journey. It puzzled me that he beat me to a village every day, no matter how early I commenced my walking. He was a tall man of, I suspect, forty years of age, with grey hair before his time. He resembled Michelangelo's David, with a serious facial expression like the statue, and I reckoned women would swoon over him. Whenever I encountered him, he was dressed in a clean white habit, a crucifix on a cord hanging over his chest with a large photo of Mother Theresa of Calcutta on his habit behind it. I noted that he did not wear boots, but sandals, which I guessed was a tradition of the Order to which he belonged. He was always kneeling in prayer, head bowed and looking neither left nor right when I entered a chapel, and continued in prayer as I left. I also noted that he was at the chapel and the Mass, but was still praying at the main altar when I attended the Pilgrim's Prayer and Blessing ceremonies. I was woken at 3:00 am in the monastery dormitory by the noise of the Italian bike riders as they packed their gear for the day's ride. Torches and headlamps flashed across my eyes repeatedly as they, in haste, prepared themselves to start their ride in the dark, before the heat of the day made their journey difficult. I figured the ride in the dark would be less hazardous for them, as not only did they have lamps on their helmets, but also on the bikes themselves. Their noise and light show we're a welcome relief, as I had been having a dark drinking dream before they woke me. These nightmares often occurred since giving-up drinking alcohol seven years earlier. This dream was in sharp contrast with the dream of the previous night – that of a beautiful maiden. I thought it strange my dream had not been of a Sword of Discernment, as my dreams on The Camino often were. Perhaps it was because I was sleeping in a monastery, or because of the influence of the Pilgrim's Prayer at the tomb of St. Juan de Ortega in the adjacent chapel. Then why the fair maiden and the drinking dreams? I never did get a proper night's sleep on The Camino. If it was not someone talking in their sleep, snoring or farting in their sleeping-bag, it was the Italian bike riders flashing lights and whispering in the dark, quite oblivious to the sleeping throng in their nearby beds.

The village of Ages was only about 3 km from the monastery, and it was far too early to have breakfast; the next village after Ages was 8 km further on, so I decided that would be a good goal to aim for to partake of my usual ritual breakfast. So I quickly dressed, being careful not to make a noise, as things were now quiet after the Italians' departure. Once my eyes adjusted to the dark outside, I could make out the shadowed silhouette of the chapel behind me, and readied my walking poles for the task ahead. It had not occurred to me, the evening prior, to check for the Camino shell or yellow-arrowed directions to determine which way to take in the darkness. I realised that my head lamp and small hand torch were in the middle of my backpack and would be difficult to find in the darkness. I stood for a moment to consider my options, whether to go back to bed until there was enough light to see or to find the light in the monastery's registry office and find my head lamp and torch - or maybe just to hand over to whoever is running this show. My dilemma was solved in an instant when, out of the darkness, a white robe appeared like a ghost in the night. It was the monk I always saw kneeling in prayer whenever I entered a chapel or church. The fact that his daily journeys began when the majority of pilgrims were either still asleep or contemplating the coming day in the comfort of their beds was also the reason he was always ahead of me, even on days when I walked fast. He quickly moved along the track ahead of me and appeared to know the exact way to traverse the darkness. The white robe was a beacon of light for me, so I quickly followed in his footsteps. Although I could now see the pathway beneath my feet, the monk's robe gave me added assurance.

I wasn't sure for how long I could keep-up with his pace, as he was so athletic and moved very quickly in the dark. I had not followed him for more than five minutes when he suddenly took a left turn onto another track; I followed in haste as he quickened his pace. No more than one hundred metres along the path he suddenly stopped, about ten metres in front of me. I, too, stopped and waited for his next move as he raised his habit, turned his head towards me while facing his body away, and said, in English but with a Hungarian accent, "I am just taking a piss."

He identified himself as Brother John of the Order of Mother Theresa. This was his sixth Camino, and he did it in the manner of the early Camino de Santiago pilgrims. He had completed each previous Camino without carrying any food, water or money. He apparently asked for food from fellow pilgrims, who shared with him during the day – a custom of The Camino. In the evening, he approached restaurant owners for food. Sometimes they refused, but he overcame this by waiting until the owner had left the kitchen and returned to approach the cook, who, in the absence of the owner, gladly gave him food.

Being The Camino, sharing both food and clothing is commonplace among pilgrims, and water is never an issue as it's always in plentiful supply at the towns' and villages' central-square fountains. Brother John's accommodation was usually in a monastery or albergue, where there was a request to place a coin in the donation box if one could afford it. Brother John picked me as an Australian and asked where I lived. I told him Sydney, and he mentioned the beauty of our harbour, the bridge and the Opera House. He had worked with some street kids and drug addicts in Kings Cross, stating that it was "a bad place".

This was to be his last Camino, as he planned to go back to Hungary for a year to teach at the Budapest University before returning to the road to assist youth in the streets and the poor. After some minutes together, he said he had to go on to pray and quickly increased his pace, leaving me to walk this pathway to Santiago by instinct. We met later in the day at an albergue in Burgos City. He gave me a prayer card with the Sacred Heart of Jesus on one side and a prayer in Hungarian on the reverse. He left me with a farewell: "Jesus is watching you and looking after you, Doug." I kept the prayer card but still have no idea what the prayer in Hungarian says.

The Missionary of Charity is a Roman Catholic religious order established by Mother Theresa in 1950. Members take a vow of chastity, poverty, obedience, and a fourth vow, to give "… wholehearted free service to the poorest of the poor." In 1963, contemplative and active branches were founded. The Brother priesthood was founded by an Australian Jesuit who became known as Brother Andrew. These missionaries care for refugees, ex-prostitutes, the mentally-ill, sick and abandoned children, lepers and people with AIDS. They operate schools, educate street children and provide soup kitchens and many other services, without charge, for people irrespective of their religion or social status. As with the Sisters, the Priests, Brothers, lay Catholics and non-Catholics constituting Mother Theresa's co-workers live a simple life without television, radio or items of convenience, and neither drink alcohol nor smoke, nor beg for food. The influence of this order of Sisters and Brothers of The Order of Mother Theresa is a worldwide way of life for many.

On the Road to Santiago

There's a story that the Christ man told,
of a pilgrim on his way
from Jerusalem to Jericho
on that fate-filled day.

Fortune wasn't smiling
when he came across some thieves;
they robbed him and they stabbed him,
left him there to bleed.

Now it happened that along that road
a priest was passing near;
he saw the young man lying there
but he passed him by.

Then came a lawyer of business mind
who had more than he could spend;
he likewise ignored the man
and on the road he went.

Then came a man both strong and kind
who put him on his back,
carried him to a nearby inn
just a little way down the track.

He shared with him some of his food,
left money for his keep
and told the hotel owner
get him well, I'll pay upkeep.

The man we call a Samaritan,
it's the name of those of kind,
who put others before themselves,
help the poor, the drunk, the blind.

Now youth today walk on The Way
to discover their own soul,
whilst those of us towards our end,
we're letting-go our load.

Suffice to say along The Way
the poor and lame just beg,
whilst pilgrims on The Camino
see naught but what's ahead.

Santiago travellers,
travelling The Camino Way,
doing their own thing,
determined to be free.

There's a man walks The Camino,
he claims no earthly goods,
lives on love for his fellow man,
carries his own cross.

The poor are slowly starving
as they hold out their beggar tins.
The unemployed cry out for help
to find a job for them.

The symbol of The Camino
is but a scallop shell;
the many road maps on its back,
many tales to tell.

Santiago travellers
doing their own thing,
walking The Camino Way,
determined to be free.

The earthen path through the Oca hills led me to San Juan de Ortega monastery and my encounter with Brother John of The Order of Mother Theresa. He had long gone ahead of me and in the dawning light I could see the village of Ages, across the remote landscape, getting ever closer. I had travelled some four kilometres, and looked forward to an early breakfast – my usual orange juice, coffee and croissant. To the south, a small detour would take me to the local church and a small bridge, attributed to San Juan de Ortega, across the Rio Vena, but I thought it was far too early to take in the sights, and all I wanted was food. As fate would have it, no café was open so I resolved to walk on to Atapuerca, another 2.5 kilometres, which I calculated would take me about thirty minutes, reassured by knowing breakfast was not far away. I had climbed a rocky pathway not long after Brother John had quickened his pace and left me in his dust. I wondered how he managed to walk this rough track in his sandals, as I was having difficulty in boots. My goal for the day was Burgos, some 23 kilometres away to the south.

CHAPTER 9.

THE DANCING QUEEN

I had planned to climb the Sierra Atapuerca, visit the prehistoric ruins, stroll along the Rio Arlanzon and take in the marvelous architecture of the Burgos Cathedral. My village-to-village guide book and topographic map showed the route to Burgos as quiet roads between quaint villages and peaceful dirt paths through pine forests, so I contented myself with the gentle pace of walking, despite the pain of my blistered feet. My mind drifted to my previous night's dreams, in the monastery albergue.

I had drifted into sleep with a visit in my dream from an angelic maiden whose beauty and figure were beyond compare. She had danced across my mind, casting a spell of mystery and longing, the likes of which I had never known. As I walked the trail to Atapuerca I wondered if she was some beauty who may have slept nearby in the albergue; if perhaps I had been half awake and had actually experienced a dancing maiden nearby albergue bunk in the dark. The dream had seemed so real, but I decided to put it out of my mind and to think about the nightmare that had visited me on my rude 3:00 am awakening when the Italians had flashed their lights while packing their bags for the day ahead.

The dream of my dancing queen had turned into a nightmare, not the first alcoholic dream I had experienced in the years since giving up the booze. I had heard many AA members share similar experiences after giving up their addiction. So, I contented myself with evaluating where I was in coming to terms with my sobriety, and thought about the AA's twelve steps. Steps one, two and three…Powerless over alcohol; woke up to a power greater than me; handing-over to that power"…oh yeah! That is the hard one - letting-go of the ego and trusting in an unknown God and handing-over all decisions, goals and visions for the future to a power greater in myth, belief or legend. It seemed a little crazy, although amazing, as every time I did just that, everything worked-out in my favour. Conversely, every time I got in the way, with my egocentric decisions, the way was always tough and stressful. Why the hell do I do that when the handing-over works so well for me?

I thought back to my recent weeks in Germany, at the beer-fest and the week of wedding celebrations I had attended in the Bavarian hills. Yes, I had been drinking non-alcoholic beer for more than a month now and it was beginning to become a habit - so refreshing, especially in the Spanish summer heat on my route to claim my Sword of Discernment in Santiago. Perhaps the previous night's dream of excessive drinking was a direct result of my social non-alcoholic binges, or maybe it was because I had not attended an AA meeting since leaving Australia weeks earlier. I resolved to get back to the meetings on my return, for an average of three meetings each week to share my addiction and my life's experiences and to listen to other alcoholics share their experiences, strengths and hopes. This decision somehow calmed me and kept me sober. I cast the thought of out of my mind as I sighted the café bar in Atapuerca nearby, and headed there for breakfast. After eating, I purchased another coffee and went to a table outside to sit in the early-morning sun and rest my still blistered feet. I gazed down the track behind me; to my amazement, the vision of pure beauty I had encountered in my dream the previous night was approaching the café, accompanied by a second stunning Spanish beauty. With joy, like a small boy, I handed her my coffee and invited them both to sit with me. At the café bar I ordered two more coffees, one for the second beauty and one for myself. Although the Spanish embodiment of my dream did not speak English, her companion did, so we introduced ourselves and talked of our Camino experiences. Juana, my vision of pure beauty, was quite reserved at first, but warmed to our conversation through her friend, Alexandra, who translated Spanish to English for me and acting as a go-between. We finished our coffee and agreed to walk together to Burgos, where this leg of the journey would end for them; they would return the next year to complete another leg. I did not ascertain where their journey had commenced this time, but they had been walking for a couple of weeks. It is common for European pilgrims to do a couple of weeks every year until they have completed the entire 800 km trek to Santiago. Some pilgrims take up to ten years to complete the walk, returning year after year until the task is done and the Compostela certificate is attained. It takes a madman like myself to attempt the whole thing in one go.

To be fair, those of us who live down-under have a long distance to travel to get to Spain, and the flights are expensive, so we like to make the most of it. At least that is what I told myself, despite the fact that I had an agenda: to release my stored-up burdens from my life's experiences and to search for a symbolic but imaginary Sword of Discernment. Perhaps, I considered, the symbol I sought was in the shape of my previous night's dream – the beauty who now walked beside me, as we headed along the track south to Burgos, like three amigos on The Way. We joked, laughed and danced, held hands, and sang our way south, in the heat of the Spanish summer's day. The constant pounding of our feet on the hard surface of the highway and byways of The Way played havoc with our blistered feet. The women were suffering just as much as I, and my Spanish beauty appeared to suffer even more. I noticed that she occasionally had tears in her eyes, and I wondered whether this was due to some past life pain that she was re-experiencing on this leg of The Camino, or because their mutual journey for this year was to end soon, in Burgos.

At the time, in the company of the two angels of the road, my journey seemed easier and my backpack felt lighter, although the constant needles of torture in my feet did not ease. Juana had talked to me through her companion, speaking of her loss of a husband after six years of marriage and the cancer that had almost taken the life of one of her two sons when he was a young boy. He had somehow beaten the disease and was now a fit and healthy young man. From the photo she showed me on her iPhone, I judged the boys to be in their mid-twenties and, although single, they were happy. Her husband had died some twenty-two years ago and she had raised the boys by herself. Our now mutual friend, Alexandra, helped me complete the picture of Juana's life. She had close family ties, loved dancing and listening to her favourite classical music – including Beethoven and The Three Tenors – which I also enjoyed in my quieter moments; but at heart I was still a child of rock 'n' roll and middle-of-the-road country music.

Juana, it seemed, loved to drive fast, out on the open roads, and her working routine, administering health products and advising women on health, took her on a daily 300 km round trip. Her husband had died many years ago while riding a motor bike, but that did not deter her from driving fast and letting her hair down. She loved to listen to music while driving between her home city of Valencia and the surrounding towns and villages. She was a medical professional, specializing in diet and exercise for middle-aged women; judging by her figure, she was a perfect specimen for her clientele to emulate.

It's quite amazing how people openly tell perfect strangers about their life, love, pain of loss, and sorrow while on The Camino. Juana was no exception, and I'm sure that if I had pried Alexandra for her story, she would have similarly responded. I recalled my journey to date and noted that I had shared, and cried over, the loss of my son Peter on a couple of occasions during this cathartic inward journey. This was nothing new on The Camino de Santiago, as pilgrims since Medieval times had taken the inward journey, shared their lives' woes, made sacrifices and let-go of their material and emotional burdens. However, right there and then I was more interested in enjoying the pleasure of the company of my fellow pilgrims, and resolved to not think too much about the past for the remainder of the day. We stopped for lunch in the quiet little town of Cardenuela de Riopico before continuing along peaceful paved roads through Orbaneja, about one kilometre away, where the road split. We had already walked some 14 km and during lunch another weary pilgrim had advised that we could leave the yellow markings along the well-worn highway to Burgos and, instead, take the unmarked, less-travelled road.

This alternate route crossed over the Rio Arlandzon and followed the river on a peaceful, shady dirt track that was easy to navigate despite being an unmarked route. I was in favour of taking this detour, but the diversion involved a longer walk into Burgos City, so I went along with my Spanish companions' decision and we followed the busy highway route, a distance of 13.5 km. This, as far as I was concerned, proved to be the wrong route, as there was no shade and the sun poured down on the hot pavement making every step unbearable. At one point, Juana stopped and quietly cried, but we encouraged her to go on despite the pain she was experiencing from her blisters and sore feet. I resolved to encourage the women to keep on tracking, and that took my mind off my own pain. The final 10 km were the most difficult, as we entered the city through the industrial area where there was no relief from the passing trucks and cars on this busy and noisy stretch of road. We were about 5 km from the city centre when my left ankle gave way, with a lot of pain, and my swollen feet made things even worse. I decided to say goodbye to the Spanish beauties who, like me, were in no mood for conversation by then and only wanted to find an albergue and rest.

I sat on the concrete at the edge of the road and ate the last piece of the fruit I had purchased in one of the villages along the route and watched the mirage of my day on the road – the two Spanish beauties – slowly fade into distance. I had only 500 mm of water left, but knew it was enough to see me through until I reached a bar or café on the city's outskirts. I entered a shopping strip on the poor side of the city, by the side of the busy highway. The shops were surrounded by blocks of residential apartments. I found my way to an electronics store to see if I could purchase a phone charger compatible with my iPhone. Although I did find a suitable charger plug in a small disposal store, I also spotted a yellow arrow on a building; that led me to the city centre and the cathedral, its inner sanctum a sharp contrast to the noisy and poor outer-city area from which I had emerged. The cathedral was the central feature of a magnificent ancient city filled with historic art and architecture, which I had read about in my travel guide.

Finding an albergue only a stone's throw from the cathedral in the heart of the city was not difficult, as the yellow arrows on buildings were always prominent. The albergue was a relatively new building, surrounded by a famous food court, the Spanish delights of which had won national food awards. I made my way to the busy register counter where many pilgrims were seeking accommodation for the night. I noted that the complex contained several floors, and was sure I would have a bed for the night. It was like a modern hotel and, after registration and the stamping of my pilgrim's passport, I took the lift to my designated room and bed on the third floor where I found, along a corridor a private dormitory containing eight bunks. Fate is fortune, as who should be occupying the first two bunks? None other than my fateful Spanish beauties, my companions of the road!

I had a shower and used the large bench area to clean and dress my blistered feet and secure a stretch bandage around my swollen ankle for support. Back in the dormitory, I was greeted by Juana, seated on her bunk and in great distress, having difficulty with her wounded feet. I sat next to her in silence and began to dress her blisters and massaged her feet with the sweet-smelling liniment I had purchased from a chemist's store a day or two before. She put her pretty head on my shoulder and cried like a child. Once both girls had recouped energy after a brief rest, they went off to dinner together. I declined their offer to join them, preferring instead to meet-up with some fellow pilgrims with whom I had walked during days past.

One of those pilgrims was Raimon, my crazy French friend of The Way. The others were a band of excited young people I had also encountered during previous days. We headed to a nearby bar and joined yet other pilgrims, exchanging stories of our individual Caminos. My mind still sensed the scent of a woman and my fingers still retained the odour of the liniment. Raimon must have sensed my distracted state of mind and seemed to grasp the essence of my thoughts and even of my desire to fulfill the mythical nonsense of my Sword of Discernment. The Spanish beauty loomed strongly in my mind, as a distraction from my journey and the real purpose of my Camino. As if attuned to my inner wondering, Raimon suddenly produced some blue balloons from his trouser pocket and inflated them, with laughter from those surrounding him. He looked at me with a smile, similar to his smile when he had found the four-leaf clover the previous day, and quickly fashioned a sword with a handle, much like my vision of the Sword of Discernment – except that it was blue, not red.

Perhaps it was his way of telling me to stick to my dream and my imagination and not become distracted again. He asked a passing pilgrim to take a photo of us together, with him holding the balloon-sword aloft. I closed my eyes and asked the God of Brother John of The Order of Mother

Theresa for guidance, in a meditative stance of respect for the young man. I thought for a moment that Raimon's balloon sword could just be a sign from God of my inner power, a sign from St. James – or that my Sword of Discernment was only a lot of hot air. My logical mind told me that it was just that – hot air – but I had great faith in my imagination and chose to hold-on to my goal for the time being. I left my companions early in the evening as they were settling into a drinking session, went off to investigate the inner city.

I had a brief walk around the shops and noticed a nice-looking outdoor restaurant with a covered balcony where I could shelter from the still hot evening sun. I found a seat with a good view of the street, ate an enjoyable meal and watched the passing parade of mainly Spanish families out for a stroll around the city's shops while waiting for the day to turn to dusk and the night to cool. After my meal I made my way back to the cathedral for a last look inside before returning to the albergue. The two Spanish beauties were asleep in their bunks and I decided to get an early night's sleep too. I read a little, from my hiking guide, looking for the route south out of the city, before realising that the yellow arrows I had found before venturing back to the albergue would be adequate to have me back on the pathway to my ultimate destination. So, I switched-off the bunk lamp – a luxury – and drifted into a deep dreamless sleep. I awoke early and decided to do some early-morning trekking before the heat of the day set in.

Passing the bed of my sleeping Spanish dream, I ruffled her hair; she turned over to face me and her outstretched hand squeezed mine. With a sleepy smile, she said, "Buen Camino", turned to her side and returned to slumber land. I thought of our previous day together on the road – our laughter, singing and hand-holding. It was true that my heart had been taken briefly by this dark beauty, but I knew that it was nothing but a passing fantasy. I wondered for a moment whether I should have taken the route to Burgos via the river, and not ventured on with the two women. I realised that if I had made the logical choice I would not now be suffering the hollow ache in my heart. My mind became distracted by the many wounds that I carried resulting from a broken heart, and I remembered the biblical story of Mary's visit to a synagogue, where an old prophet told her, "Thy own soul a sword shall pierce". I was in search of a Sword of Discernment, and here I was, in my imagination, with one additional notch in the dagger within my heart. Putting all thoughts out of my mind, I headed for the nearest café for my usual breakfast of freshly-squeezed orange juice, croissant and coffee before once again continuing on the road. There, I contemplated the confusion in my head and the feeling that seemed to be in my heart. "There is no fool like an old fool", I thought.

The Spanish beauty was nothing more than a temporary distraction of the mind on a hot August day on my Camino – a way of relieving the burden of my soul and of keeping my thoughts away from the pain in my feet and the ever-present weight of an unneeded backpack weight. Reality had dawned, as plainly as day follows night. I resolved then and there to not allow any more angels of the road distract me from the inner journey that I was coming to terms with.

We met each other in a dream
the night before I met you;
it was like some movie scene
as you flashed across my mind.

A vision of pure beauty,
you were a dancing queen
floating to some ancient rhythm…
then you faded away!

I shouted you a coffee
somewhere along the track;
you smiled and sipped it slowly…
placed your hand upon my lap.

So we walked along together,
smiled and laughed a lot,
sang our fair share of songs
to beat the blisters and our packs!

No, we did not talk the same words,
it was signs and symbols that
became a big attraction
as I straightened-up your hat!

We sometimes held each other's hands
with childlike fun at that;
danced ourselves along The Way…
the Santiago track!

We parted when in pain and sweat
I stopped to rest my feet,
drinking warm fresh water…
watched you walk on in the heat!

As fate would have it
we met again
later on that day;
you cried upon my shoulder…
said goodnight and went to sleep!

I woke early at the albergue
to start walking before the heat,
ruffled your grey-golden hair;
you held my hand and smiled
yourself back to sleep.

A day or two I came upon
a note in my backpack;
it was written in Spanish,
so I asked a guide to quote:

"Thanks for making me
a princess on a difficult day;
a kiss for you in friendship,
Buen Camino on your Way!"

Sometimes when I cannot sleep
I think of that fate-filled day,
hand-in-hand with the dancing queen;
was it real or just a mirage
on The Santiago Way?

Leaving the majestic city of Burgos, its Medieval grandeur and the promenade on the banks of the Duero and Arlanza Rivers, the pilgrim enters the Meseta, walking among immense crop fields, through small woods of holm oak and conifers to the Medieval stronghold of Hornillos del Camino. Then, another day of walking vastness of the Meseta before the gradual climb up to the plateau then descending to the valley of the River Bol and the pretty town of Castrojeriz; and its 9th-century hilltop castle. The final walk on the plain of the Burgos region leads to the highest point of the Meseta, Alto Mosterales. After crossing the Pisuera River, The Way enters the Palencia plains of Tierra de Compos, a land of fields and the Gothic architecture of its 14th-century church.

The Way then approaches Formats and the 18th-century Canal de Castilla. The scenic route at Poblacion de Campos follows the peaceful banks of the Ucieza River to Carrion de los Condes. The natural track then proceeds along the old Roman road, with its original paved surface, which was historically used by French pilgrims on their way to Santiago. The walk then passes through many little valleys, making the route more difficult, but then emerges into peaceful oak woods and cereal fields. Here the pilgrim crosses the Valderaduey River into the province of Leon, to the Medieval town of Sahagun, in the heart of the Meseta.

Negotiating the long and winding road through the maze of city streets out of the city Burgos would have been almost impossible if not for the yellow arrows pointing the way south. Although they deface the walls of ancient buildings in most cities, towns and villages on The Camino, the roughly-painted yellow arrows are regarded almost as sacred by the population and accepted by municipal councils because they are symbolic of The Camino. I shared a coffee break with a young Belgian pilgrim as we saluted the magnificent city of Burgos and its immeasurable architectural wealth and historic art – a place of myths and legends.

Like me, the young Belgian boy had seen enough of art and culture for a day, and we just wanted to regain the mystic sense of walking our respective paths, in our own space. We had a final laugh together as he noticed a pretty, South African girl passing by, wearing his favourite top. He had left it in the albergue when packing his knapsack, and remarked that it looked better on her than on him, so he let her walk on without any comment to her. Such is the charity of those of us on The Camino de Santiago pilgrimage, as the relevance of material possessions seems to pale into insignificance while walking the mystic madness.I had traded the urban city streets for the peaceful but monotonous landscape, and did not hire a car, ride a bus, bike it or ride a horse – preferring to lug my backpack. Many of us had started the journey on foot, with a mission to complete the journey in the traditional way, not relishing the option of any other mode of transport. The sound of distant ringing of church bells faded as I reached the city's outer limits; I knew for whom the bells tolled as I took each painful step on the peaceful Meseta. This was the path of the pilgrimage reportedly taken by the prophet Mohammed while in a meditative state as he prepared for a battle of the faiths – his mission being the desert awakening to a belief that God is One and Mohammed is His prophet.

CHAPTER 10.

PILGRIM'S PROGRESS

Like St. James, it is unlikely that Mohammed had ever set foot on Spanish soil, but the armies of his followers certainly did. And those of the Christian belief of a Christ who had lived seven hundred years earlier marched against and fought the Moors to regain the territory and The Way that I now walked upon – The Way of St. James, the apostle, preaching of a carpenter and His miracles.

The Christ, a carpenter's son, never spoke of himself as being a prophet, but was reported by his followers to be the son of God. The Christ never spoke of being God, but only of his Father in heaven, for he was speaking to simple people in sacrificial love. St. James reportedly preached on this ancient path of the kingdom of heaven within, as Jesus had once done, teaching of charity and simplicity; of faith without works being dead; of action speaking louder than words.

This was the pathway of the great king-warriors: the Frenchman, Charlemagne, the general who fought for territory and for peace; Napoleon and his troops; the peace of one destined for war; St. Francis of Assisi, the man of simplicity fighting an inner war in search of peace. This had been the pathway of pilgrimage for more than a thousand years – for pilgrims who walked for penance and pardon; peace and understanding; seeking guidance; letting-go of burdens; for vision; for companionship. This was also the pathway for modern-day pilgrims, and for this particular old pilgrim too, seeking a mythical Sword of Discernment and letting-go my burdens, with an imaginary goal to keep ever-present as I walked The Camino Way, across the great silence and peace of the Meseta.

The journey was occasionally broken by walks through fields of wheat, some of which was being harvested as I passed, leaving me ever so briefly with the sweet scent of hay in my nostrils, soon replaced by the dryness of the desert air. Here, with the grace of God within me, I would walk the next 31.4 km to my destination for the day, with the vision of an outer Sword of Discernment rising ahead of me like a misty mirage in the sun-lit haze.

I looked forward to soaking my feet in the San Bol fountain in which, legend has it, pilgrims who soak their feet will be cured of all foot pain. I also wanted to visit the ruins of the nearby 11th-century monastery of San Boadilla and relax in the adjacent luscious green yard; something that someone living in a city of parks and gardens in Australia would normally take for granted was now a luxury to look forward to. It would prove to be a long stage to walk this day, but my guide book mapped-out many small villages for intermediary stops for food and water.

Hontanas, my goal for the day, across the desert wasteland under the ever-fiery presence of the Spanish summer sun, was, for me, a bridge too far. However, I did make it to Hornillos del Camino, 11 km short of my day's objective. The constant pounding of my feet on the hot, dry, hard surface of The Way proved to be too much by late afternoon, so I decided to stay in what appeared to be the only albergue in the small village, to soak and treat my blistered feet. I was also looking forward to the local pilgrim's meal that I'd seen advertised on a rough tin sign by the roadside at the entrance of my home for the night. The spring fountain of San Bol was only 6 km away, and Hontanas another 5 km after that, so I thought that a day of feet-soaking followed by a leisurely walk south in the morning was a sound idea. It did prove to be a wise decision to stay at the albergue, and I enjoyed a single room and a three-course meal. The fresh salad, veal and the curd dessert, all washed down with a couple of alcoholic-free beers, followed by an early night to bed, were just what the doctor ordered.

I woke at 6:00 am to the sounds of other pilgrims in an adjoining room repacking their knapsacks for the day ahead. I washed, dressed and was on the road again at 6:20 am. I found the only café open at that time of day, and had a clone of my usual breakfast – this time, a preservative-filled pack of orange juice, a cellophane-wrapped croissant and instant coffee made with boiled water; I hoped that the milk was natural cow's milk. When there is nothing else that is wholesome to eat, beggars can't be choosers.

The early morning inner light of the café gave me the opportunity to once again dress my blistered feet. The morning was again hot and dry as I entered Hontanas and found a real breakfast of toast and coffee at the first café I came across. It had been too early and dark when I passed through San Bol to do the feet-soaking I had planned. I dispensed with the idea of taking a day off, and arrived in Hontanas in broad daylight.   This old man had crossed the desert wasteland and reached another oasis, an ancient village of numerous springs and abundant water. I had been warned about the dangerous wild wolves that hunted in packs around the village. They were said to lay hidden in the valley of a little river, so that one scarcely saw then until it was too late. Legend has it that they roamed around the village at night, attacking sheep and even humans. Because of that, in Hontanas my fellow pilgrims and I were advised that it was safest to cross the river and the desert in the middle of the day while sheep were guarded by non-ferocious dogs. I took all this with a grain of salt, as being another myth or legend, much like my Sword of Discernment. I was beginning to muse and laugh inwardly at the folklore. I was not afraid of dogs, even wild ones. And as for river crossings, well, I was born near a coastal river and the ocean, had swum where sharks were always a threat and had walked barefooted where red-bellied black snakes lay, and being bitten by poisonous ticks, spiders and bees was nothing new.

I had once stepped on a black snake curled-up asleep in the grass during the mating season. My boyhood mates and I had been hunting birds' nests in snake-infested swamps, searching for rare eggs for our prized coloured egg-shell collection. The snake had woken suddenly, disturbed by the pressure of my foot on its body, and darted out from behind me. It headed for a friend, following closely behind him, and we quickly departed the scene as the snake slid into the watery swamp before coming around to have another attempt at biting one of us. That was not the only encounter I'd had with snakes. Once, eating wild berries on a property with a group of boyhood mates, one of them called out, "Snake!", and everybody ran, except me. I just thought he was having a lend of us all. My mate's dad, whose poultry farm property we were on, advised me to stand perfectly still, and, looking down at my bare feet I saw the snake, no more than a centimetre or two from my toes, sliding towards me. I was really scared at the time and could not have moved even if I'd wanted to; my body was frozen to the spot.

The poultry farmer chased the snake with a whip, a hook and a stick; with the hook he caught it by the tail as it headed into a hole, then bashed the living daylights out of it until it was dead. Over one-and-a-half metres long, it was the largest snake I have ever encountered. The farmer, my friend's dad, showed no mercy as he killed that thing. He was obviously thinking about his livelihood, as snakes are known to kill fowls and eat the eggs. I thought at the time that it would have been easier to confront the snake than to take a hiding from my friend's father.

Many a time on my bush walks in Australia I came across snakes – some of the more poisonous variety and some not so dangerous. My last encounter was not long before walking The Camino; I was walking alone in the bush, near a river, thinking about the word "live", musing that if I wrote in on a piece of paper and held it up to a mirror, it would read "evil". No sooner had I manifested this thought that a large red-bellied black snake emerged in front of me from behind a large rock as I rounded it. I quickly got out of its way as it slid off the track and into the river. I resolved at that point to not think about evil or snakes ever again.

Of course, reality is a different story when one confronts the real deal. I still don't like snakes, but dislike them less than dangerous spiders, which don't seem to be a phobia of mine. However, my deep-seated fear of snakes possibly derives from being indoctrinated during childhood with the biblical stories of Adam and Eve, in which the snake is the devil's instrument of evil, tempting Adam with the apple from the tree of knowledge and power. This image, used by the religious teachers of my childhood years, became forever embedded in my subconscious mind.

While the Christian teaching that the snake tempted Adam to eat the forbidden fruit did leave an indelible message on my brain as a thing of evil, some ancients regarded the snake as a positive force. Images of snakes have been found in rock carvings dating back tens of thousands of years. A 70,000-year-old carving of a rock python is evidence that the San people of Botswana worshipped the python as a creator spirit. The indigenous Australians also show reverence for the great Rainbow Serpent, a giant snake that carved-out features of the land. My thoughts turned briefly to the beginning of my Camino and the first shell marker at the base of the Pyrenees, near St. Jean-Pied-de-Port, where a dead asp lay curled on the ground. Poisonous snakes, dangerous spiders, ticks, crocodiles, sharks and wild man-eating wolves, I considered, had no place in my mind, here on my Camino.

Continuing my journey, I dismissed all fears of the dangers in nature. The possibility of encountering a wild wolf was very unlikely, and I shrugged my shoulders at the thought that nature can be both cruel and kind. I did not see a sheep in this desert country, nor any wolves, which I guessed had died-out before the village's 14th-century protective walls began to crumble. I knew I had ample time to explore the area so, after breakfast I purchased some more band-aids and a jar of sweet-smelling ointment with illustrations of a Camino pilgrim and a shell-brand stamped on its lid. I applied the "ungento traditional mundi Camino" cream to my swollen ankle and blistered feet, once again dressed my wounds and put on a clean pair of socks. I assumed that the directions read something like, "traditional urgent treatment for the journey", noting that it contained petroleum jelly and Aloe Vera – with other ingredients written in Spanish which I could not understand. Tightly lacing my boots, I continued on my Camino.

This routine became a daily habit, and fitted in with the well-earned rests as I explored the countryside along The Way. I intended visiting the church of San Anton, where the remains of the 3rd-century hermit are kept. He is supposed to have cured a young girl of a disease known as St. Anthony's Fire, which caused a terrible burning sensation, loss of blood circulation and, eventually, gangrene. The 11th-century Order of St. Anthony developed a reputation for healing the disease, so, I figured that if by some miracle or past mysticism I could be cured of my blistered feet and swollen ankle, a visit was well worth a shot. The church had long been in ruin, so my hoped-for cure had to wait until another day. In truth, all I really needed was to rest my feet in cool water.

The trail continued along the paved road of the village, past the church ruins which featured a high archway across The Camino pathway. I followed a pleasant, quiet, shaded road to Castrojeriz, another 9 km further south. I got to thinking about the two Spanish women I had walked with on the road to Burgos. My day on the road with Juana had been something like Peter Pan chasing after Tinker Bell, who was always just a little out of reach, and her beauty always fascinated other lost boys on their journey to Never-Never Land. I regarded the quest for my Sword of Discernment as being analogous with the quest of Peter Pan and the lost boys. It had always been a hidden quest to follow some mission in life, and forces yet unknown to me had driven me through much pain, sorrow and regret to The Camino Way. I certainly did not need the distraction of a beautiful woman, knowing from bitter past experience that it would only bring pain and sorrow; it was far better to walk The Camino, cross deserts, streams, climb up hills and down dales, write some poetry, sing a song or two, keep a journal – rather than bring ultimate sorrow and pain to another human being.

Why was it that men always looked to the Tinker Bells for the fulfilment of their Godly quests? It was more than obvious that it was far better to engage in the warrior thing – of adventure and exploration – and save the womenfolk for the day when the boy became a real man of substance, a man who cares more for his woman than chasing a golden dream at the end of a rainbow. Alas, I had learnt this through bitter experience, but was still a boy at heart, and just knew that some of us never grow up despite being successful in the eyes of the world.

The hill proved to be especially steep after leaving the desert plain in the heat of a midday sun. The heavy backpack and nurtured but still-painful feet made my journey much slower than usual. As I walked ever upward, I was glad to have reinforced myself with the little food I had carried in my backpack. I was again reminded of an old bush-walking mate, Peter, back home in Australia, who had told me a story of striving ever onwards. Peter related a story to me during one of our more arduous mountain-climbing walks in The Snowy Mountains. The story had apparently been told by an American preacher ten years after the Columbia space-shuttle disaster, in which the seven astronauts on board had been killed when the shuttle disintegrated on reentry to the Earth's atmosphere. An enquiry into the accident prompted the then-President, George W. Bush, to retire the NASA space-shuttle fleet – although the space programme was renewed two years later with – of all people, the Russians.

The Reverend Dan Gullles, of the Smithville Church of Christ, related stories to his congregation, attempting to make sense of the death of the astronauts, and to encourage climbing into space again. He told of a mountain climber who fell to his death while climbing a dangerous peak. Friends later returned to the peak where he had fallen and erected a sign, which simply said, "He died climbing." When Peter related this story to me, we made a pact that we would never quit, no matter how slow or difficult the path forward was, or the pace of the journey. Our mutual decision was, at that time, that the epitaph engraved on our headstones would be, "HE DIED CLIMBING."

I made it to the top of the mountain, where there was a road-side stall set up with food and water for pilgrims. The enterprising Spanish trader had transported the supplies of food and water in an old wagon which was perched not far away on the other side of the mountain. Prices were not stated; there was only a simple cardboard sign with "Purchase by donation" in English on it. He probably got more money from pilgrims than he would have with fixed prices. Besides, he had a guaranteed market; after such a climb we pilgrims were definitely in need of food and water. The stall-keeper had erected umbrellas to shade pilgrims from the sun and had also provided bench seats for all to rest upon. I sat near, and struck-up a conversation with two pilgrims, Nino and his daughter, Lauren, whose goal was to film and interview people on The Camino, documenting the reasons why they were walking The Way.

The project was simple but, I thought, a great idea to later sell into the market. Nino was on his second Camino, accompanying his fourteen-year-old daughter on her first pilgrimage and film adventure. Lauren asked if she could interview me, saying that all I had to do was state my name, the country I came from and why I was doing The Camino. I agreed, saying, "Hi, I'm Doug, from Sydney, Australia. When I started The Camino, I had in mind to believe as I walk The Way that it is a journey of the spirit – the power within me – my spirit." They both seemed to like what I said and I gave them poetic licence to use it as they saw fit in the film.

The climb down the other side of the mountain was just as steep as the climb up; it dropped away sharply from the 200 metre level, then up again before running level, and then easing to another 800-metre drop to the valley floor below. The dirt track had no give and my right toe felt as if a devil with a pitchfork was poking at it with every pain-filled step. I struggled, with toes pressing to the front of my boots whenever there was a dip in the terrain. I became distracted by the enjoyment of being in the company of other pilgrims as we made our way together down the track. One such pilgrim was Christa, a mid-seventy-year-old retired German ballet-dancing teacher. She had given up teaching ballet a couple of years before walking The Camino, and had retired to help her husband on their farm, as he was very ill. He had died recently, so she was on The Camino in his memory and to overcome her sadness in losing him.

She still carried her business cards, and handed me one. It read, "Tanzapadagogin ballet teacher". I was amused by the inscription on the reverse side, "O Mensch, lerne tanzen sonst wissen die Engel in Himmel mit dir inches anzufangen"; roughly translated, it means, "Oh Lord. I learnt to dance so the angels in heaven know that they should not mess with me". Christa and other pilgrims had fallen behind me, so I walked on alone for the remaining 18 km to Boradilla de Camino and, as I entered the village, noted graffiti on a viaduct wall: "Escape to here is similar to hell. Turning from our roots we go into 2013, which is the best idea". The small hamlet resembled a scene from an American western movie; there was one dusty dirt street with two albergues, an eating-house with outdoor seating and another with an undercover verandah. I went to the two-storey municipal albergue and placed the donation for my accommodation in the charity box. The receptionist stamped my pilgrim's passport and I secured a bunk upstairs, with six other pilgrims and a balcony overlooking the film-set street below.

The surrounding plain and the strange place made me feel as if I had been cast back to The Wild West; I half expected two gunmen to emerge from a saloon as I watched from my lofty verandah. The movement of the locals, the pilgrims on the café's verandah partaking of food and drink almost made me feel as if I were in a dream. I noticed a large crowd of locals making their way to the building attached to the albergue at the other end of the street. Music rang out and singing began as I headed for a shower before changing once again into clean clothing and washing my sweat-laden clothes of the day. Refreshed, I ventured to the nearest café for pre-dinner drinks before going to the far-off diner for my evening meal. There, I was greeted by Christa, the German ballet teacher, and Jane, and English language teacher. While enjoying our evening meal we talked of our journey to Santiago, recounting our own personal reasons for walking The Way, and discussed many subjects including our mutual interests, cultures and the habits and customs of our countries of origin.

On return to my bunk, I had a brief conversation with an old Italian man whom I had met at the albergue in Burgos, he understanding some words of my English while I was able to interpret and understand some of his Italian – the rest we achieved by sign-language and making unusual sounds. My stay in the municipal Titas Albergue proved to be a God-send, as the other one, 500 metres away at the far end of the town's only street was and next to a crowd of local revelers who raged all night, celebrating the annual festival of the harvest. I managed to get some sleep despite the very loud noise, and and was grateful to be relatively far removed from it.

The music was still playing when I woke at 5:00 am; in fact it seemed to be even louder in the light of day that it had been during the night. Back in the street, I found that the eating-places didn't open until 9:00 am, so satisfied myself with some cheese, dry bread and a peach that I had been carrying for such an emergency. I drank a little water and refilled my water flasks from a nearby tap. I managed to catch-up with Jane, the English-language teacher, a young New Zealand girl and the old Italian. Because of the noise during the night, Christa had decided to stay behind to have some badly needed sleep. I did not envy her, as the music could still be heard for quite a distance after leaving the country film scene.

Jane was in deep conversation with the old Italian, who was telling her that the village we had left resembled the set of the movie "High Noon". Now I knew why it seemed so familiar to me. He attempted to sing the theme song – as sung by Frankie Lane - from the movie, which starred Garry Cooper and Grace Kelly. However, he could not remember the melody or the lyrics. I was able to recall and recreate the movie from beginning to end, and explained that it was my father's favourite film when I was growing up. I had learnt the words, and knew the melody of the song, "High Noon" and sang it to them in typical Frankie Lane style as walked along together. The song, the pilgrims I was walking with, the film and the countryside all seemed to be in unison as we went along. Jane was quite taken with the fact that I knew all the lyrics and could sing a melody without losing a beat. The old Italian hummed along in the background and appeared to be enjoying himself. The singing and ensuing conversation kept my mind from my inner pain and the devil that continued to pin-prick my big toes. It was a journey of 24.5 km to Carrion de los Condos and we all decided to take break at a café bar in Fromista, where I ate some more food, redressed my feet, ordered a second cup of coffee and waited for Christa. She had cried the night before about missing her husband and had considered abandoning her Camino to return home to Germany.

Wounded Love Heart

Now my heart beats to a drummer
that's not quite the same as the rest;
it's where I ling to be free,
attuned with the sound in my chest.

Listen to the rhythm of the heart beat,
the sound of a different drum,
not the beat of a heart for another
nor the weary heart wounded by love.

It won't be found in worldly values
where money's the ultimate quest;
not the beat of a heart in battle
where they pin a medal on your breast.

It may be found in tune with nature,
where man is at one with the plan,
climbing a rugged mountain range,
tilling and planting the land.

Sailing the blue of the ocean,
viewing the flight of a bird;
hearing the sound of a cicada
deep in the forested wood.

Catching fish for survival,
cooking it on one's own fire;
sleeping out in the open
watching the star-filled sky.

Seeing the universe at dawning,
plainly being in tune;
living the now when it's crowded,
being still in a room.

It's being in tune with one's senses,
the music you have in your heart,
conscious of each passing moment.
The wounded love heart's where you start.

Jane and the other pilgrims said their "Buen Camino" and walked on. I proceeded to write in my journal, as had become an obsession, having made a decision to write about the spiritual aspects of my Camino. I had not intended writing it for any other purposes than for my own mental release and thought process; a record of my physical and spiritual journey. It never occurred to me at the time that I would write a book of prose or a novel centred on The Camino de Santiago and my heart journey – much less an album of songs inspired by the chance meeting with a young German rock musician later on my Camino. I was distracted by a view of many solar windmills on a distant mountain as I made my way alone. Christa had not appeared, despite my long wait, and I wished her all the best in my mind and continued on. Seeing the windmills, I began to think of Don Quixote chasing after windmills.

My good friend, Kevin, had been the first kidney-transplant recipient in Australia in the nineteen-sixties. Although from Brisbane, he had no choice but to move to Sydney for the operation and subsequent dialysis treatment. We worked together for a time before he headed north again, and I lost contact with him. Kevin was quite artistic, and he summed me up quite well by carving a bronze plaque depicting me as Don Quixote astride his skinny horse, Rocinante, with a windmill in the background. Kevin had implanted the plaque into a timber background and decorated it in the Spanish style.

I had spent a lifetime, it seemed, tilting at windmills, lady loves, business interests and embarking on many quests, both mental and spiritual. The thought depressed me a little, as here I was, once again on another quest to find a symbolic representation of a mythical Sword of Discernment. I forced myself to lift my spirits and laugh at my foolishness and the notion of finding some silly sword awaiting me in Santiago at the end of my journey. Yes, it was true, I thought once more – there is no fool like an old fool, and gave that thought some worth by calling out, "Boys will always be boys". I never did discover what happened to Kevin, but he had made a brief visit with his wife and child when I was working in the New England ranges. The last I remember was a short conversation we had, when he phoned to let me know that his marriage had broken down and he was now divorced. I lost contact after that and thought little about him until my own misfortunes took hold a decade or more ago and I, too, got divorced. Maybe he died because of kidney failure; I made a promise to myself to investigate government records on my return to ascertain whether he was alive or dead.

A brief rest just outside the village of Castrojeriz was another necessary pause in the journey for me. I removed my boots and socks and soaked my fiery feet in a stream. A young man and his girlfriend sat down with me and copied my actions. Earlier in the day I had given him some of my magic Camino liniment which he had massaged into his feet. He said it had worked well for his swollen feet, and I had to admit that it had worked for me, too. I wondered what the Spanish ingredient was that provided the mixture's healing power; perhaps it was the presence of the ancient symbolic pilgrim on the lid with The Camino scallop shell in the background.

As we sat there talking, a feather floated down from the heavens above and landed at our feet. We three looked up into the blue, but there was no bird in flight to be seen. This was typical of many strange occurrences on The Camino, and there were to be many – even stranger – happenings to follow down the track. Here we were, three pilgrims, total strangers, enjoying a chat with feet in the stream by the path of The Way, and nature was calling, "Birds of a feather flock together". At least that's what I was reading from the experience.

I arrived at Castrojeriz early in the afternoon and calculated that I had walked for 21 km during the day. Considering the state of my feet and the many rest stops to treat them, I thought I had done well to get as far as I had. The next day was to be a 19 km walk to Boadilla del Camino, and normally would have been an easy day for me, but with a heavy backpack still weighing me down, and foot problems, a good rest before tackling the next leg of the journey made a lot of sense. The albergue inn-keeper did the usual passport-stamping, in this case, "Casa Rural El Veredero", and I went for a hot shower, followed by two soft-drinks and a packet of potato chips at the bar. Before heading out for dinner, I returned to my room for a twenty-minute nap, the proprietor's mother, who was eighty in the shade, volunteered to do my washing, for which I was happy to pay the asking price of three Euro.

After my nap I ventured out into the street, I noticed my washing hanging on an outdoor clothes-line and, as the evening was still very hot, figured it would be dry on my return. Making my way to the only café bar still open in the little village, I enjoyed another pilgrim's meal. The Spanish daily eating habit during summer is to have a light breakfast, mirroring my own taste for freshly-squeezed orange juice, a croissant and coffee. The midday corrida (lunch) is usually had between 2:00 and 4:00 pm and is typically a large meals consisting of many courses, usually starting with something light, like a salad, a sandwich or traditional tapas or soup. The second course could be fish, chicken or a meat dish, followed by a dessert of fruit, Spanish flan or a sweet pastry or cake. Wine and bread are supplied free with lunch and the evening meal. The Spanish usually eat dinner late in the summer evenings, between 9:00 and 11:00 pm. Traditionally, it's much smaller than the midday meal, and will consist of a salad, sandwich or a selection of tapas.

Everywhere in the towns and villages, and to some degree in the cities, meals are today-fresh and the wine and bread are usually locally produced. Spanish meal traditions are altered on The Camino, primarily to suit the pilgrims' eating habits and the opportunity to market a pilgrim meal deal in the evening. So the cena, the evening meal, becomes lunch for pilgrims on The Way, usually looking for something light to eat whilst walking the trail, and therefore preferring dinner to be the equivalent of the corrida, the Spanish lunch. The "menu peregrine", or "pilgrim's menu", is usually priced around nine Euro and is a great way the end the day and restore energy for the next day's trekking.

At 8:00 pm I was an hour early for the evening meal, and as the bar had Wi-Fi I hired a computer for an hour to contact friends back home and catch-up on a backlog of emails. Two of my old fellow rugby team members had sent a school rugby photo with the caption, "Which team is this?" I had a string of emails from some school buddies, advising of the death of some of the favourite boarding-school teachers of my youth. I assumed my fellow classmates of five decades or so were coming to realise, as I was, that we are of that vintage – in the afternoon of our lives. Recent deaths of our favourite teachers and fellow classmates and the realization of our fading youth were good reasons to make contact again.

Approaching the midnight of our living on this earth gave us another good reason to join social media, such as Facebook and Twitter, to maintain our contact before the deal is done. I made a mental note to attend the next reunion of the old brigade, whilst I still had life within me.

I enjoyed my evening meal, finishing with the local cheese and biscuits and a couple more "OO" SIN alcohol-free beers before retiring for the evening. The escape to my emails had helped a little to ease my sense of isolation, as I could find no-one in the village who spoke English. I had used symbolic sign language and the little Spanish that I understand seemed to work for me. However, I thought it was a shame that the proprietors of businesses, especially in the cafes and bars, do not speak any English; I'm sure that if they did, they would sell more produce and souvenirs than they did. Then again, I did feel that it was a little insulting on my part to assume they should change. After all, I was in their country, not my own, and here I was making a judgment on what I saw in villages along The Way, based on my own upbringing in Australia and our commercial way of life in a big city. The meals, I noted, were always fresh produce, probably locally-grown, and maybe they were making better profit margins than many city business owners do. So perhaps they not need to sell tourist souvenirs to make a living – as I with my money-making mind had assumed. It did not really matter much in the scheme of things, as a pilgrim on a letting-go mission, eating the best of foods at bargain prices. The priority was not commercial; it was primarily a sense of tradition of The Way that our Spanish hosts honoured. There was always a healthy respect for the pilgrim, the tradition of The Camino and the spiritual significance of the journey.

"Round like a spiral, like a wheel within a wheel'
never ending or beginning on an ever-spinning wheel,
like a snowdrop down a mountain, or a carnival balloon,
like a carousel that's turning running rings around the moon,
like a clock whose hands are sweeping past the minutes of its
face, and the world is like an apple whirling silently in space,
like the circles that you find in the windmills of your mind."

Lyric by Alan and Marilyn Bergman

I started walking the next morning at 7:30 am but stopped for breakfast at the café where I'd had my meal the previous evening. It appeared to be the only eating-house open day and night, and I had decided that the Spanish in this village café should try a little harder to learn English. On reflection, I was the tourist in this country, so it really was my obligation as a pilgrim to make more of an effort to understand their language. I settled for a banana, bread and water as my "Spanish breakfast", thanked the proprietor with something like, "Muchas gracias, amigo" and he gave me a big toothy smile. Once again I was on my Way, having made a little note in my journal on compassion and judgment.

It was 8:00 am, later than usual for to get moving along The Way. I had journeyed 24.5 km along the Canal de Castilla and followed the road less travelled, a route by the Rio Ucieza; a happy wandered, tramping the track from Villacazar to Carrion de los Condes. The heat on the road today took some getting used to, but I was enjoying meeting-up with fellow pilgrims en route and the time seemed to fly by, and I arrived in Carrion de los Condes in mid-afternoon. I made my customary visit to the local church, found a refugio – a hostel reserved specifically for pilgrims - for the night, showered, washed my day's clothing and headed back to the narthex of the church and joined the throng of young people singing in unison with the nuns of Carrion de los Condes. It was a true narthex, or vestibule – an area inside the church but separated by a screen from the nave, the "body" of the church. In modern times, narthex has come to mean the entry, or foyer, but originally it was an area used by those seeking penance for their wrong-doings, or by those being instructed into Christianity. These people were restricted to this entry area until their reconciliation or baptism into the faith. The simplicity of the Spanish Catholic churches I had visited displayed the influences of so many foreign powers dating back to Medieval times, having been torn-down and rebuilt so often. In some cases, decay had necessitated replacement, and the cost of rebuilding meant dispensing with some of the former architectural symbolism. Catholic vision traditionally assigns symbolic meaning to various parts of a church building – as it does to pretty much everything else in the world. The roof symbolises charity, which covers a multitude of sins; the floor symbolises the foundation of the faith and the humility of the poor; the columns represent the apostles, bishops and doctors; the vaulting represents the preachers who bear-up the dead weight of man's infirmity heavenwards; and the beams signify the champions of ecclesiastical right who defend it with a sword. The nave – the "body" – symbolises Noah's Ark and the Barque of St. Peter, outside of which no-one is saved.

The orientation of the church itself is to the east, towards the Heavenly Jerusalem, and the direction from which the Messiah will return in glory. West represents death and the devil. Whilst all this symbolism has been either forgotten or largely unknown by modern-day Catholics, the basic traditional symbolism of a sacristy, by which the priest enters on the Gospel side and exits on the Epistle side, still exists in some churches. The priest may well utilise this space to dress in his vestments to offer the sacrifice of the Mass, and it's also where the relevant items and liturgical vessels are usually stored.

Traditionally there is a special sink that – unlike an ordinary sink - drains straight into the earth, by-passing the sewer; the purpose is to preserve the dignity of sacred things which can no longer be used. The sacred vessels used to be rinsed there so that no particle of the concentrated host and no precious blood of the Christ will end-up in the sewer. I suspect that the sink is rarely used nowadays, as it seems to be the practice of the priest to ask the altar server to pour more red wine into the sacred vessels before the priest swirls it around and drinks the residue; he then wipes the inner vessel with a clean altar linen. This was the procedure at any of the Mass church services I attended in Spain and, with wine so plentiful and given free with every meal, it made a lot of sense to me. Indeed, why would you wash the vessel with water when you can clean it – and the palate – with wine!

The plain and simple church architecture I experienced along The Camino resonated more with me than did the grandeur of the cathedrals at Burgos, Leon and Santiago, my final destination. At those places the majesty and mystic symbolism dating back to Medieval times still remains, as I suspect it does in most cathedrals throughout the Christian world.

The little-known town of Carrion de los Condes once had as many as 10,000 residents and no fewer than fourteen pilgims' hostels during the 8th century. A beautiful old building, known as Iglesias do Santiago, on a garden square near the nuns' quarters, still had the 12th-century façade although the rest of the original building had been destroyed by fire. I attended another pilgrims' Mass in the new structure. Here, the legend of one hundred virgins, demanded by the Moors from Mauregato, the Christian ruler, is celebrated. I wondered if, except for the nuns, there were any virgins left in the town. The Moors' leader must have had a voracious sexual appetite - he demanded one hundred virgins every year! The Christians prayed for this travesty to end, and some Christians had the idea of chasing the Moors from the town with a herd of wild bulls; I noted that signs depicting two bulls appeared in dark hidden corners of buildings – but no sign of virgins. It is well known that Charlemagne, the French warrior chief, set-up his camp at Carrion de los Condes when fighting the Moors. It made good sense; with so many hospitals and virgins on hand, it was a perfect place for rest, recuperation and lovemaking. This was also the home of Sem Tob (The Spanish version of the Hebrew "Shem Tov, meaning "good name"), the 14th-century Jewish Rabbi and poet, known locally as Sem Tob de Carrion. His writings were a deliberate attempt to express Jewish thought and wisdom in a romantic tongue. His most memorable work is the epic poem, "Proverbios Morals". I thought about how I found it easier to articulate poetically rather than through prose in a journal. Poetry seems to me to be the surface of the words – just as music gives depth to lyrics. I mused that those who think logically, unemotionally and with quiet intellect seem to get to the "head" of a matter, while we crazy poetic types dig under the surface to the heart; but in truth, we all may well need both head and heart. I guess we all can't be the same when expressing the stories of our lives' lessons. Our words come from such a variety of sources, nature, the light, the dark, good and evil, smart people, drunks, criminals, the birds and the bees, the fish and the sea creatures, the mind and the heart – and even mad people like me.

The next day I was awake at 5:00 am and took the opportunity to treat my blisters once again, with iodine and band-aids. I met-up again with John and Jill, the English honeymooners, who again provided me with anti-inflammatory tablets. I had enough medication now to relieve my pain and see me through to the next port of call, Terradillos de los Templarios. The 26.6 km route was straight, relatively level, with fields of blooming sunflowers everywhere to relieve my boredom. As I stepped back in time along the pathway of the Knights Templar, I looked forward to completing this 17 km section - the longest stretch of road without the relief of food or water - of the well-worn route of the Camino Frances (as The Camino de Santiago is sometimes known). It was indeed a relief to ascend a hill and come to an oasis offering, in exchange for a small donation, drinks, seasonal snacks and sandwiches. The saviour who ran the old wagon-stall was in his mid-thirties carried twelve kilograms of water twice a day, on foot, in two large buckets, and made his own brand of home-grown lemonade. He rang a bell every time he saw a pilgrim approaching and, although he never requested money, he did stand next to a large donation box. The mountain trekking had been tough, but now on the plateau I was again feeling the extreme heat and suffering much more with my blisters and the swollen ankle. I was buckling under the weight of the excess weight in my backpack, and made a mental note to dump at least five kilograms at the first opportunity, at a post office, and send the superfluous items forward to Santiago.

The heavy weight of a full backpack had never been a problem for me during a four- or five-day walk, but on this 800 km journey it seemed heavier every time I shouldered it. Coming from an era of "keep it for a rainy day", I had been indoctrinated into holding-on to material possessions – quite the opposite of The Camino philosophy of "less is more". The modern generation has the easy come, easy go attitude when it comes to belongings, whereas we of baby-boomer vintage cherished the accumulation of material possessions, as did our parents after the depression of the 1930s and WW II. It could be argued that we baby-boomers had also spoilt our children, by giving them things to use which they just dumped when something new came along. So the idea
of just leaving my prized possessions on the path for a passing pilgrim didn't cross my mind. At least it didn't until I arrived back in Australia and, still in the spirit of giving, dumped most of my Camino extras with a "paying it forward" attitude, putting most of the items in the local charity bin. My will to continue striving occasionally weakened, so at those times I distracted myself with positive affirmations, much like those I had used when training salesmen years earlier. The 1st-century poet, Perseus, came to mind: "He conquers who endures". I thought of people who had endured despite setbacks. Abraham Lincoln was the best historical example that came to mind. When he was seven, his family was forced out of the home and he had to work to help support them. His mother died when he was nine, but he continued to work. By the age of twenty-two he had lost his job and had no work at all.

At twenty-three he went into business in a small-store partnership, but his partner died, leaving Abe with a debt that took years to repay. He fell in love, but his sweetheart died; his heart was crushed and he suffered a nervous breakdown. At the age of thirty-seven, after two failed attempts at Congress, he was elected, but lost his seat two years later. Eight years later he ran for the Senate, but lost. Aged forty-seven, he failed in his attempt at the Vice-Presidency. At age fifty-one, he was elected a President of The United States of America, then endured the civil war, claimed victory for the north and encouraged the southern states to join The Union under The Stars and Stripes. At age sixty-five, he was assassinated. A tough life and a tragic ending for a man who suffered defeat for much of his life. One thing he did not know was how to quit. (Later, the "Lone Star" state of Texas joined The Union, and is the birth-place of Presidents Lyndon B. Johnson, Dwight D. Eisenhower; it's also the home-state of George H. Bush and his son, George W. Bush, the former born in Massachusetts and the latter in Connecticut, both states having had pivotal roles in The Union formed by President Abraham Lincoln.) Abraham Lincoln once said, "I am a slow walker, but I never walk backwards", and this became my slogan for the difficult days ahead. I thought of the epitaph for the Swiss mountain-climber who fell to his death some years ago, and the shrine, erected by his friends, bearing the words, "He died climbing".

I knew that I had not arrived spiritually, but I would keep on keeping-on despite the difficulties, blisters and swollen ankle. It was after the steep hill at Castrojeriz that I had fallen and twisted my ankle. I was walking down a steep slope and slipped, fortunately not hitting the ground because of the support of my walking poles and boots. I'd made it to the bottom of the slope and stopped to examine the injury. I quickly massaged the area that was swelling, applied a tight bandage and continued walking despite the pain, repeating to myself, "I am strong. I can beat any pain". Just outside San

Nicolas I came across a small pilgrims' hospital by the side of a roadside chapel, outside of which hung a Spanish flag and a sign which I translated as, "San Nicolas hospital, a peaceful chapel". The scallop shell and the St. James' Sword of the Knights Templar were on the wall nearby. I entered the small alcove, which had been a resting place for pilgrims for decades, and took-in the vista.

In the obviously historic vestibule of the chapel was a large wooden table, where a nurse attended to a pilgrim, administering some tablets and water, whilst a man whom I assumed to be a doctor was tending to another pilgrim's injured hand. I gathered that this foyer, the entry to a small traditional church, now served as an emergency hospital for weak, weary and injured pilgrims, some of whom just sat on bench-like seats along a far wall, appearing to be in a meditative state. I assumed they had come in to escape the heat, as it was nice and cool inside. Perhaps they were there in penance, awaiting reconciliation or baptism into a dying but traditional faith. In a corner stood a large medicine cabinet housing all types of liquid medicines, tablets, medical equipment, bandages and gloves, all of which could be seen through the glass doors and in the drawers, which were half-open.

CHAPTER 11.

GAUVAS' ADVISE

Gauvas, a small man of Arabic appearance with shoulder-length hair, dark beard and piercing eyes, looked at me as he busily attended to a young female pilgrim with a hand injury. He wore a full-length white robe and could have passed for Lawrence of Arabia if not for his small stature and skin colour. Pilgrims' bags were piled near the entry by those awaiting treatment, those merely escaping the heat and those awaiting their traditional Catholic indoctrination. Gauvas introduced himself in English while continuing to attend to the young girl's hand. He enquired after my health and I explained about my twisted ankle and blistered feet. He left the young woman and instructed me to remove the bandage and to not use it again. I was rather puzzled by this, and even more so when I asked what the treatment would cost. He merely shrugged his shoulders and continued to examine my ankle and blisters. I was not aware at that time that the Spanish Government picked-up the tab for all pilgrims' medical costs, and even helped fund the local municipal albergues on The Camino. This explained why, in the main, albergues worked on donations and were run by volunteers. After cleaning my blisters with water from a large bowl on the cabinet, he treated them with iodine and applied sticking-plasters without padding directly on and over the wounds. He then led me outside the building, to face the entry wall where the Spanish flag, the sword and scallop shell hung – all reminders of what I was doing on The Camino. Gauvas taught me exercises, using the wall as support, to relieve the swollen ankle and strengthen the area of the injury, and told me I would have no further problem with it and that my condition would improve – on the proviso that I did the exercises every time I took a rest stop along The Way. I have to admit that the swelling did begin to subside almost immediately after I'd repeated the exercises every two or three hours along The Way. Gauvas also had warned that if I did not do as he'd instructed I would not make it to Santiago. The toughest part of his instruction was regularly administering the iodine and sticking-plaster treatment directly on and over the blisters.

A further recommendation was to bathe my feet in warm salty water whenever I could in hotels. I determined, then and there, to do that at least once a week until my blisters healed. Not content with the advice regarding my wounds and injury, he also said that I was strong in body and mind and did not need to take western medicines – including antibiotics; I should drink more natural juices and plenty of water, eat more natural foods such as raw vegetables, fruits and nuts , and give-up coffee altogether! He placed particular emphasis on giving-up anything that contained sugar and its substitutes. I did my best to adhere to his advice, but it did not last. I had a fix in my mind when it came to western medicine, and needed my daily fix of coffee. I decided to make his suggestions a New Year's resolution the following year.

"And he said unto them, ye will surely say unto me this proverb, 'Physician, heal thyself: what so ever we heard done in Capernaum, do also in thy country." (King James Bible Luke 4:23).

The many blisters, sore feet and shin-splints had cause me to falter and stumble many times on The Way, but continuing the exercises that Gauvas had taught me were not complicated and proved effective. I wrote them in my journal for future reference and also passed-on my new-found exercises to anyone who cared to try them. I made a special note to advise those who may be more susceptible to injury, or who had some physical handicap, to check with a medical professional before actually doing the exercises. On The Camino, finding a professional medico was never difficult; there was at least one in most villages.

Gauvas' Exercises

Exercise 1. Find a wall and stand facing it.

"While standing upright, place one leg about 45 cm behind the other, keeping the back foot flat on the ground. Now, while still keeping the back leg straight, with the foot remaining firmly on the ground, bend the front leg at the knee, towards the wall, with the heel about 6 cm from the wall and toes touching the wall. Repeat this three times, changing the legs so both get the benefit of the stretching."

Exercise 2. Fold arms and, while standing upright, cross legs and place feet side by side.

"Bend forward from the waist, as far as possible, with head down, looking between your legs. Repeat three times."

Exercise 3. Place hands on buttocks and lean backwards.

"Keep both legs straight then straighten up and repeat three times."

Exercise 4. Stand upright and lean body to the left and then the right, from the waist.

"Place one hand below a knee and, once into the stretch, raise the other hand upright, look up towards that hand without leaning backwards or forwards. Repeat three times on both sides."

The Zone Therapy Lifestyle. The zone therapy lifestyle proved effective in working the pressure points of the feet to affect all parts of the body, and also effective in keeping the feet in good order. Take a new tennis ball, still somewhat firm, and while rolling it under the balls of the feet, apply pressure on the ball. This also is effective in giving relief for body, mind and spirit during long walks.

Of course, I learnt most of these lessons after my Camino and my return home. Often in life we have to go through our own pain before there is gain. We may listen to others and take their ideas in at any given time, while thinking subconsciously, "This does not apply to me". It often takes one's own Camino before we realise that to be forewarned is to be forearmed. My lessons on The Camino taught me a lot when it came to health, fitness and how to get through the 800 km of The Camino with an overweighted backpack. Later, I included "Tips for walkers" in my website www.caminoway.com.au. This was after my return home, to help those who may make their own Camino in the future.

Breath and Meditation. Through my many travels, and after so much depression, pain and anxiety, I turned to all sorts of gurus and tried mindfulness meditation in a purpose-built tepee. I tried it with the sweating caused by the heat of a fire while focusing on glowing hot rocks in the centre of the enclosure. I turned to prayer, meditation, long walks on beaches, to screaming therapy and sand therapy, as well as spending time at live-in counselling. The combination of these roads to recovery reached a crescendo with listening to music as I got in touch with my misspent youth and rediscovered the 1970s. However, the best was yet to come, when I would discover yoga breathing exercises.

When we come to the practice of meditation, we don't yet understand the truth of how things are or what is right and what is wrong, so we first have to make ourselves calm and, with practice, come to understand what is what. It can be very confusing for our western minds to grasp the essence of meditation, so it is important to not think too much, for where there is knowing, awareness will rise and become wisdom. I relate the lessons of the practice of meditation that I sometimes practise – although perhaps not often enough in my daily life.

So, calm first; awareness will rise from within the calm and it will contain both thinking and wisdom. So let it all go to nothingness, otherwise it will only cause confusion. This is the time to work with the mind and nothing else. Stop trying. Just allow the mind to be calm and don't let thoughts turn you to the right or the left, forward or back, up or down, above or below. You are not going to do anything other than practise mindfulness or breathing. Fix your attention to your head and then move the sense of breath down your body to the tips of your feet and back to the crown of your head. This is to gain an initial understanding of the way your body is, before beginning your meditation.

You may be sitting, or walking your Camino while observing the inhalations and exhalations of your breath. No pressure on the breathing is required; just allow your circumstances to dictate the breathing pattern. You will find your own pattern and it will be natural to you alone, even if you are climbing a hill, so just be mindful of it; let all thoughts and ideas drift away. If they are important to you, they will return in some form later. Don't worry if you think you have lost the idea. I promise you won't lose it; it will come back, although perhaps in a different form. How important is it at the time, anyway? If you make this a daily practice you will feel much better able to handle life's tasks and your long walking treks will prove to be easy. Life always presents difficulties, but breathing meditative practice will help you cope, irrespective of circumstances. Don't think about this, just do the practice every day and you will view life differently.

Just be aware that the mind will play tricks on you, and you will find that it often wanders, particularly during early practise. Don't suffer because of this, just get back the practice of focus on the breath. Remember, your mind has not gone anywhere, it's still there, and it's only your imagination and change occurring in the mind. In a flash, you are back with your breathing focus. You are the one who knows you are not craving anything during this mindful state of breathing. You are not trying to do anything. You just are, wherever you are in the physical world at the time, focusing on your breathing. That's it! Practise breathing and focus on breath and you have the perfect meditation tool.

Of course, sitting in a quiet place will get you into a calm state quicker than if your body is moving, but it is also possible to attain that inner sense of calm while in movement. Everyone is able to know; everyone is able to understand. It is not something that exists in a book; it exists in you, for you, because of you. Just reflect right now on you; you're breathing. Maybe you are in the midst of some trial or tribulation, experiencing sadness, happiness, joy, a sense of loss or a sense of gain. Feelings are not facts, they are merely feelings. While you are doing the practice, just do it and listen to your breath; return again and again to the practice until it becomes second nature.

For those of us who are new to the practice, the lifestyle practices of meditation of the devoted live by five principles:

1. Unconditional love towards all beings.

2. To be honest and refrain from impinging the rights of others.

3. Be moderate in all things, including sexual relations. To be moderate is to be pure.
4. When you speak, be straight, truthful and upright.

5. Refrain from intoxication in all forms, that is, refrain from substance abuse, family, friends and material wealth and in fact everything.

Then belief is pure and a form of honesty, kindness, contentment and freedom from bondage of any kind will eventually be fact. These principles are of course fact for an ideal world, but we don't live in one, in our modern lifestyle. We can only be mindful of the principles, live by them as best we can and continue to breathe! We live in a world of human beings, animals and plants which are subject to the forces of nature and events. Some bring joy, some sadness, others suffering and hardship. Nothing in our natural world is free of pain in some form. We tend to shy away from difficulties, pain and sorrow, preferring to take the soft option, but no growth comes without pain and difficulty. If we accept the fact that pain is good, that is teaching us and making us strong. In the long run, we can live this life with whatever comes up and make the most of this one, long day called life, before we leave this mortal coil.

I am not advocating that we look towards the darkness in preference to the light, but both are equally true, just as night follows day. So let's embrace it and get on with it as best we can right now. The pilgrimage of this Camino for me has been a journey, a long walk, moving from one place to another – in body and in mind – and with a spirit of adventure I did not expect to experience. It has been, and will continue to be, a holy, long work long after I reach Santiago. It has been a chance to encounter and glimpse the mystery – and to just breathe!

    Note in my Journal (on the road to Leon).

Leaving the vast " Tierra de Compoa" behind, the pilgrim continues across more corn grain crop fields to reach the plateau of Leon. Along the way, the pilgrim will pass the pretty village of Reliogos and take the " Via Traiana" trail past more crop fields and on to the first of industrial activity in approaching the city.

Leon, the historic capital of the kingdom in the middle ages, is an historic enclave on the pilgrim's route to Santiago de Compostela. The Pulchra Leonina in the Leon Cathedral is the "Sistine Chapel"of Spanish architecture. Gaudi's neo-Gothic Casta de Botines and the Hospital de San Marcos add to the decor and sense of luxury. The cottages, museums, food outlets and character of the locals all evoke a vista reminiscent of a poor man's Paris.

CHAPTER 12

THE ROAD TO LEON.

It was Sunday morning and I once again woke late after a good night's sleep. Stomach satisfied after my usual morning sidewalk café breakfast, I was on the road again. I was now tramping the path of Roman history, after leaving the majestic Burgos, the folklore of "El Cid" and the Gothic architecture of the heart of the city. The villages and towns of Castrojeriz, Fromista and Carrion de los Condes had introduced me to the vastness of the Meseta, with its wide, open landscapes, the sounds of nature's wildlife and endless crop fields as my companions when not walking with other pilgrims. The Medieval towns of Sahagun and El Burgo Ranero and other picturesque, sleepy villages and hamlets were pleasant distractions from the immense Meseta plateau I was traversing.

The last 19 km to Leon were as painful as my entry into Burgos had been. Once again, it was as if hot pokers were penetrating my toes with every step. John and Jill, the English honeymooners with whom I enjoyed a meal a day or two previously, had caught-up with me over coffee in "Villamore de Mansilla", on the outskirts of Villarente. I had run out of anti-inflammatory tablets and they gladly gave me enough to ease my foot pain until I reached Leon. I sat for a long time, redressing and treating my feet with a bucket of ice-cubed water supplied by the café's owner before returning to The Way. The only Sword of Discernment I could feel was the one that pierced my feet, but the treatment did help a lot and the anti-inflammatory tablets kicked-in within an hour and I felt much better as I approached Leon.

I had been walking on the quaint paved roads of Cantas and occasional old Roman roads into Mansilla de las Mula, admiring the remains of the city that was fortified by a Roman walls which had been rebuilt in the 13th and 14th centuries. The walls were now in decay but the two original gates to the tower's staircase stood in a condition appearing as new as the day they were installed. As Leon loomed closer, the final 7 km involved a lot of walking through industrial areas on the city's outskirts. However, this was relieved by bridges and overpasses making the walk safe, despite the trail-marker detours and the heavy traffic. I stopped just short of the city to eat some sardines, dry bread and cheese, the remains of the food in my knapsack from the previous day.

The city's outskirts were very run-down, with slum buildings, old posters or graffiti on dirty shop walls and dirty windows; ragged people were hanging about with nothing better to do than stay in the shade of alleyways. I ventured into a general store for water, but thought better of it, despite my thirst, and continued following the painted arrows towards the inner city. As I came closer to the city's centre my spirits lifted and the scenery improved immensely. The first local resident I encountered was a middle-aged Spanish lady who approached me and offered me a bed to stay with her. I did not know if she was offering to share her bed or asking if I wanted to be a lodger; either way, I was not interested as my mind was on the heart of my spiritual quest of my outer Sword of Discernment – a faint expression of it in my head manifesting into something in this ancient city; a city established as a permanent settlement by the Roman military as far back as 29 BC, to protect Galician gold during its transport to Rome. I was stunned by the ancient beauty of the place, with an eye to my quest and in a mindful state despite the ever-present blisters on my feet and the history surrounding me. Could this be the city of God – that source of fiery spirituality that would bring me to the place of peace, the outward manifestation of the inner Sword of Discernment which I had set my mind to achieve? Maybe I had listened far too much to other pilgrims on the journey speaking glowingly of this ancient city, or perhaps I had taken too much notice of others' viewpoints on belief and understanding, and maybe I had always been brainwashed, even from childhood. Perhaps this seemingly impossible dream was merely a motivator to keep me moving forward with a quest, like some Don Quixote, living an impossible dream and chasing yet another windmill!

It had proven so many times in the past to be so, and the realization of letting-go of it all was beginning to dawn on me. I would at least take time out to rest and explore the wonders of the past of this great monument to man, and the vibrancies of its ancient and modern culture and history. The route to the centre of Leon took me to a place I had never previously visited during this lifetime; I felt I was being transported back in time as I slowly wound my way through an ancient laneway past an historic wall which, I later discovered, had been built by the Romans in 29 BC when they had first established the city as a military encampment.

The city was alive with pilgrims like me, all exploring the side streets, which all looked daunting but exciting to visit. I made a mental note to spend an extra day there to further explore its ancient historical sites and get a feel for its beauty. I was now in a state of exhaustion, but my spirit was lifted by the sights I saw as I neared the inner sanctum of Leon. As my feet suffered with blisters and the heat, I was keen to find a refugio for the night. As luck would have it, I met a pilgrim who directed me to the El Burgo Ranero Albergue, the most beautiful sight for this weary traveller. This refugio (or albergue) did not open for new pilgrims until later in the afternoon, so I contented myself with lining-up with fellow pilgrims, waiting for the huge courtyard doors to open so that we could register and have our pilgrims' passports stamped. I purchased a cool drink from a restaurant bar opposite the albergue; it had a neat, ancient cobble-stone courtyard bounded on three sides by buildings. It was shaded and cool, providing a refreshing relief after walking on predominately hard surfaces all day with the sun beating down relentlessly and temperature in the high thirties.

The refugio opened on the dot at 6:00 pm and I filed in with the rest of the pilgrims to obtain a bed allocation. The dormitory-like facilities held a great many beds, and were clean and comfortable. It provided a unique service: guests could make themselves a cup of tea or coffee and have a biscuit without charge and, better still, it was a monastery, attached to the adjacent church, and pilgrims were allowed a two-night stay.

This fitted perfectly with my plans: explore this great and ancient city, give my feet a holiday from my boots for a while and rest and recuperate. After settling-in, I quickly showered, did some washing and hung it in the rather large clothes-line area. While waiting for my clothes to dry I joined some fellow pilgrims at the outside bar for drinks and an early dinner. It was time to reflect on the day's activities before taking a brief nap and then returning for another drink. It had rained during my nap, so I left my wet clothing on the line. A number of my friends from the road had turned up, and we compared notes on our journey to this point. I again caught up with Julia who, notably, unlike the previous times we had met along The Way, was not drunk. However, she seemed to have taken a vow of calmness and sobriety now, and had left the rowdy friends behind to spend some time on her own. She joined me for a non-alcoholic drink and we talked of our mutual experiences along The Way. Later, I learnt that, as a consequence of her Camino experience, she took a job as a volunteer in albergues on The Camino as a service to other pilgrims.

She had been touched by some inner spiritual experience on her Camino, and it showed. We talked until 8:00 pm when we noticed our fellow pilgrims had assembled together with the albergue's volunteer staff to attend Mass at the chapel attached to our lodgings. I, like my fellow pilgrims, including Julia, joined them and we made our way to the adjoining church for a pilgrims' Mass. This was the second time I had attended Mass since commencing The Camino, and a record for the number of times over the past two decades. The only other times had been at my son's funeral a decade earlier and, prior to that, the only other I could remember was at a classmate's funeral. I mouthed the words of the service without taking too much in, but sang along with the throng to some sacred melody. The usual pilgrims' blessing was performed, this time by a nun instead of a priest, and the blessing was handed out to each of us in our own language. I felt overcome with a heaviness that I could not explain and, at the end of the service, returned to the albergue with a kind of body-shuffle and weariness. I was sound asleep even before my head hit the pillow.

Leon, a Roman military outpost for the locally-mined Galician gold in 29 BC, was overtaken by the Visigoths, a Germanic people whose descendants and their influences still remain today. They were separated from the Ostrogoths in the 4th century, repeatedly invaded Roman-held territories and established great kingdoms in Gaul and Spain. They took the city of Leon by force in 586, establishing it as a centre for agriculture and, no doubt, the mining of gold. The Muslims (Moors) took the city in 712 and held it until the Spanish regained control, reconquered in 856 by the great King Ordono I, who initiated a building boom. In 988 the city was once again taken over by Muslims under the leadership of Al-Mansurs, who rebuilt more of the city, and it flourished as a centre of the wool industry. As I weaved my way along cobble-stone pathways and narrow streets, I was taken by the morning shadows of the buildings that spoke to me of Roman, Gothic, Muslim and Spanish peoples who had walked these ancient streets centuries before me. I somehow felt as if I was viewing the city as a reflection, like someone who gazes into a river and sees images upside-down.

The sheer depth of feeling surrounding those streets engulfed me; it seemed I had walked back in time. As I walked towards the main square I was returned to the present time of modern shops, coffee houses and restaurants. I found my way to Leon's finest treasure, the sublime Gothic cathedral, with its magnificent stained-glass windows allowing the light to stream inside to steal the show. This is the fourth church to stand on this spot, begun in 1205 and taking 100 years to complete. The building's serene Virgen Blanca statue welcomed me from below the central tympanum. The seats in the choir are carved with biblical characters and creative, humorous depictions of the vices, reminding me of the cheek of Michelangelo's murals on the ceiling of the chapel in Florence, visible only by climbing the steep stairs to the ceiling. The seven chapels within the Leon Cathedral contain Gothic tombs, including that of King Ordono II, with a scene from the crucifixion. In the centre of the cathedral, Rodrigo Diaz de Vivar, the Medieval Spanish military leader known as El Cid – "the master" – is buried.

My Camino journey was not about returning to the hustle and bustle of any modern-day central business district, so I quickly retraced my footsteps, stopped at a café where I sat outside to eat. There, I watched the movement of the passing parade of tourists, enjoying the pleasure of a light Spanish lunch and the noonday sun. Leon is a pleasant, laid-back place and, being joined by fellow pilgrims for a chat gave me a sense of somehow being free of life's responsibilities. The afternoon was topped off by strolling across the plaza from the basilica and taking a long walk around the city's outskirts to take in more of its beauty. I vowed to myself to one day return to this great city and spend more time visiting the sacred art museums, Romanesque structures, and to return once more to the cathedral, perhaps for a Mass on a Sunday.

The second night at the Albergue Leon Benedictina was a fitting end to my stay in the city of my dreams on The Camino. Although I had an afternoon siesta for around an hour, in the tradition of the Spanish locals during the summer heat, I was still weary. I went back to the street around 6:00 pm and headed for a nearby bar for an evening meal. Sandy, a retired Canadian Airlines employee, joined me and we had an enjoyable chat over food and drink. Sandy had walked The Camino the previous summer and had returned, to give back to The Way and to pilgrims by working as a volunteer in the albergue in which I was staying. He worked a ten-hour day, allocating beds, ensuring that each pilgrim was issued with bed-linen, and keeping a watchful eye on pilgrims, like a dormitory master in a boarding school. During my afternoon nap, it had rained for the first and only time during my journey. The rain had lasted long enough to soak my washing again but, to my surprise, it was all dry when I returned from my evening meal with Sandy. I ventured out once again, met with other pilgrims and attended the pilgrims' Mass next door before returning to bed early.

I woke at 5:00 am, quickly dressed, packed, joined fellow early starters for complimentary tea and toast, quickly washed-up and commenced tramping out of Leon. The walkway on the outskirts of Leon was similar to revisiting the Champ de Mars in Paris, but without the Eiffel Tower and The Seine. My mind flashed back to a fancy tablecloth that my mother put on the dining table when we had visitors when I was a child; it was clean, plain and white with a crocheted frill around the edge. I pictured that tablecloth without the frill and, to me, that was Leon: Paris without the frill. The pathway leading out of the city meandered past museums, parks, gardens, over bridges with flowing streams and on to a lovely outdoor café – the last opportunity to grab another bite to eat before leaving the city limits. It was whilst enjoying my second breakfast, of coffee, croissant and orange juice – now a daily habit for me – that I met Dan. He was from Prague, in The Czech Republic, and proved to be great company for me on the next leg of my journey towards Santiago. We commenced walking together to Chozas de Abago, and at Dan's suggestion we set our sights on staying at the Refuge de Jesus, some 21.5 km south. Dan had stayed there the previous summer, when he had completed the same leg of The Camino from Leon. On our breaks for lunch and an afternoon snack, I noted that Dan did not eat anything, but merely drank tonic water or coke. He said he didn't eat during the day and, to cap it off, ate only a light meal in the evening. He claimed to get all his energy from the bubbles and didn't need food. After that, I nicknamed him "Bubbles." In truth, it had become a lifelong habit of his, a consequence of the discipline imposed by his father when Dan was a child. Times were tough under communism when Dan was a boy, and it had been a regular treat for Dan and the rest of his family to accompany his father on his educational excursions. The family could not afford food after paying their transport costs, so they went without, and this is when Dan developed the habit of eating only one meal a day. Dan's dad was an academic who had written about and taught the history of certain areas of The Czech Republic – aspects of history which were not commonly known by the locals before he began to educate them, and he was considered to be the expert on the history of those areas.

We arrived at Villar de Mazarile and paid our dues for the night at the Refuge de Jesus. It was a fascinating place, a little off the beaten track and at first glance could have been mistaken for a boat-builder's premises. At the entry stood an ark, possibly a replica of the one built by Noah, and may have once been a tourist attraction, although it was now in disrepair. I was more eager to dress my blistered feet than to spend time examining the spectacle. The refuge's walls were covered from floor to ceiling with writings and drawings, no doubt scrawled by pilgrims over many decades. Among the scrawls of youthful comments on the wall, I was attracted by the following quote from Jack Kerouac's famous novel of the nineteen-fifties, 'On The Road'

"They danced down the street like dingledodies, and I shambled after, as I've been doing all my life, after people who interest me, because the only people who interest me are the mad ones, the ones who are mad to live, mad to talk, mad to be saved, desirous of everything at the same time, the ones that never yawn or say commonplace things, but burn burn burn like fabulous yellow roman candles exploding like spiders across the stars, and in the middle you see the blue centre light pop and everyone goes "Awww!" ("Dingledodies" is a word coined by Jack Kerouac affirming weirdos he was always drawn too.)

The refugio's proprietor stamped our pilgrims' passports, asked for a small donation and directed us to a spare room on the first floor. Like every other room in the place, ours had graffiti from floor to ceiling, but it was reasonably clean. I showered, and dressed in clean clothes, hung my washing out and joined Dan outside in the courtyard for some bubbles. The night closed-in as I sat talking with a free-thinking English girl named Nicole before going off to bed. It was Nicole's second Camino, and we found ourselves in a deep discussion about the strangeness of the experience and the fun and laughter derived from meeting other pilgrims along The Way. I was struck by her infectious laughter and her intellect, but more particularly by her childlike innocence. She taught pre-school children, and I mentioned that I had had my fair share of failed so-called love relationships with school teachers in the past. Her response, that perhaps a good idea would be to think of a future relationship with someone who wasn't a teacher, caused me to laugh aloud, although I did file that suggestion away in the back of my mind for future reference. Nicole had walked The Camino with her sister the previous summer, and we talked of strange happenings she had experienced. She explained that since their Camino together, they had a saying; when talking about strange events affecting their lives, they now always said, "Well, that's the Camino." I was beginning to resonate with that! Dan had already settled-in for the night and was fast asleep when I returned to the room. We had two room-mates, a young couple who were also settling-in for a night's sleep; they were both quiet, which was a blessing. It was nice to have some quite pilgrims with whom to share a room, and a change from others with whom I had stayed albergues on The Camino. I wrote a poem about my boots while giving them a clean in readiness for an early start the next day, then, once again, I was asleep within five minutes of putting my head on the pillow.

You are my soul companion
as we walk The Camino Way,
faithful from morning to nightfall
tramping in step with me.

You're just an old pair of boots
worn weary, just like me
greeting my toe, feet and blisters
as we start the day.

Yesterday you were there for me,
today is the same on The Way;
in the evening we part company,
tomorrow you will be here I pray.

The Camino from Leon to Ponferrada is almost level, and easy. One walks through fields of grain, corn, potatoes and apple orchards, along footpaths and dirt tracks to the prettiest village on The Camino, Hospital de Orbigo. Here the pilgrim will cross the famous bridge - Puente de Orbigo – with the distant scene of the Leon Mountains as the pretty hilltop city of Astorga, the capital of Margateria, is reached. The "pink" cathedral, the Gaudi-inspired Episcopal Palace and the city walls are unforgettable, as are the local chocolates.

Gradually, the pilgrim makes his way to the Leon Mountains and the El Bierzo region, surrounded by broom, heather and oak. The climb to Mount Irago among the broom and heather is in stark contrast with the iron cross on the mountain's top, a good point for contemplation, before descending to the lush area of El Bierzo. The mountain village of Acebo is a peaceful place to stay, before entry into the city of Ponferrada.

CHAPTER 13.

PLAYING THE CHILD'S GAME

It was early morning and still dark when Dan and I made our way south, planning to reach Villavante, 10 km down the track, before the heat became too severe. This leg of the journey was to be the last of the flat Meseta scenery, before The Way became more rolling and, we hoped, green, in preparation for the Cantabrian Mountains during the next 5 km to Hospital de Orbigo, for the enjoyment of Medieval ambiance and the excitement of the history of Medieval jousting.

The long, flat, tar road we had walked in the dark was not so difficult, despite limited distance vision. We could see only a few metres ahead as we marched along, thinking we were the only souls on The Way so early. However, as some angel in the sky above pulled back the curtain to allow the dawn, we were surprised to see a long line of pilgrims, in single file, spread along the road ahead, as far as the horizon; likewise, a similar line behind us. It resembled some ancient ritual, walkers silently pounding the pavement, each one alone, yet there was something mysteriously beautiful about the experience. Somewhere near Villavante, we veered away from the beaten path for about five hundred metres, heading towards a village café we had sighted from the road. I ate and drank my usual breakfast and Dan settled for his bubble-water. We had a long chat during the break, and Dan decided to move on, taking a different route. Once again I tended to my blistered feet and stretched and massaged my swollen ankle before taking to a dirt track with views from a slight hill overlooking the last of the wheat fields and the flat, dried, parched land. The track slowly wound downwards beside tall grass to a railroad crossing, with no warning. I realised that it could be dangerous to cross, as it was on a bend in the tracks, allowing a limited view for an engine driver. I was later proved right, when I heard on the news a few days later that a pilgrim had been killed at that crossing.

Arriving at the entry to Hospital de Orbigo, I stopped at a pleasant little café where I enjoyed coffee and cake, and meeting again with two new friends, Robin and his good mate Roland. My chance meeting with Robin was to have a profound influence on my life in the future – something I was unaware of at the time. Robin was a rising music star and accomplished guitarist whose rock group, "Uritup", was making headway in the charts back in Germany, along with their second album, "Overcome". Both Robin and Roland worked with refugees in government-paid employment. Robin wrote heavy-metal rock songs, recorded with his group and performed live concerts outside his working hours.

We both agreed that it was important to hold on to paid employment, as making a living out of what pleased us most was often not practical in the long run. Before my two new German friends left the cafe we agreed to meet later in Hospital de Orbigo, in the main street on the other side of the impressive Gothic bridge over Rio Orbigo, at the site of a Medieval jousting competition. Young, a New York-born Korean, and earlier companion of the road, joined me and we crossed the bridge together.

We recalled the story of Don Suero de Quinones, a wealthy Leonese knight who had been rejected by a woman he loved; he sent out a call to knights of the Medieval kingdom in 1434, for a jousting competition to determine who was best of all the knights of the realm. Apparently the good Don locked his neck in an iron collar and swore not to remove it until he had defeated all the other knights. He defended the bridge and succeeded in his goal, freeing himself from the torment of lost love. He took the collar off and made a pilgrimage to Santiago, where he left a jewelled bracelet, which can still be seen there in the cathedral's museum. The bridge, known as "The Honorable Pass" after that event, overlooks a grove of poplars, and I imagined the display of brilliant flags standing where they now stood, trumpets blowing and the excitement of the Medieval joust! On the other side of the bridge, I again met with Dan and introduced my new German friends. My little band of brothers, Dan, Robin, Roland, Young and I made our way through the town and on to the track towards Astorga.

I had walked 31.5 km that day as we crossed the zig-zag overhead pass of train tracks at the entry to Astorga, now weary, but boosted with a zest for life in the company of my young friends. I resolved to shake off my lethargy, and enjoyed the legendary pathway of St. James and St. Paul, who both reportedly preached in this old city. Astorga, a city of historic buildings and an awe-inspiring cathedral with an impressive Baroque façade and retablos, is a very enjoyable stopover. The Celtic-influenced city was an important trading centre for the Romans, early Christians, and for the Spanish; it had been destroyed by the Moors, then rebuilt by the Christians in the mid-9th century. It flourished with the pilgrim traffic and trade, and housed many pilgrim hospitals; St. Francis of Assisi stayed in one of them during his pilgrimage in 1214. My usual end-of-day ritual, of cooling-off in a scared and beautiful place made my cathedral visit even more worthwhile.

My new-found little band of brothers and I left Astorga in the early morning light, on a slow climb to explore the mysterious Maragato culture. Our goal was the vista of Gaucelmo's pilgrim hospital in Foncebadon, and to experience the ambiance of a tiny stone village nestled in the mountains some 26 km away. The landscape and building-style changed as The Camino wound its way into the wild hills of Galicia. As I passed through a small village I noticed, written on a wall, in English: "The fellowship sucks! Fuck it.

Yeah!" This reminded me once more of the dangers of drinking, and was an obvious sign that some poor fool had had enough of AA.

We had lost Roland the day before, and decided to leave some motivational signs by the wayside to encourage him to keep on with his Camino. He may have found that he just wanted to be alone on his Camino for a while, or perhaps the extreme heat had affected him and he found the going too difficult. In case it was the latter, we used a black marker-pen that Robin had purchased in a village store to write encouraging words and notes along the way. In hindsight, I think Roland may have understood the messages even better if they had been in German, but Robin may have taken pity on us, as neither I nor Young could write or speak German.

I was happy with the company of my two young friends, and had long since given up on seeing Dan, our Czech friend, again; as was his practice, he had started out on the road before us. I felt like a young man again as I joined in with the fun and laughter of youth. Their company somehow reminded me of my quest for direction and freedom when I was in my early twenties, like them – except that I was conditioned to convention and was ever seeking freedom of expression, while they seemed to be living their Camino as a rite of passage. I, instead, was letting-go of burdens that derived from my life of ingrained conditioning, and which held back my true inner freedom. My youth had been one of acting-out through burial of all that was fearful and painful. I had lived a philosophy of burying it all and moving forward.

Risk-taking, whether when sober or under the influence, had become the norm for me during my younger days: climbing into a boxing ring with no ring experience to fight a professional fighter; climbing the mast of a ship, while drunk, during a cyclone, with a Dutch photographer, to get a photo of the bow of our ship disappearing into a wave on the high seas; playing "chicken" in cars while driving at dangerous speeds, prepared to die, and not give in. My hero back then was James Dean, who lived his life the way he acted on screen – and, of course, the maxim, "He who lives by the sword, dies by the sword", came to reality for him when he did die, still in his youth, while driving at high speed in his sports car. It was only by some spiritual grace that I did not follow his path to glory!

There are many instances of my taking huge risks in the cause of either freedom or climbing the mythical ladder of success. All was risk-taking, and my constant burying of fear and pain finally had come to an end when I crashed into the hell of depression and alcoholism. I could blame my depression on tragic life events, the dangerous ways of my youth, many concussions caused by head knocks while playing football or in the boxing ring, or on the physical stress I chose to endure in corporate and in my own business situations. However, I had no answer for my uncontrollable drinking episodes that finally led me to the AA and The Twelve Steps. Yet, here I was now, walking my Camino, but somehow enjoying a new-found freedom of companionship with young men who were letting-go of issues of their young lives on this journey inward; a journey during which I, in my old age, was only now coming to understand the reasons for my letting-go – and for living. Here they were, with this old guy they seemed to want to be with, to share their experiences, their joy, their pain, their strength, their vision for the future – and to have fun with while on a mutual pathway to the spirit. In my case, it was still the search for an outward expression of a Sword of Discernment that I was coming to terms with on a daily basis. My goal was not far from being realised; it was slowly coming to reality with every step along the path of my Camino.

I had fallen behind my young companions and thought that perhaps Roland would catch-up to me before I reached Foncebadon, which I hoped to do before nightfall. Robin had warned me that there was limited accommodation in the Monte Irago Albergue there. I had told him that I would definitely try to get there and if he saved a bed for me I would kiss the foot of his bandaged leg. I didn't see Roland, but did manage to catch-up with two wonderful Italians – Marcus, who manufactured cotton fabrics in Italy, and his gorgeous girlfriend, Marfuaus, who worked in the consulting world. Marcus did not speak English, but Marfuaus acted as our interpreter. The three of us enjoyed discussing our mutual business interests and a late snack and drinks at a sidewalk café in Rabanal, a beautiful isolated village where many pilgrims had stopped to either rest prior to climbing the steep mountain ascent at the end of a long day, or to stay for the night. The Knights Templar had initially established a fort here in the village, to provide refuge for pilgrims from wolves and bandits. In Medieval times, it was influenced by both the Christians and the Muslims, as one of Charlemagne's knights had married a Muslim woman from the village.

I said my goodbye to my Italian fellow pilgrims, who were tossing-up whether to stay in the village for the night or to venture on to Foncebadon where they had already booked beds for the night. In the early evening I made the slow, steep ascent towards Foncebadon, 4.5 km further, at the top of the mountain trail. It was still very hot when I reached a point about half-way up the mountain and realised that I had run out of water and was feeling rather parched. As luck would have it, I turned a corner on the track to find a water trough and a tap, with refreshing mountain spring water. I drank my fill and refilled my water flasks, soaked my feet in the chilly waters of what was possibly a drinking trough for livestock and then, after a rest, thought about camping for the night under the stars. I was free in body, calm of mind and relaxed of spirit, with no fear of the possible consequences of sleeping out in such an isolated spot. However, after a short time, I thought better of it and decided to catch-up with my young friends, make my way to the mountain to and seek out the Monte Irago Albergue, to see if Robin had in fact reserved a bed for me.

Foncebadon was another movie-set experience, similar to the village in which I had stayed a few days previously and like something out of one of Clint Eastwood's spaghetti westerns of the late 1960s. The Roman road went through this pass, and it had been another stopover point during Roman times. However, it had died as a main route after the Romans left and later became a hermitage for monks of the 10th century. It remained practically deserted until the 1980s, when the village's crumbling rustic stone cottages, cafes and albergues made a comeback as a stopping-point for modern-day pilgrims. Foncebadon is where Shirley MacLaine describes her encounter with vicious dogs in her book, "The Camino".

I entered the Monte Irago Albergue and encountered many pilgrims seated, waiting to share in an extremely large paella; in a giant pan was a combination of what appeared to be risotto, capsicums, onions, garlic cloves, squid, peas, and possibly parsley. I could not recognize the other ingredients, but the aroma made my mouth water as I was by now extremely hungry.

The kitchen also contained the registration desk for pilgrims, but the young long-haired Spanish guy preparing the paella over the open flame chose to ignore me as he went about his business. I filled the time by looking at an old photo on a nearby wall of an Indian sage in long robes with a large crucifix adorning the walking staff held firmly in one hand. The picture was very faded, but unmistakably had been taken outside the front entrance of the albergue. The photo's shabby wooden frame matched the dirty walls of the small entrance, where I waited patiently until another young, greasy-haired youth in a long, dirty robe and holding a mangy-looking cat under his arm enquired of my needs. When I explained that I wanted a bed for the night, he waved his free arm at me and, in broken English, said, "No bed left". I said I was Doug, from Australia and that Robin, the young German, would have asked for a bed to be reserved for me. He exclaimed, "Awww! Senor Australia, you have a bed!" I made my way to the back of the albergue, dodging sheep, goats, chickens and a mule, and found Robin on his way to an outside basin to wash his clothes. I could not help myself, and fulfilled my promise to him by leaning down and kissing his bare tattooed leg, as I was so grateful to have a bed for the night.

The albergue accommodation adjoined the animals' stalls and the chicken coop, and I got the last of the this rubber mattresses and proceeded to dump my gear on the floor before making my way back to the kitchen to join the rest of the pilgrims for a meal. I returned to the mattress to lay-out my sleeping bag for the night, and was surprised to find my Italian companions, whom I had met during the twilight hours in the village of Rabanal in the valley below, on the mattresses next to mine; they had decided to venture up the mountain for the night after all.

Young was having some pain in his leg muscles and tendons, so I showed him Gauvas' exercises and some yoga stretches to help him to a quick recovery. I happened to turn around while instructing him and saw my Italian friends also copying the exercises, as were a dozen or so other pilgrims in the room. I felt a little like the sage of the photo I had encountered in the albergue's entrance. After a shower, I joined Robin and Young across the pathway from our basic accommodation for a communal sing-along. Robin had borrowed a guitar and began to play some great old rock 'n' roll songs and some ballads of his own creation. I was surprised to see Dan join us, as he had arrived earlier in the afternoon. My band of young brothers and I were now together under the stars on the top of a mountain.

The next morning, it was a fond farewell to my Italian friends, with Marcus' comments translated by Marfuaus, "I will never forget your friendly smile, and will always remember your snoring!" We heard, days later, that the albergue had been closed-down for ten days by the authorities due to unhealthy conditions, and had to be fumigated. We left the Monte Irago Albergue after a complimentary breakfast of bread, jams and fruit. Dan was already well ahead on the dirt track. The sun had not yet appeared and the morning was cool and full of silence; no sound of crowing roosters, of sheep, goats or mules and not a sound of wild dogs. This surprised me a little, as I had heard so many mystical stories of encounters with vicious dogs around Foncebadon, but maybe it was the time of day when the animals, and the dogs, were enjoying the peace and cool before the heat of the day set in again. I was joined by Robin and Young as we climbed our way towards Cruz Ferro, the high point of the Irago Mountains before the steep descent to Ponferrada, some 27.5 km away.

We passed horse pastures and the ruins of the Guacelmo's Medieval pilgrim hospital, ascending through scrubby heather and gorse to arrive at the highlight of every pilgrim's journey on The Camino, the Cruz Ferro. The Cruz Ferro, almost the highest point of the entire Camino Frances, consists of a tall wooden pole topped by an iron cross. This ancient Celtic monument was first erected by the Romans in dedication to their god, Mercury, the protector of travellers. It was later crowned by the cross and renamed as a Christian site in the 9th century by the hermit, Guacelmo. For centuries, pilgrims have brought a stone, or some icon of personal significance representing their burden, to this place; those from foreign lands bring something from their homeland. The stone, or the item representing the burden, is left here, leaving the pilgrim lighter – both literally and figuratively – for the journey ahead, The decaying rocks now form a small hill at the foot of the pole, although why pilgrims now pray, let-go of their burdens and pay homage here to whatever it is that attracts them to such a desolate place is beyond comprehension.
I watched as many pilgrims climbed the mound at the foot of the pole, stand in silence while letting-go their burdens. Some cried silently, wiping their eyes; others, like me and Young, just stood, watching, in a kind of vacuum of nothingness. I had no rock or

symbol to leave there but, instead, asked Robin for the marker pen and wrote my son's name and the date of his birth on a rock wall near the base of the pole: "Peter 17/7/1977". He would always be with me and in my heart he wasn't dead, so I felt right in engraving the date of his birth – not his death. I had already cried a couple of times on The Camino, and saw no need to leave any symbol of my burden – not even a personal rock, only a symbolic marker for the spirit of my son.

The place did seem to have a heavy energy, surrounding us all with its presence. It was neither good not evil, but a powerful force-field that engulfed us for the entire time that we stood on top of that mountain pass. The silence was broken by three women who climbed to the base of the pole and sang in unison, "We shall overcome some day". The old folk song and hymn touched Robin's heart deeply, as he cried out, "Oh! Fuck!" and began to weep. I had noted that he had a tattoo, in Spanish, across his chest: the word, "Overcome". I was later to find out that this was the name of his rock group's second album. We slowly picked up our backpacks and made our way down the steep slope to the base of the mountain. Neither Robin, Young nor I spoke during the next half hour. The experience of that place was so moving, and we all later agreed that there was something strange about the energy of the place.

Our journey's pathway passed the little Refugio de Manjarin, hosted by Thomas, who considered himself a modern-day Knight Templar – the last of the Knights - serving drinks and snacks to passing pilgrims. The rustic appeal of Thomas' humble abode, with no running water or electricity, made our brief stop another memorable experience. The rough signs on the verandah of this strange Spanish Knight's abode detailed the distances to Santiago and other cities on The Camino. We walked through fields of heather, arriving at a wide path up to a large cairn for a breathtaking view of Ponferrada in the valley floor below. We then commenced our sharp descent for the next 3.9 km to El Acebo. Once more, we had lost the seriousness in our nature and, falling into step along The Camino, began to tell stories and jokes to each other as the sun beat down on us, once more ignoring our discomfort, inner pain or aspirations, just living in the moment.

My young companions were now spread a great distance apart. We got word from Roland, by his mobile phone, that he was about six hours behind us, still climbing the trail to Foncebadon. Dan, on the other hand, was possibly an equivalent distance ahead of Robin, Young and me; we had made frequent stops and taken time to contemplate the aspects of life that we considered worthy of discussion on our personal journeys. We were making a steep descent to the next small village, El Acebo; my blistered feet began to act up again and, finding the going rough on my knees, I cursed the fact that I still suffered from the old rugby injuries of my youth. The Medieval town, like so many on The Camino, had a church in the central square surrounded by houses with wooden balconies flanking the trail, like a town in a western movie. The central point, as always, was a water trough with running water for bottle refills. Robin and Young were already eating and drinking coffee when I caught-up to them. After I ate and drank my fill we once again set out on the track together. Apart from the image of John the Baptist in the 15th-century church, the only monument of significance was on the village outskirts, where a statue stood as a tribute to a seventy-year-old German cyclist, Heinrich Krause, who died there in a bicycle accident in 1987.

It was at this point that we began to talk about music, as a consequence of our previous night's sing-along under the stars. Robin had demonstrated how he could play fifteen or thirty songs using the same chord, running one song into the next with a few verses from each. He seemed to make guitar-playing so easy; he was obviously skilled as a guitarist and had a pleasant voice which, to my mind, suited ballads more than the heavy rock he was engaged in. He had sung a song called "The Mountain Side", which depicted the story of a refugee child running from a village when planes flew over to drop bombs. He later told me that he wrote the song after hearing the story from one of his client refugees back in Germany. I said he should consider turning to singing folk ballads, which I thought would be more his style. I was later to find, on my return to Australia, that he had in fact formed a new folk group called "Master Mint". The fact that the music trend was changing to folk once more in Europe and the United Kingdom was the prime catalyst for forming the new group and, I suspect, the real reason for his venture into folk music – not some off-the-cuff suggestion by a weary old man on The Camino.

I showed Robin my "Boundary Rider" lyrics, which he liked. This meeting, and our discussion of those lyrics, actually was the catalyst for my sudden burst of creativity when I returned to Australia, our chance meeting setting the vision for my future down a completely different pathway. Whilst I made entries in my journal every day, they were more of a letting-go, and a cleansing of a past life that I needed to commit to paper. The chance to journal at every opportunity had become a necessity, and I often stopped for some hours at a time on The Camino to make my daily entry. I had no idea then that I would establish a website, www.caminoway.com.au, write a book of prose centred on The Camino, write this journey of the Sword of Discernment, or even write an album of songs – and all as the result of meeting Robin. As well as our sing-alongs and in-depth discussions on the road to Santiago about what our lives are all about, we did fill hours during our journey thinking of slogans to help motivate Roland to keep on keeping on.

The words we had left for him along The Way to give him incentive to continue created interest among other pilgrims, to the point that people who joined us later, in bars and cafes, asked, "Who is Roland?" and "What is the point of the signs?" I think Robin wrote the first, "Roland walks this way" and this was followed by Young's and mine, "Roland knows" and "If Roland can do it, so can you".Robin wrote on a rock seat, "Roland sat here" to encourage Roland to take a rest occasionally. I guess his

"Roland land = Fatherland" gave the exercise a personal German touch, as did his motivational wall sign on a downhill run, "Roll on, roller coaster!" Our stop by a river, to cool off later in our journey, resulted in me writing on a steel upright, "Roll'n' River" and, much later, when Young and I took a different track to Samos, we left a sign on a high post, "High rollin'!"

No doubt Robin created other signs on his track. I was happy during my hours with Young to listen to his ideas of setting up a Roland Kingdom on some island paradise and minting our own currency called "The Roland". We thought of having a postage stamp made, bearing the Roland motto, and using these to stamp pilgrims' Compostela certificates at Santiago rather than with the official traditional stamp for those completing the entire journey. However, we concluded that the Spanish might take a dim view of this idea and regard our act as a lack of respect for the pilgrimage. Of course, it was merely a joke we were thinking about, but I'm sure that, in our fun mood, a dare would have done the trick. It was not until I had completed my walk, and was walking through Santiago, that I awoke to the significance of our signs for Roland along The Way. Roland, the nephew of the great French warrior, Charlemagne, had marched The Camino along the French route of our markers for Roland. The monument to Roland at Alto de Ilbaneta, at the base of The Pyrenees, honours his battle to the death during the French retreat. The signs we had made with Robin's marking-pen would weather many a storm over the ensuing years, and pilgrims making their way along the way of St. James and seeing those signs of encouragement to our friend, may think, in their ignorance, that they are some sort of tribute to the great French soldier.

Well, they did help to pass the time for us during our long walk together, and also helped us recapture some of the silly things we did in our younger days. In truth, it caused no harm to anyone, and I discovered later that Roland quite enjoyed our efforts as he marched his weary way towards Santiago, like Roland the French warrior.

The Loner (James Dean)

When I was a young man
I watched the silver screen;
my hero was a loner
by the name of James Dean.

Now Jimmy was a wild one,
gave his heart to every role;
he had trained in method acting,
and acted with his soul.

James Dean, James Dean,
larger than life on the silver screen.

It is said the good die first
whilst the living just get old
and their hearts just get harder
and their living is controlled.

It was not that way for Jimmy,
he was a candle in the wind;
he burnt it in the middle
and he lit it at both ends.

James Dean, James Dean,
larger than life on the silver screen.

Now I am old and weary,
having joined the crowd at large;
trying to fit in…
you should see my scars.

CHAPTER 14.

WHEN IRISH EYES ARE SMILING

Memories of the impressive Templar Castle in Ponferrada fade as the pilgrim walks through the lush pastures of the El Birzo, nestled in the mountains. Flavours of exquisite cured meats and delicious cherries from the local villages and a visit to the garden of Iglesia de Santiago at Villafranca, and Puerta del Pardon (the "Forgiveness Gate") all nourish the body and the heart. The Way follows the valley via the Valcarca River before a challenging ascent to the ranges of Os Ancares and Sierra do Courel, passing through the Ranadoiro Mountains and across the Alto do Polo, descending into the village of Triacastela.

The San Xil Camino offers scenery that fortifies the pilgrim's spirit, whilst the optional narrow forest track slices through typical Galician oak woods; an alternate route to Sarria, through Samos, with its impressive monastery. This is perhaps the first town in the region where the pilgrim can enjoy the delicacy of freshly-cooked octopus. Walking across the valley to the river and following the path of the river to Sarria is a wonderful acknowledgement that man cannot duplicate that which nature provides.

Roland had fallen far behind us and Dan was nowhere to be seen as we entered the Celtic settlement of Ponferrada. The city had been a Roman mining town, later destroyed by the Germanic invaders and the Visigoths before being rebuilt by the Romans. It was again destroyed by the Muslims (Moors) and recaptured and again rebuilt by the Spanish.

We entered the city over the pilgrim bridge, built originally by the Romans but unusually reinforced by steel beams zig-zagging above the modern railway. The city's modern name, Ponferrada, derives from the Latin, Pons Ferrata, meaning Iron Bridge. Ponferrada had been a booming pilgrimage town, with a diversity of merchants, including Franks and Jews who were protected back then as the town rejected the call for segregated communities. The railway came to Ponferrada in 1882, and in the 1940s the town grew with the boom in the coal industry. Joining my ragged band of brothers, Robin, the rock star and Young, the artist, whom I was later to learn was an accomplished classical musician, we made our way to the historic Templar Castle on the town's outskirts. The castle, built in the 12th century, had also been destroyed by the German invasion in the 13th century; it was constructed over the remains of a Roman fort, which, in turn, had been built over a pre-Roman Castro.

The Knights Templar duties were, traditionally, to protect pilgrims and give them refuge. However, soon after the castle was built, the Templars were banished and the site in later years became a tourist attraction. We went across the drawbridge and through the main gateway, with its impressive Templar coat-of-arms above the door. Although fascinated to be walking in the halls of the brave knights of old and viewing the relics on display to attract the tourists' Euros, we were unable to see more of the historic parts of the castle, Those areas were closed to visitors, and are reported to hold all kinds of secret Templar symbols – particularly inside the twelve towers, which represent the twelve months of the year and the twelve disciples of Christ.

We left the urban area of Ponferrada and followed the trail into the scenic green of the vineyards, cherry orchards and wildflowers towards the mountains of Galicia and the beautiful Villafranca del Bierzo, among the foothills of the Rio Burbia. We had covered a distance of 27.1 km, in high temperatures, to Ponferrada, and then headed on towards Villafranca, another 24.7 km north. The 16.7 km to Cacabelos, which had been the administrative centre for the Romans' gold mining, was the goal for the day. Nearing the town, both Young and Robin got ahead of me as my weary soul and torn feet got the better of me. I decided to find an albergue for the night. I had missed the free Wi-Fi connection, café and mini-market, preferring to take the gravel path through a picnic area into the town, crossing the bridge on the far side of town, viewing an old mill and a wooden olive-press as a landmark with a direct route to the albergue.

The walled entry to my ranch-style abode had a most curious folk-art painting of young Jesus playing cards with San Antonio de Padua. The famous Saint from Portugal, born in Lisbon in 1195 and educated into The Order of St. Augustine, spent eight years in the convent in Portugal to which the relics of five Franciscan martyrs had been brought from Morocco. These relics inspired him to follow in the footsteps of those heroes of the faith and, after extreme opposition from his Order, he finally obtained consent to join the Franciscans. He was granted permission to go to Africa to preach to the Moors, but after severe illness at sea he returned to Assisi where a chapter of the Order was in progress. We was ignored by the Order and remained in obscurity, but providence revealed to the Franciscans what a treasure they had acquired, and San Antonio (St. Anthony) was made professor of theology and successfully taught this subject at Bologna, Toulouse, Montpellier and Padua. He later gave up teaching to work as a preacher and as an accomplished orator, travelling through France, Spain and Italy.

He was regarded as a legendary hero even in his own lifetime, and many miracles were attributed to him. As a child, I was taught of St. Anthony's miracles, and to pray for his intercession if I'd lost something. Strange as it seemed to me on my Camino, I recalled that the many times I had prayed about a missing item, he always managed to find it and return it to me. Throughout my adult life, despite giving up my traditional Catholic religion, I never forgot St. Anthony and, to this day, still ask him for help when something goes amiss; he has never let me down, although it may just be a coincidence, or a superstition on my part. I prefer to think not, but I did wonder, on my entry to that ranch-style albergue, what on earth was symbolized by the picture of St. Anthony playing cards with Jesus, on a wall in a remote village on The Camino.

I was too foot-sore and weary to ask while the proprietor stamped my Camino passport, and then I went to the kitchen for an evening pilgrim's meal. Returning to my room, I showered, took an anti-inflammatory tablet for my now swollen feet and, once again, was asleep before my head hit the pillow. I had not bothered to secure the door or to hide my money, phone or any other possessions. After all, San Antonio de Padua, the St. Anthony of my childhood, was protecting me and all that I owned that night. The night's stay at El Albergue de Mercadoiro was exactly the break I had needed. Mercadoiro was isolated, and little more than a desert oasis consisting of a restaurant and the albergue.

The old albergue structure had been built in the 18th century, and since restored. It was cheap, clean and comfortable and the four-course pilgrim's meal, including beer and wine, cost nine Euro. I had a SIN (non-alcoholic) beer and enjoyed a long hot shower in a private room before going to bed. It had been a long and difficult walk for me, but there was now less than 100 km to Santiago, as had been my aim that day. I decided to not push myself too hard, as my feet had been hurting all the way. Frequently walking with foot pain, despite having taken an anti-inflammatory tablet the previous night, in Sarria, did not help my mood or my motivation to push on. I was weary from lack of sleep, as the albergue in Sarria had housed seventy small bunks, and the after-effects of waking in pain, coupled with being woken many more times by snoring and movement from fellow pilgrims had not helped matters.

It had been good to start walking early, after a quick breakfast. Because I had wandered off the beaten track the day before and gone quite a few kilometres in a wrong direction, I was now determined to focus on the yellow arrow markers and plod on alone. Sarria is famous for its antique fairs, but as none had been scheduled for that week, and as the reconstructed tower of a Medieval castle held no attraction, I had decided to keep walking. Although I had already jettisoned 2 kilos a week or two earlier, I calculated that my backpack still weighed around 13 kilos and, still thinking about the excess weight I had carried for the better part of 700 km, I resolved to mail at least 3 kg to Santiago when I reached the next larger village with a post office.

The blisters had all but healed, but my feet were hot and swollen from the constant pounding and the effects of an extremely hot summer's day. Many lessons I had learnt about long-distance walking while on my Camino: to wear only cool clothing in the heat; drink plenty of fluid; keep energy levels up with healthy food; wear sandals whenever possible; carry no more than 10% of one's body weight. I made a mental note to write this information in my journal for future reference when next I stopped for a break. I kept myself content by singing songs, composing poems, stopping frequently to cool my feet and updating my journal. I had crossed the Medieval Ponte Aspera Bridge and the River Celerio when leaving Sarria then climbed the peak to Alto de Paramo, which had been difficult in the heat. Then came the trek through an oak forest to the hamlet of Vilei and on to Barbadelo, a distance of 6 km which had been slower going for me, taking a couple of hours. The days of Barbadelo being a thriving commercial centre was mentioned in the Codex Callixtinus, a 12th-century manuscript attributed to Pope Callixtinus II, but believed to ave been arranged by the French scholar, Amyeric Pilaud. The days of its commercial heyday were no more; I could find only a small snack stand, where I purchased a bottle of water to supplement my own two bottles which I filled at a nearby fountain. The snack stand sold fruit, mixed nuts and some cake, all adequate enough to see me through until the evening meal.

Reenergised, I walked a further 12.7 km on a gradual downward slope, regularly passing small abandoned hamlets and several small towns before arriving at Mercadoiro, another desert oasis. I had walked 16.9 km that day, and now had the fire in my belly to push on to Santiago. I had passed the marker indicating the final 100 km to Santiago, and recalled the rocks, notes and photographs that lay in a pile near the marker. On a stone fence nearby, a sign had been erected, reading, "Lay down your sorrow". This was obviously a monument for those who had not walked the entire Way and let-go their burdens at Cruz Ferro, near Foncebadon. Many pilgrims were content to walk only the final 100 km to Santiago, have their passports stamped at albergues, museums and churches along The Way, walking only that distance to qualify for their Compostela certificate at Santiago! While I was walking the entire 800 km to collect my certificate, other pilgrims believed they had to walk another 90 km from Santiago to the Finisterre coast to lay-down their burdens, burn some prized possession or throw a symbol of their burden into the ocean. As the saying goes, "Whatever floats your boat!" I was certainly not intent on walking a further 100 km after I had arrived at Santiago and collected my certificate of completion.

I awoke early the next morning and was out on the road at 6:00 am. The road dipped down for the 3 km to Vilacha, passing the only albergue there, a restored building draped with flags from around the world. As it was too early in the morning for the café bar to be open, I pushed on. Soon, Portomarin could be seen across the river, so I made a detour across the long bridge over the Rio Mino and climbed the stairway into the village. I had run out of money and needed to find an ATM to replenish my supply, and to pay for breakfast. The climb up the steep stairs to the small village was worth the effort. Formerly, the town had stood on both sides of the river, but had been flooded when a dam was reconstructed in 1956. The old stone buildings of the historic part of the town were removed, stone by stone, and a modern township had been erected high on a hill near the river.

The bridge I had crossed to reach Portomarin had been rebuilt many times; it was wide-spanned, crossing the river at a strategic point from which ruins of the ancient Roman city could be seen during low tide. Al-Mansur destroyed an early bridge during his campaign of devastation in 997. It was later rebuilt by the Spanish, but again destroyed during the war between Queen Urraca and her husband. She had the bridge rebuilt, along with the pilgrim hospital. The Church recognized that the bridge needed protection, and the role fell to The Order of Santiago, and later to The Order of San Juan de Jerusalem. It's great that the bridge still stands, as it was a wonderful feeling in the early morning to cross the bridge, climb the steep stairs and enter to town of Portomarin.

The modern main street had protective stone walls on either side, with covered sidewalks to shade shoppers from the sun's heat. I found the ATM and returned to a busy eatery on the covered sidewalk for breakfast. All along the street were bicycles belonging to pilgrims who, like me, were intent on having an early breakfast; many sat around me, chatting in Italian. As I sat eating my usual freshly-squeezed orange juice, croissant and coffee, I was distracted by a small car stopping on the edge of the road, and watched with interest as the driver alighted from it. I immediately recognized the lady as a pilgrim I had met and walked with a couple of days previously. She was a fit-looking French woman, possibly in her early fifties, and had at the time been walking with another equally fit-looking woman who, at a guess, was in her mid-seventies.

  Both women had set a quick pace and were keen to chat as we walked side by side. The younger woman spoke fluent English, but with a Parisian touch in her speech. I had commended them on their fitness at the time, but they fell behind me when they stopped for a break. I never saw either of them again until this moment, when the younger of the two stepped out of the car. She, too, had come to have breakfast and to buy some supplies for her friend. Apparently the elder lady had been hit by a car and had torn ligaments, although thankfully nothing broken. She could not walk, so they had rented a car to finish the remaining 100 km to Santiago. They were both disappointed that they could not complete The Way on foot, but thankful that the accident had not been more serious.

I was reminded of the dangerous rail crossing I had encountered some days back when Dan and I had taken different routes. The fact that a pilgrim had been killed there the day after we had passed had been part of the conversation on the road with these two women. It was ironic that we had also discussed the potential danger of walking too close to the edge of the road when trucks passed by. They both had discussed their misfortune and had already resolved to return during the next summer holidays to the point where the accident had occurred, and walk the remaining distance to Santiago.

I made it a point from then on to stay away from main roads, seek accommodation on the outskirts of large towns where traffic was not so heavy, and to find a tourist information centre somewhere along the pathway to book my accommodation ahead in Santiago. It was becoming the height of the holiday season in Spain, and there were to be more cars than usual on the roads; more push-bikes, too, usually with an Italian calling, "Buen Camino" as his companions followed, as in a peloton during the Tour de France. The number of pilgrim walkers content to walk the last 100 km to Santiago to claim their Compostela certificates had certainly increased that day. The increased number of holiday-season bike riders anxious to complete the last 100 km, with proof of accommodation stays stamped in their passports to qualify for their Compostela certificates, was becoming like peak-hour traffic in a city.

I was once again alone with my thoughts and the pounding beat of my feet, practicing a six-in-six-out breathing pattern through the nose, which I hound to be the best method for getting my mind into a "theta" place of mindlessness. The "beta, alpha, theta" helps quieten the mind, and the constant walking helps quieten my soul and the rhythm of my heart. Put briefly, the "beta" represents the walking experience of the mind in full flight; the "alpha is more like the state of mind whilst meditating or in relaxation; and the "theta" is the ultimate – the mind non-thinking, or what for some strange reason is known as mindfulness. It is in fact more akin to mindfulness, as it is like a deep meditation, or the state of mind when one is asleep. The mind relaxes, unwinds the thought process and relaxes physical tension and pain. One might argue that a good sleep achieves the same outcome, and this may well be true. However, if you seek to be awake, take-in information without deep thought, or just open the mind to another "power", this is definitely a great way to do so. Sandy MacGregor taught me this method when I attended his CHI live-in meditation seminar, and I used it successfully during my deepest sense of pain and loss a decade ago. It takes a Camino to remind one of the power of eastern methodology, which we in the west have only recently begun to understand and accept.

I walked the next 8 km slowly in the heat, climbing a gradual slope to the tiny hamlet of Gonzar, walking beside some impressive oak trees, then on a dirt path to Castromajor, resting from the heat there in a Romanesque church where a wooden statue of a virgin stands. A traditional legend recounts that a basket of pig snouts was left as a sacrifice at the church during the time the Moors controlled the area. When the offeror returned the next day, the snouts had turned into coal. Amazed, the Christian pocketed one of the lumps and later found that it had turned into gold. She hurried back to the church to find the basket empty. The locals could not tell me what the lesson to the story was.

As I passed through lush forests and traversed rolling hills, alternating between dirt bush tracks and quiet country lanes, I recalled my two days walking along The Way with the Greek men. We had enjoyed a meal together, talked of life, difficulties with the Greek economy and how difficult it was to get payment from clients in business or working for wages in their home country. Many people on The Camino had the time to walk because there was limited work available in most southern European countries. I appreciated how fortunate we had been to date with our Australian economy. I managed to keep up with the Greeks for a day, but on the second day they said a fond farewell, increased their pace, and slowly faded into the distance ahead of me. Now I was alone again, and thought about the many pilgrims I had encountered on my Camino during the past month, knowing that some would write and remain friends long after this Camino. My young band of brothers was no doubt a long way ahead by now, and I was resigned to thinking that perhaps we would meet again before the end of The Camino.

I had walked 25 km in extreme heat, and whilst the route was mainly across rolling hills, nothing had been steep and, all in all, it was an enjoyable day in the country. I reached Portos in the cool of the evening and stayed in its only, small, albergue. Knowing I had a long, 28.4 km journey the next day, I had the evening meal early and set off for bed for a good night's sleep, I was more interested now in reaching Santiago, and resolved to content myself with conversations along The Way with fellow pilgrims instead of becoming distracted by historical monuments. Leaving my little bunk house in the darkness, I decided to try an experiment and walk by instinct in the dark. It was only 5:00 am, and sunrise would not be until 7:20 am. It was pleasant in the cool of the early morn, catching what little breeze there was before sunrise, and wishing it would rain a little to soften the blow of the heat that each day provided. I was thankful for the sunshine, but the heat became almost unbearable after 9:30 am, and persisted for at least another twelve hours. Still, I had two hours of early morning walking in relative cool conditions, and was grateful for that.

Proceeding by instinct involves switching-off the mind and focusing on every step along the path. My LED torch was near the top of my backpack but I chose to not use it; instead, I felt my way along at a steady pace, like a blind man with a white cane.

My instincts sharpened with every pace, and I actually closed my eyes from time to time as I gained more confidence in the experiment. I became mindful of the swinging of my legs, the sound of the earth beneath my feet as my boots hit the surface, which changed from tar to rough stone and then to a dirt track; I repeated, in my head, "Cobble-stone, gravel, rough, rock, pebble-stone".

Once I knew I could move by instinct, I decided to hand-over my thoughts to instinct when I met someone who spoke a foreign language I did not understand. This also proved to be successful as I listen intently to the words, watch the movement of the speaker's mouth, body and hand movements. I began to understand, and could engage in conversations with people along The Way without effort, even though oblivious to their native tongue. This was demonstrated later down the track when I encountered a young deaf French girl while taking a detour with Young two days later.

I was thinking over the previous 700 km and of the people I had met during my pilgrimage: my meeting with the young German backpacker when we ran out of water and found a well in The Pyrenees; enjoying the company of the Irish mother and daughter and their stories of the land of my forefathers; the spirituality of the two Canadian schoolteachers; times with the Danish artist and his actor son; laughing with the Dutch kids; singing with the Belgians; listening to the beauty of the South African brothers and sisters; being poetic with the young German rock star and my band of brothers; eating with the Greeks and Italians; passing time with the French and the two Spanish beauties; influenced by the English teacher's freedom and the determination of the retired German ballet teacher; appreciating the kindness of an albergue volunteer and the charity and goodwill of the North and South Americans. There seemed to be so many other pilgrims to be grateful to, and all crossed my mind.

Yes, The Camino is truly a step back in time and a letting-go of burdens, but it was also the experience – more often than not for me – of being influenced and impressed by the people I met along The Way. My journey was drawing to a close and I trusted that I would get to meet many more people, hear their stories, share their joys and lend an ear to their pain and suffering – as had been done by others for me. My Sword of Discernment had already been expressed in the outward signs and experiences I had experienced – and would continue to – as I wound my way to Santiago.

As I walked through the green vista of vineyards, cherry orchards and fields of wildflowers, the mountains of Galicia loomed before me. It was but a short trail of about 8 km to the Villafranca del Bierzo where the final and most beautiful town of The Camino would be a brief oasis and rest stop before I trod the happy path of destiny once more; a well-earned rest stop before I set out to complete the next stage of the journey to La Faba, some 34 km further. The pathway from my overnight albergue climbed steadily for the next 32 km, and I calculated that my plan to stay in Villafranca del Bierzo should take no longer than an hour if I was to make it to La Faba at a reasonable pace this day. However, I was not to venture too far that day. Stopping at a small

albergue and entering a café bar for some lunch, I took a seat at the bar next to an attractive young blonde woman who was in deep conversation with the barman, speaking perfect Spanish and wearing a colourful cotton dress and fancy sandals. I assumed she had arrived by bus or car, as she was by no means in the attire of a pilgrim.

The barman left to prepare my order and she sat sipping a local wine while I was lost in thought and rather intrigued by the fair-skinned Spanish beauty who talked and laughed with the barman who was also preparing he lunch. He came back to the bar with a large board on which was a plate of tapas. She turned to me and, in a perfect Irish-American accent, asked me to join her in her feast while I waited for my own order. She introduced herself as Anne Marie and began to tell me her story and tales of her ancestry. I thought of the two Irish women I'd had conversations with at the bar in Pamplona, knew it was going to be a long day and that I was not going to get very far that day on my Camino. I ordered a SIN beer and enjoyed my Spanish pie and a fair share of Anne Marie's tapas before we moved to an outside garden, where she proceeded to tell me some of the reasons why she was walking The Camino.

It turned out that she was staying the night at the albergue opposite and had taken the time to shower and dress-up for lunch before I'd arrived. I made a mental note to book into the albergue if I got talking too long with this Irish-American beauty. To my knowledge, there was no other place to stay before Villafranca del Bierzo, another 6 km along the track. As it happened, Anne Marie was a New York restaurant owner who had lost the business in the flood that had washed through the city nearly a year before her visit. She was battling changes in the law, to reopen her business in the future, close to where her former popular and successful restaurant had been. It had originally been her dad's business, but he had become gravely ill and had died some twelve months before the flood, and she was left to run it. By her own admission, she had done that very successfully. Every time she spoke of her father, she shed a tear, and it was plain to me that she needed the Camino journey, like many of us, to let-go of her burdens.

As a young girl she had taken off to South America and spent a year in a village, learning Spanish, which she enjoyed using during many broken conversations with the barman whenever he came to bring us another drink. A lag in our conversation occurred when three female walkers with whom I had walked briefly during past stages of my Camino, appeared in the beer garden. Now surrounded by beer-drinking Irish women, I took the opportunity to quietly slip across the road to book into the albergue for the night, but there were no vacancies. This was the first time on my Camino that I was stuck without accommodation. I returned to rejoin my Irish womenfolk and decided to sing them every Irish song that I could remember from my childhood and beyond. They enjoyed every minute of my efforts to entertain them, and they each gave me a farewell kiss as I left them in the twilight, determined to find a bed somewhere down the track before dark. I did not have to go very far, as less than 2 km away I came across the small village of Valtuille de Arriba, and secured the last bed in a twelve-bed albergue.

"When Irish eyes are smiling, sure 'tis like a
    morn in spring.
In the lilt of Irish laughter, you can hear the
    angels sing.
When Irish hearts are happy, all the world
    seems bright and gay,
and when Irish eyes are smiling, sure, they
    steal your heart away."

Chauncey Olcott & George Graff, Jr.

CHAPTER 15.

STRANGE HAPPENINGS

"The relaxing atmosphere of the Rua Major in Sarria's town centre, with its fine food, cafes, churches, chapels, monasteries and pilgrim hospitals – and a visit to the castle fortress and the Magdalena Monastery – makes the pilgrim's stay a nice respite before the final destination.

The Camino takes the pilgrim through pretty villages and peaceful hamlets under the shade of many old oak trees on quiet country roads. The Way passes the beautiful Romanesque church in the village of Barbadelo before crossing the River Mino and a rise uphill to Serra de Ligonde.

The pilgrim passes the hamlets of Gonzar and Ventas de Naron, the Romanesque churches of Santa Maria in Castromajor and Eirex, where a statue of Daniel with the animals, and one a pilgrim, are featured. The trail continues downhill, past the village of Casanova, steeped in myth, and on to the village of Leboriero and the lively markets of Melide for local octopus, the most classic dish of Galicia.

The Camino crosses several streams and follows a forest track to the village of Boente and its church of Santiago. The Medieval village of Ribadisco and the town of Arzua, with their churches of Santa Maria and Magdalena, are a fitting way to prepare for the final leg to Santiago. The remaining pathway to Santiago takes the pilgrim through woods, sleepy villages and across streams. En route, the unique statue of Santiago and the lovely hamlet of Rua are worth a visit. The rest of the route is a mix of country roads and forest tracks.

Lavacolla, on the outskirts of Santiago, is where pilgrims wash in the river in preparation for their arrival in Santiago. Rows of eucalyptus trees line the way to Monte de Gozo, where the pilgrim catches the first glimpse of the Cathedral of Santiago." .It is traditional to attend the Pilgrim's Mass at the cathedral, while delighting in the stark architecture and the spiritual and cultural "Mecca" of Santiago. Entering the township of Villafranca del Bierzo, I was struck by the beauty of this Medieval town with its Renaissance touch, despite the blemish on the landscape of modern hotels and office buildings. I had entered the main gateway, past the Iglesia de Santiago, with its doorway for pilgrims who were too sick to walk to the main entrance – considered to be the essential way to enter if you hoped to gain indulgences from the church. This holy place of worship and recovery was, according to legend, built by Saint Francis of Assisi himself on his pilgrimages. He must have had the support of his maker, because he seems to have achieved so much during his brief time in Spain.

The town sat on the remains of a fortified Roman encampment, at the meeting-place of the Burio and Valcarce Rivers, in the shadow of a mountain pass. It later became a city of merchants, or Franks, more accurately described today as foreign merchants or traders. It also became the home of numerous pilgrim hospitals after the outbreak of The Plague in 1589, and was destroyed by flood in 1715. The French soldiers who overtook the city in the 19th century improved it architecturally, but they were driven out by British soldiers who ravaged the town, destroyed its castle and stole valuables from the churches. Today it is a great place to rest before the ascent towards the nearby pass of the O Cebreiro Mountains.

In the town's lush botanic gardens, I found a great place to eat my take-away sandwich and enjoy a cool drink. After resting my feet for a spell, I took a walk down memory lane, wandering the picturesque streets. I noticed that the mansions built in the 19th century bore the coat-of-arms of the original inhabitants and the castle, although not open to the public, had been restored to its former glory. I left Villafranca and slowly strolled the remaining kilometre to a fork in the road. Although I knew that the more challenging route was apparently more beautiful that the lower route, it did involve a steady climb up another 500 metre slope, so I chose the lower road, knowing it would be quicker. I assumed that Robin and Young had more than likely chosen the high track, which was 1.5 km longer to Trabadelo where the paths met, and I would make up some time. Robin had communicated with me earlier via SMS messages, and I knew that he and Young were only about an hour ahead of me. We agreed to meet in Trabadelo at the base of the pass where both paths rejoined. I could understand why pilgrims took the more scenic route, as my day's walk was mainly on a track parallel to the highway, with crash barriers providing protection from the traffic. Because of the super highway overpass above, the traffic on this highway was mostly very light, and I had peace and quiet of the countryside to myself. This was the historic route, passing through Pereje, and was the site of the old pilgrim hospital donated by Dona Urraca for the O'Cebriero monastery in 1118. The hospital was decommissioned during the land reforms of 1835, and is but a monument today. Apart from that, there was little to be seen and I continued my non-eventful bypass to Trabadelo.

After the view of the highway along which I had tramped for the last 10 km, the pathway into Trabadelo was pleasant. The entrance to the town featured immense chestnut trees and the activity of a modern timber mill which reminded me of my early childhood on the north coast of New South Wales. Back then, there were three timber mills within the boundary of the small town and another three within a seven kilometre radius; to my knowledge, all had ceased operating - except one, a small, privately-owned hardwood mill. I noticed that the Tabadelo mill had a pile of freshly-cut logs and the aroma was heavenly.

This sight would not impress any tree-hugging enthusiast, who probably had no understanding of the nature of regrowth or the effect on small tree growth dwarfed by excess shading by larger trees. The argument for cutting-down the larger trees to allow photosynthesis to do its job of allowing the natural growth of the young was always used by timber men. Those of "green" persuasion argued that the number of years it takes to grow a large tree and cutting it down did not justify the men's reasoning. The timber men always have a rejoinder; that big trees suck-up less carbon dioxide and expel less oxygen into the atmosphere than a large number of small trees growing in their shadows. I guess both arguments have their points, but I bent more to the view that the timber industry was a vital part of the community. The timber mill closures since my childhood left many men on relying on social security payments, which have continued to the present day in my old home town. I did have time on my Camino to reflect on personal issues, spiritual outlook and community. It was a time for reflection; a time for rethinking beliefs and attitudes; and a time for letting-go.

As I walked in the cool of the early morning, I was mindful that these mild conditions would not last; that the heat of the day would soon descend upon me. Content with the time of day and my walking pace, I began to move into a zone of awareness, as in a good set of tennis between two professionals. The constant hitting of the ball back and forth, with one player moving without haste and consistently positioning himself or herself to receive the ball, while the opponent's focus is to place the ball where the other player isn't, becomes a mind game, and the first to break their concentration and step outside that zone of awareness loses the point, the game, the set, or even the match. My walking was now in this zone of awareness; my feet doing the walking while my body and mind did nothing but stay on course for the ride. I was mastering feelings and emotions, intent on kindness to myself and compassion for other pilgrims on The Way. Outside my zone, my feet ached and my body was wracked with the pain of the strain of what now seemed a never-ending journey. Just for now, my soul loved and my ego was in check, content to merely roll with the ever-constant drumming of my feet. It is said that the brain knows three steps ahead of where your feet will land. In my current state of mindfulness, the brain was in neutral, the body relaxed and the feet were in charge.

I was intuitive of the ability to connect with a power greater than and beyond my mind and senses, now sensitive to the flow of energy coming to me from beyond - the energetic system that drove my body, like the power of a light-bulb when switched-on. The connection was deeper now; the flow of energy seemed to be coming from nature and the universe surrounding me. The connection flowed to fellow pilgrims, this place and this moment in time. I was no longer a beast of burden with a heavy backpack; I seemed lighter and my mind was open to guidance. I was now connected to a nature of divine oneness and a consciousness of higher awareness. The thought of poems I had written on my journey once again entered my head and, for a moment, I was guided by the intention to write it all as a book. I quickly dismissed this idea as I did not want to lose the flow of energy that had come over me. Perhaps it was my ego and mind rejecting guidance, as the thought of writing a book was, in my limited belief, developed through fear and a need to express inner feelings. It was not something to publish for the world to see, I thought. At the time, I was not attuned to the fact that I would in fact write many books, including poetry and, in fact, write songs about The Camino. I buried the thought as my feet continued to march to the beat of a different drummer. However, the seed had been planted, and it was that seed that would evolve into my true Sword of Discernment long after I completed The Camino de Santiago.

I had heard it said that some people receive intuitive guidance from ascended masters; others access it through daily, automatic writing, dreams or past-life regression. Whatever the technique, this day I was open to the lessons that applied to me at that time: the handing-over to a power greater than me, without definition; a pathway to higher awareness. It surprised me that I did not do this more often – allowing my brain do the hard yards. The brain's manner of treading life's path had led me to depression and misery. Here and now, I had found a new way; I had now come to believe that it was always the way. The choices I had made in my life had been driven by fear and the need to control; now there was a different pathway.

My task now was to transcend my own limits and those of my greater consciousness. I had an inner warning of the dangers of illumination. It was now a time for letting-go of all that the world had taught me and to focus on training my mind and body to be open and conscious of higher awareness, otherwise the power to transform would be blocked. It was coming to me now that this higher consciousness is a gift, and in that state of being I needed less and would not ever be afraid again. It was a means of expressing love in a blissful state of generosity of the spirit. I would do what I love to do best, share myself with life and with other people. The need to be connected to this higher awareness would require openness to learning; to be open to what is, not to the ways of the world any longer, but to the ways of the spirit, my spirit.

The sense of the higher awareness had left me and I had walked a long distance without actually being conscious of it. My belief had been tested and had come up wanting. I resolved then and there, from this experience, to continue to test my beliefs. In the cool of this Spanish morning the spirit had revealed to me the vital need of evolving to higher awareness. My logical mind told me that I still needed to be in this world – but not of it; to do the things I had to do, but to hand over to this inner awareness, this higher power; to be truly alive; to have faith; to be strong and spiritually powerful. It was the lesson of The Camino. Doing all this would be my Sword of Discernment. I once again felt the burden of my backpack and the constant pain in my feet.

The fly-over traffic above the small village could not be heard, making my entrance into the town peaceful. It was mid-afternoon when I sent an SMS to Robin to ascertain whether he and Young were ahead or behind me. They had indeed taken the longer, scenic route over the Camino Duro and had reached Pradela, near the pinnacle of the mountain, with another 2.7 km descent down a steep track to Trabadelo, so I knew they would be at least an hour behind me because of the slow pace needed on the steep downhill path. I walked on to La Portela de Valcarce and sent another SMS to Robin to let him know where I was and that I would find a private B&B for us. As luck would have it, I actually found a lovely home with three bedrooms at the entrance of the town, and booked it, hoping that Robin and Young would agree. The owner, living in the house opposite, across the main route, assured me that she would only charge me for a single room for the night if the boys didn't show up. I busied myself with a fresh shower, made a cup of tea and ate some nuts I had kept for such an occasion. The laundry had a washing-machine, but I opted to hand-wash my gear, as was the case during most of my Camino. After hanging everything out to dry, I attempted to reenter the premises, but had accidentally closed the door, which had locked automatically. The keys were on the kitchen table. I went back to the owner's house across the road and found that she was having an afternoon siesta, but her house-maid assured me that she would be awake soon and would then give me another key.

I sat on the front verandah, content to just sit and take in the passing parade of pilgrims still on the road. To my surprise, a familiar voice startled me and, standing at the front gate was Dominic, the Italian tiler. The last time we had met was at a bar

200 km back along the track. Robin, Young and I had been sitting at the bar which, to all intents and purposes, resembled a movie set, both inside and from the outside. As a matter of fact, all the businesses on both sides of the street were built of timber and stone, and the bar's doors were not unlike the swinging doors you see in the westerns. I half expected to see Clint Eastwood or John Wayne come strolling through the doorway into the saloon. So many villages and buildings along The Camino appeared similar to western movie-sets. Of course, there was no Clint Eastwood, but instead, in marched Dominic to buy drinks for his girlfriend, Francesca, who was outside, seated in the shade of the building.

Dominic insisted on buying us a round of drinks, which we graciously accepted. We all stepped outside to meet Francesca, an olive-skinned Latin beauty. Dominic introduced us and we all sat on the ground in the shade of the building opposite the café hotel bar. We were soon joined by a middle-aged Swiss woman who had walked almost 3,000 km across the French Alps to The Camino Way. As we sat laughing and joking, we decided on a group photo; later along the track I had a look at it. To my surprise, the photo had come out perfectly, except for a single beam of sunlight, shining directly on me, and on no-one else on the picture.

I thought it strange that this had happened, and remembered John, of The Order of Mother Theresa, and his holy card with the Sacred Heart of Jesus and his comment, "Jesus is looking after you, Doug", rung in my ear. I also remembered my evening meal with the gracious Nicole, from England, who, in her free way had said to me when strange events occurred, "That's The Camino". Who knows what laws of nature or other unknown forces influenced the outcome of that photo? But I had made a mental note to not delete it from my phone camera.

Dominic had noticed the sign on the fence, advertising "Accommodation available. Apply within", and I told him that the lady of the house was having a siesta and I was waiting for her to bring me a key. I enquired after Francesca and he said she was about 100 km back, with shin splints and needed to rest. We agreed to meet later, at 8:00 pm, for dinner together at the restaurant behind the house when Robin and Young had arrived and had some time to recover from their day's walk. The house owner emerged, gave me a spare key, and I left her in conversation with Dominic and returned to my abode.

I sat on the verandah again, facing the main road, and wrote in my journal, detailing the day's thoughts and activities. In the distance I could see Robin and Young approaching, and I greeted them with glasses of cold water from the kitchen refrigerator; they were both feeling the effects of the heat – the temperature still being in the high thirties in the mid-afternoon. I gave Robin the spare key on the instruction by the owner, who had told me that we could all settle-up for the accommodation cost in the morning. She said breakfast would be available in a side café she had converted at the rear of the restaurant. It also housed a bakery, so fresh bread and croissants would be available from 7:00 am. I marvelled at her business skills, as she had income from the house, which had been renovated, a restaurant operating in the garage area behind the house, a bakery which I noted in the morning had locals lining-up for her fresh bread and croissants, and she served a continental breakfast in the café bakery. All her takings were in cash, and I reckoned that some people, irrespective of economic conditions, could make a good living with ingenuity and hard work.

The youth unemployment rate in Spain was 53% and overall unemployment was 25%, but this woman, through hard work and providing a service for the passing pilgrims, in a little village on The Camino de Santiago, was raking-in the Euros. It struck me as strange that with the number of pilgrims on The Camino, more people did not take the opportunity to do business. I came across only two enterprising merchants outside the main cities and larger towns, during the entire 800 km, willing to sell their products and services, and both of those worked on donations, not fixed prices.

Dominic joined Robin, Young and me at an outdoor seating area in the back yard of the house. To our surprise, he had a very elegant, tall Italian woman with him, who looked at us all with horror and a "look down the nose" expression of judgment. She was dressed like a princess on an important date, with jewellery, a studded head-band, a long soft plain cotton dress and fancy shoes. Her attire seemed so out of place on The Camino; her dinner companions, Robin, Young and I were dressed just like Dominic, in walking pants, short-sleeved shirts and sandals, feeling quite at ease. We did our best to include her in our conversation, but it was obvious that she was not interested in talking to us. Dominic, on the other hand, was as effervescent as the sparkling wine they drank with dinner. My young brothers settled for the local beer I, as had become my habit, drank a non-alcoholic beer or two. The woman, whose name escapes me, left the table as soon as she finished her meal and Dominic stayed for another drink before shaking hands with us and wishing us "Bien Camino". Dominic and his new-found partner were as different as chalk and cheese. After finishing our meal we went back to the house and sat on the verandah for another chat, which lasted until after midnight, when the temperature had dropped far enough to ensure a comfortable night's sleep.

I woke during the night in a half dream state, sensing that my mattress was being pulled away near my feet. I raised my head from the pillow to see three little boys in the half-light tugging at the mattress, suddenly startled by my comment, "I am not afraid of you". They stood quite still then, and did not reply. I said to the one nearest the left side of the double bed, "Don't be afraid. Come closer so that I can see you". He advanced about half the bed's length and I caught sight of a beautiful small boy in the moonlight shining across the bed. He was three or four years of age. I said, "Who are you?" and he replied, "My name is Douglas". In an instant, I recognized a mirror image of myself at that age. Suddenly, I was that little boy standing by the bed and, as that little boy, I recalled the exact same situation when I was three or four years of age. I had been standing next to the bed of an old man all those years ago but, now, in the present, I had not recognised him; both the child and my aged self seemed to be carrying hidden burdens and, as an innocent child, I knew I was looking at a spiritually sick man trying to get well. I sat up in the bed, switched the light on, but there was no-one there. Looking down to the end of the bed I saw that the mattress had been moved away from the bed by about one-third of its length. I got out of bed and pushed the large mattress back into position on its base, turned out the light and went back to sleep.

Some time before dawn I awoke again, this time startled to see my mother standing on the right side of the bed with a knowing smile on her face. She never spoke, but I did hear her words: "Love many, trust few, always your own canoe". She looked deeply into my eyes with an understanding, sad gaze and the smile remained; I heard her say, again without opening her mouth, "I am alright now; I am in a safe place". I was in shock at her appearance, as she was ghost-like, but she left me with an inner peace as I watched her slowly fade away. She had been dead for more than a year now, and I wondered why she had come to me after such a long time and, indeed, on the other side of the planet, in Spain of all places. I had not turned-on the lights this time, and just drifted back to sleep. I awoke late, around 8:00 am, and walked upstairs to see if Robin and Young were still there, as it was their usual habit to be on the road before this time of day. They were both fast asleep, so I went back downstairs, had another shower, dressed and collected my dry clothing from the outside line. Even after being in the night air they were completely dry when I took them down. I repacked my backpack, made a cup of tea and, while sipping it, considered my previous night's close encounters.

"Feel the flame that forever burns,
teaching lessons we must learn,
to bring us closer to
the power of the dream.

As the world gives us its best,
to stand apart from all the rest,
it is the power of the dream
that brings us here."

CHAPTER 16.

DREAMS & REALITIES

I woke Robin and Young from their slumber and encouraged them to join me for breakfast at the bakery. I was packed and ready to get back on the road again, but they still needed to wait for their washing to dry, and had to shower and pack before being ready. We enjoyed our fresh croissants and coffee at the bakery, paid our bills and I said "Buen Camino" to my young brothers. On the road again, I began my long, final uphill quest to La Faba, some 14 km of mountainous, heather-linked earthern tracks. I was thankful that the weather report was for a fine day, as the trails are often muddy and slippery after the tar and cement roadways have been left behind, around 4 km from the peak. I took some photographs of young pilgrims seated in a group near a stone fence at the edge of a village, as a memento of my stay in La Portela de Valcarce, and began the long slow climb on this mountain pass.

I was on my own road less travelled on this Camino to Santiago. Thousands of travellers had walked this pilgrimage before me, and no doubt many would do so in the future. This was a time for reflection and introspection; unexplained happenings; logic giving way to myth and legend. In the clear daylight of this plodding journey, towards the end of my Camino Way, I found myself recalling the events of my Camino journey and the events of a past life that was now but a dream; a film implanted in my memory, that no longer held emotions – just simple recall. Visions of which, had I reentered, would have resulted in feelings of joy, pain, sadness, love, hate – or, in fact, any of the deadly sins that are biblically spoken of. I resolved to not go there now, but rather to focus on the steps of my travel on this hot Spanish morning.
My thoughts somehow drifted to my inner Sword of Discernment and who I really was and what I am now all about; the mindful

image that I had logically determined and sought to have some outward symbol of, had seemed to be a worthy quest to fulfil on my journey. It was to be the outward fulfilment of a myth at the end of the rainbow at Santiago Which, through accomplishing my inner mission, would result in me completing and producing a result that would be worthy of my cause. It was proving to be another myth, buried upon yet another myth. The inner movement of my thoughts, emotions, feelings and desires were, in fact, more of a mindfulness of sharp spiritual perception and judgment. My becoming sensitive to my ever-changing movements and understandings were questions that came from I knew not where, nor, in fact, to here they were leading me in a spiritual sense.

In my head I heard, "Trust in the slow work of God", but I was still in the darkness of my way, stumbling like a blind man towards some unknown light, perhaps to some new enlightenment. I began to hand-over, and felt as if I were being asked to walk a tightrope without a safety net. Maybe this was so, and the spirit within me, which I was beginning to understand really runs the show, was taking me from my head to my heart, and was taking hold. So my pace slowed as I made each painful step on what seemed a treadmill of repetition. I began to recall that a sign I had been given many times in the past, and which I had chosen to ignore, was the real purpose of doing my Camino de Santiago. I had thought that it was all about letting-go past burdens, seeing if I still had any affinity with the religion of my childhood. I had set out to discover whether my vision of love would manifest itself on The Camino Way, and to get in touch with an outward symbol of my inner-self discernment, a sword of honour that I would carry forth like some knight of old in a modern world. The Way had, for me, become all those things and more, for it was leading me down a pathway from a well of darkness where the dragon of my fear existed and from where, in time, a lotus flower of creative ideas and actions would spring.

My mind wandered back to an event five years earlier, when I was walking on a suburban street in Sydney, Australia, and I had picked up a medallion from the footpath. It held an image of a stick-man walking a mountain path with arms outstretched in a gesture of being free. Above his head was a black raven flying away, and the sun was beaming brightly in the sky. The border of the image was a river, with turbulent flowing water, but with elements of calm, deep water. At the base of the medal was a symbol, a Christian cross. I had turned the medal over to find an image of a pilgrim's staff. I was depressed at the time, in a deep

cloud of despair, and the small prophetic medal held little meaning for me then. Now, here on my Camino, all that was on that medal had now come true as I walked the same path in fulfilment of its images.

Now, with a pilgrim's staff in my hand, the message of that medallion would come back to me again, long after I had completed the pathway of my life. Just for now, I reflected upon its meaning and recalled many other strange coincidences as I walked my weary way towards my heart. There had been many signs during my past life, and now, many more on The Camino. I recalled my meeting with the two Canadian school teachers who encouraged me to attend Mass on two occasions during my journey – something I had not done for decades. Their gift of the wooden Rosary beads which had been blessed at Lourdes, a symbolic gesture by these two young Canadians, had resonated with me at the time. That gift was accompanied by the Mysteries of the Rosary, each of its five Mysteries introduced by a vision and mantra to focus on whilst praying to God the Father, the Son and the Holy Spirit and reciting the Hail Mary on each bead. It was a very personal gift from these devout young women and, at the time, I appreciated it. I never did get to praying on those beads, despite my attempts to do so, always falling asleep prior to beginning. However, for some reason I could still recall the Mysteries, a memory extending all the way back to my childhood.

I lost the beads somewhere along The Way, and briefly thought of how the girls would be disappointed, no doubt still praying for my reconversion and the renewal of my faith. My immediate justification allowed me no guilt for the loss, as I felt that the hand of fate had taken its course and that some other more deserving pilgrim would derive more mileage from the beads than I ever would. I had checked my backpack and could find only the sheet of paper with the Mysteries and decades of the Rosary neatly written out for me in a typical chronological order for the cyclic days of ritual. I made a mental note to get a new set for myself at Santiago, on the slim possibility that I would take up the practice, and a set for my son, Sam, who had asked me to buy him a set there. I had thought it a strange request on his part, as he had shown no particular interest in religious services or doctrines of faith and morals, despite having attended a Catholic school. Sam had

always been the quiet one; perhaps he prayed to himself, something I rarely did – at least, that is, until I began to learn the lesson of handing-over to a power greater than self. That lesson was a consequence of my path to recovery from alcoholism through attending AA, and not from my religious upbringing. I cast my mind back to the two strange coincidences: meeting Ramone, in Burgos, and his fashioning a sword from balloons for me, as if he had an insight into my vision of a Sword of Discernment; and meeting of Brother John of the Order of Mother Theresa and the card with the flaming heart of Jesus, and his parting remark, "Jesus is protecting you, Doug".

I recalled the photo in my iPhone of myself with fellow pilgrims, and wondered about the beam of light that shone on me and on nobody else. I thought of the party at home, the week before my wife left me for another. Every photograph of me taken at that party also showed friends, but a lightning-rod of light cut me in half in each of them. It was like a premonition of what was to follow. I thought of my powerful friend, Patrick, spending every night of his life giving his energy to others who suffered; he was recalled by hospitals throughout Sydney, at least three times a week, to help others pass to the other side. A group photo with mutual friends from a decade before showed Patrick as nothing but a ball of light. Everyone else in that photo appeared as normal. I had shown him the photo on my iPhone immediately after it was taken, and he merely looked at it in a matter-of-fact way and said, "Yes. I am full of extra energy tonight". I could fill a book with the wonders of Patrick, but for now, it was all just my source of wonder. Once more I recalled Nicole's voice, "Well, that's The Camino, Doug. "I thought of the miracles of Lourdes, where the Virgin Mary had appeared eighteen times to Bernadette Sourbirous, a fourteen-year-old peasant girl, identifying herself as the Immaculate Conception, giving Bernadette a message for all, "Pray and do penance for the conversion of the world". Lourdes, ever since the miracles were first reported in 1858 – and like The Camino – attracts more than a million pilgrims each year. It is said that no-one leaves Lourdes without a gain in faith. Moral and spiritual cures are more well-known than physical cures, although there are many reports of amazing bodily cures having occurred at that holy place. Some go to Lourdes with lifetime prejudices, yet their minds become suddenly cleared. Frequently, skepticism gives way to faith, and coldness and antagonism become a whole-hearted love of God.

Many books and movies tell the story of Lourdes; even Hollywood made a movie in the 1940s of the remarkable event, entitled, "The Song of Bernadette", which won six Academy Awards. It was the Christ who is reported to have said to the Jews, "If you do not believe me, believe the work that I do". Christine used to say, "We are all light workers for the kingdom". Occasionally though, she would say to me, with a curious expression on her face, "You are a dark magician". I guess I had to be taken-down to the dragon's mouth, the pit of hell, before returning to become the light worker that the Light of all Lights had destined me to be – perhaps.

As I've recorded previously, it had become a regular ritual for me to visit any church that I sighted at the end of a day's walking on The Camino – not visiting for religious reasons, but as a means of cooling down after the severity of the extreme summer heat of the day. The church buildings were usually small, just large enough to house a small community of local and pilgrim worshippers, primarily for the Sunday Mass. During the week, visitors were mainly pilgrims like me, interested in the historic significance of these houses of worship more than their religious rituals. I took advantage of these visits, and enjoyed them more than any museum along The Way.

Arriving with a weary body and damaged, aching feet was such a regular occurrence for me. The sense of arriving in a relaxed state, of just being in the historic places and taking-in the architecture of Roman, French, English and Spanish origins, was awe-inspiring; I could unwind, both physically and mentally, while under the influence of Muslim patterns in the roofing, or while viewing the sharp contrast of golden altars and iconic images of Christ, the apostles and the Virgin Mary – all of which left a lasting impression on me. They may have been places of worship for some, but to me they smelled of a past way of living worship that was steeped in tradition, but not spirituality, a way that for me was now dead. I thought of the kings, queens, princes, saints and sinners, and the many pilgrims of the past and present who had perhaps either sat where I sat or kneeled in the hope of God's influence over whatever their cause or pain may have been. The thought of these visits had become a reparative event and a recurring act for me, and all the churches somehow became blended into one.

The strange happenings of my Camino were not yet over, but for the time being I put aside all thoughts of strange events, miracles, historic churches and the reasons for my own journey as, with every step, I now focused only on the determination to complete this journey of discovery. I was again reminded of the words of my friend, Norm, "Alcoholism is a hurry disease", and I vowed to myself that I would do my best to slow down. I had been brought to stillness through depression and alcoholism; the closing-down of the computer within my brain and the crippling pain that ensued had caused my body to rest for a long period of time before ultimate recovery. It was perhaps the only way that the God of my own true nature and understanding could get me to stop running around in the pit of hell.

Here I was now, living without an agenda. I had come to The Camino without either a map or a real goal. Eventually I had had to succumb to the need for a map, after twice becoming lost along The Way. However, I had no map for the spiritual way, only blind faith in a God of my own understanding, a belief that could be either real, or merely a myth. I knew only that I had to trust in my instinct; trust in an inner belief and act according to a guidance that could not be defined by logical or sequential reasoning; trust in a power beyond explanation - all with the need for great courage and for an imaginary Sword of Discernment to keep one's focus on the path ahead, one step at a time.

Robin and Young had caught-up with me at Vega del Valcarce, the largest town of this day's trek. A small shop sold souvenirs of The Camino, and I purchased a Camino shell with the red Sword of Santiago painted on its outer shell, but could not find a symbol of what I had hidden deep inside. My outward symbol of a Sword of Discernment was something of my imagination, but I had not thought to let-go of logic, sequential reasoning and trust in a power greater than the one true God that was my personal guide. If only I had left reason to chance, like I did – in the main – on my Camino, I may have had the answer to my outward goal of what was now manifesting within me as a seed of creativity and which, given time and patience, would flower in God's good time, not mine.

Although I was learning to let go, and to allow God to lead, the ability to actually do so escaped me; I was still caught up with using the head, and not the heart, when it came to this mythical Sword of Discernment. I so wanted, and needed, outward proof of a sword; perhaps it was to identify myself as a warrior, or maybe only that I needed something to hold onto in my mind to help drive me ever onward. Who knows, my many adventures into the unknown, climbing great mountain ranges, crossing rivers, attempting to live the way of men of the road in past history may all have been nothing more than an ego thing.

The Camino somehow was different than any of those things; it resonated with the darkness within and attempted to shed light on the dark soul of my inner child. This journey was like spiritual rain on parched earth, helping to germinate the seed that had always been there, a seed of creativity waiting to break open and sprout into the world above, breaking through the crap and crud of the artificial dream of the world that had been cast upon me, the one that I had mistakenly embraced. I was now on a different path and, with time and patience; perhaps I would see the discernment within my heart flower into that which I was truly meant to be.

The pilgrim's shell and the sword symbol of St. James of Santiago that many pilgrims wore to indicate that they were on the pilgrimage were not my symbols, but those of all who had walked the many routes to Santiago from Medieval times until this day. So many pilgrims wore this shell, symbolizing that they were walking to Santiago either for their own inner journey of discovery or merely to take a long walk, to meet new people and enjoy The Way. I chose to not wear the shell identifying myself as a pilgrim; this weary, dust-laden old man with his heavy backpack and walking poles was a modern-day model of the traditional Medieval pilgrim who walked for penance, pardon and meditative enlightenment. I identified more with that symbol of the road than with any other symbolic emblem purchased from a shop, church or museum, or with any religious statue or even the road to

Santiago itself and, maybe, just maybe, even the Sword of Discernment that I so desperately seemed to need. I was on an inward mission, from the head to the heart, like so many of my older comrades on this journey. The youth were perhaps taking their Camino journey as a rite of passage, but for me it was more about letting-go of the past; letting the God within take hold; letting-go the religious indoctrination of my childhood; and doing my best to be free. As a friend back in Australia would say, "Just get on with it and stop trying to work it all out."

For its protection, I carefully wrapped my Camino shell, with the Knights Templar emblem on its outer shell, in some clothing. Its outer shell was the emblem that leads pilgrims from all over Europe and the Americas to the road to Santiago; it was the official signage of the many routes to Santiago; the many ridges on its back, a map of The Way. I noticed that the inner shell resembled a hand, the one we use to recognize and acknowledge our fellow man. So I wrapped and carefully stored the symbol of my Camino, reached for my journal once more and wrote down a poem relating to the shell. I planned to hang this shell-symbol, with my Santiago Compostela, in my home office on returning to Australia. Robin and Young now joined me, and I was transported back to the reality of the journey as we headed for a café to partake of some food and drink to fortify us for the next leg of the walk, to Herrierias.

What was left of my small band of brother, Robin, Young and I, continued climbing the long weary road to Herrerias. The numerous quaint villages along The Way provided respite, as we always managed to find a shaded location under an awning or a large tree for a drink break. The Galician influence was evident in the landscape and architecture, and even in the villagers' hospitality, although we had not yet officially entered Galicia. I had not yet had a meal of the famous Pulpo Gallego, boiled octopus served with olive oil, paprika and a hunk of bread, all traditionally accompanied by the refreshing local Ribeiro wine in a cold ceramic bowl. I put the thought of the red wine out of my head but my mouth watered for the octopus. We restored our energy with frequent stops to escape the sun's heat, and savoured the shade of the many chestnut trees along the route.

We thanked the Lord that the weather was dry and that the earth beneath our feet was not muddy or slippery. We arrived at Herrerias, traditionally an iron-working town on a river bank. The iron was once excavated from a nearby hill and transported to the village where the furnace smelter, large iron hammers, forging tongs and bellows can still be seen. It reminded me of my childhood visits to the local blacksmith, where I watched him forge horse-shoes; twisting the iron into shape, cooling it in a vat of water while holding the white-hot metal with tongs in one hand and beating it into shape with a huge hammer with the other. The need for such an industry was now, like so much of life's journey, lost in change.

Near the edge of the small village, some straw-roofed huts could be seen, yet another symbol of a past life now gone forever. We stopped for another drink break and filled our water flasks at the La Fuente de Don Quinones fountain, named after the famous jousting hero at Hospital de Orbigo, which we had heard about earlier on The Way. We were tourists in these small Spanish towns and villages, and contemplated out lot as we sat and ate in a small picnic area by a creek, greeted by a welcome sign for visitors in the old Galician language.

We were now entering Galicia, the last of the autonomous regions of The Camino and home of the much anticipated Santiago de Compostela. The official language of Galicia is Spanish, but more than 90% of the population speak the Galician dialect (which seems to be closely related to Portugese). While excavations have shown evidence of megalithic prehistoric culture in Galicia, the region was later settled by Celtic tribes who later became known as Galicians. Much of the Celtic culture remains, even the bagpipe music, which we would experience along The Way and at our destination. The people, although friendly, displayed the Celtic nature of fierce independence, much like the Scots, and similar to what those of Basque background had displayed during my time in The Pyrenees on this inward and outward journey of the spirit. The people of Galicia had conquered the Romans, the Muslims and the French invaders and, while practising Catholics comprised the majority of the population, the region has a reputation for witchcraft and pagan beliefs. There are many rituals and traditions in which pilgrims are encouraged to participate, including the drinking of 'aquarama,' the idea, as any alcoholic beverage had the opposite effect on me.

We had completed the steady climb together, and shared an evening meal and accommodation at one of the many small albergues. Somehow, we had lost sight of Robin, who had drifted behind to walk with some other pilgrims he had met. We had agreed to meet again in Triacastela, but that didn't happen. Young and I ventured forth along the Galician bypass through Samos, "the country of a thousand rivers". We talked of a Roland kingdom, a myth dreamed up by Young. We stopped frequently, to erect more signs to encourage Roland to continue his Camino, and delayed our journey in the hope that he would catch us and our band of brothers would again be united.

Climbing the challenging O'Cebreiro, we were rewarded with breathtaking mountain views, then descended the steep track to Triacastela, where we saw the coat-of-arms on a castle door – the only reminder of days gone by, when three castles were there. Nothing remains today. Passing through O'Cebreiro, the first officially Galician town on The Camino Way, we were reminded that this was the birth place of Father Elias Valina Sampedro, the local priest who was instrumental in the 20th-century revival of The Camino de Santiago; the man who created the painted yellow arrows and the cement markers – the arrows which had kept me on track. In the village stood the Iglesia de Santa Maria la Real, a reconstruction of the Medieval church, in which the baptismal font, Virgin and chalice reliquary are still housed. These relics were found during the reconstruction of the pre-Romanesque church ruins.

Local tradition claims that the Holy Grail, the chalice from which Jesus drank at the last supper, was hidden in O'Cebreiro. An event in the year 1300 brought fame and pilgrims to the little village. The story of a local parishioner trudging through the snow to receive communion annoyed the priest, who mocked him for going to so much trouble for a bit of bread and wine. At that moment, the bread and wine were transformed into real flesh and real blood. The Virgin statue, on display at that time,
is said to have turned her head to have a better look. The event was later declared a miracle by Pope Innocent VIII. When Queen Isabel passed through, two hundred years later, she donated an ornate reliquary for the remains; the Galician coat-of-arms, incorporating the chalice and host as a central symbol, remain to this day. We also noticed many old oval stone buildings with thatched roofs, well suited to Galicia's harsh environment. Peering inside one of these, we saw that it was divided, for animals and humans, with lofted ceilings. There was no chimney in the kitchen area; smoke could only escape through the thatch. Similar structures, in various stages of reconstruction or decay, appeared throughout Galicia along The Camino.

We had last set sight on Robin at Triacastela, 15 km back. Our phone communication indicated that he was now about an hour behind us, so we decided to walk the remaining 23 km to Barbadelo where we planned to find accommodation for the night. Arriving at crossroads, we had two options: the shorter, direct route via San Xil, saving 6.5 km and passing through some small hamlets, or the longer route, passing through Samos, and visit the historical monastery which incorporates a pilgrim albergue. We erected the last of our motivational signs for Roland and took the road less-travelled, to Samos, following a paved road for a few kilometres past some pleasant rural scenery, and caught our first glimpse of Samos, in the valley below.

The beautiful countryside was overshadowed by the large Benedictine Monastery standing above the tiny village. An expansive stream running through the middle of the hamlet created a perfect picture postcard, the image reminding me of a typical painting of John Constable, the English artist who always depicted quaint outdoor scenes. We meandered down a road that entered the village and found a perfect place for lunch.

A little kitchen inside displayed octopus and other delicious local concoctions. I asked for a meal of octopus and Young joined me with a similar order. We ordered a cool drink and went outside to sit in the shade as the cook busily cut up the octopus with a sharp knife and put a pan of water on the stove to boil our first full local meal in Galicia. The meal arrived in a large bowl, with paprika and olive oil already applied, no doubt to the cook's liking. He left us abruptly after placing a bottle of
olive oil and a flask of paprika by its side, and more hunks of bread than it was possible to eat at one sitting. I applied more olive oil to my meal and enjoyed the local delight. Young, likewise, was busy eating, and it was not until we had both finished our meal that we spoke of our immediate plans.

We made our way to the Samos Monastery, which had been founded in the 6th century as a monks' hostel. It was now a centre of wealth and prestige, controlling more than three hundred other monasteries in the region. The pilgrims' hospital, attached to the abbey, was built in the 11th century, is still in commission. We wandered around the ancient site, taking notice of the historical plaques indicating that the abbey had been destroyed by fire in 1537 and again in 1951, the latter causing significant damage, although the building still stands. Samos was the seat of power of the Benedictine Order in the early 19th century and produced seven bishops for the Catholic Church in Spain. We walked around the exterior of the 9th-century Mozarabic Chapel, noting that the monastery's imposing façade was in the late Baroque architectural style. Young wanted to do the guided tour with a friendly monk, but we were told that the next one would not be held for two hours, at 4:30 pm. We didn't relish waiting around, so we entered the building via a staircase to a cloistered courtyard featuring a rather ornate fountain in the centre, then found the gift shop attached to a library. Although the library was closed at the time, a plaque near the door bore a Latin maxim: "A cloister without a library is like a fort without an armory". This library was armed with more than 30,000 volumes, but I could see no weapons displayed. As Robin was nowhere to be seen, and we had been in Samos for approximately two hours, we thought it was time to get back on the pathway to Sarria, the gateway to the final 100 km to Santiago. Leaving the monastery, we crossed the river and followed the paved road past a piazza with pilgrim sculptures, then along a park and recreation area. I took some photographs of buildings on the way out of town, and enjoyed a rest and a swim in a beautiful flowing stream on the outskirts of Sarria.

Young was like a small boy again as he continually appeared and disappeared into the refreshing waters of what was, for the moment, our ideal lifestyle. He was like a dolphin, appearing for a brief moment with a cheeky grin and then reappearing with a smile and a glint in his eyes. The water was very cold, and I ventured into a nearby fast overflow stream, although never plucked up the courage to dive in as Young did. I washed in the stream, dried and, while still in my swim shorts and boot-free feet, went to the other side to refill my water flask with clear water.

Close by, a Spanish family sat, eating a late lunch, their food laid-out on an old wooden table. They were seated side-by-side, with father, mother and children lined up like roosting chickens. The father was swigging red wine from a glass jar the size of a small drum. He was a little intoxicated, and offered me a swig of his heavenly nectar, but I shook my head as I passed them by. Returning to the river, I had occasion to pass them again, and the drinking man once again offered me his drum of fine wine. There had been a time in my life when I would have gladly joined him in his quest to empty the contents, but those days were long gone. I thanked him again, but declined his offer.

The path alternated between pavement, cobblestoned and dirt as we took an alternate route to reconnect with the main route to Aguiada, 20.6 km further north. The lush forest of cypress trees and ferns adorned the sides of the track, which followed a stream for the next 12 km until we reached a dirt road leading to a bridge, where we sat on the rail. The heat was again extreme, and we were drinking our water in great gulps to quench our never-ending thirst. Young rolled a cigarette while I communicated with a young French girl who had arrived at the bridge a few moments after we had. We seemed to be the only pilgrims on the road at that time of day.

The girl could not speak English, and had a small whiteboard sign and marker hanging from her neck. She indicated that she was, in the main, deaf, and asked people to write words on her whiteboard so she could communicate with them. She spoke from the roof of her mouth, and sounded as if she were speaking in an echo chamber. I indicated with a wave of my hand that I spoke no French, and suggested we might lip-read. I gathered from her voice, lips and hand movements that she had fallen on the track about 100 km back a few days earlier. She had been alone at the time, suffering from heat exhaustion, and understood why we had stopped to rest. Other pilgrims had found her, delirious, and took her to a doctor at a nearby hospital, where she stayed the night and recovered sufficiently to continue her lone quest on The Camino. I guessed she was in her early twenties and quite alone, although not all lonely. I wished her well, said, "Au Revoir", that being about the limit of my French vocabulary, and watched her walking away and disappearing in the distance. Young was amazed that I had known exactly what she said without actually understanding a word of French and that, likewise, she had understood my English. He said, "You understood every word she said. How did you do that?" I merely answered, "It's the miracle of The Camino." In truth, I did not really know how I had understood so clearly, but surmised that it was through her hand movement, tone of voice and the movement of her mouth that I understood her story.

Young decided to walk on alone and try to catch up with Robin before reaching Barbadelo. We figured, due to our two-hour stopover in Samos and an hour enjoying the peace and having a swim, that we were now about two hours behind him, as he must have taken another route to Sarria. I was suffering with swollen ankles and new blisters, so decided to stay behind for a time and redress the blisters and rest my aching feet. When I finally began walking again, I climbed a rather steep hill and continued along an upward path for the next 8 km until reaching a main road near Aguiada and an albergue, about 17 km north of Sarria. Walking from the road to the grassed verge and then to the albergue's verandah, I was surprised by the melodious sounds of a piano playing Tchaikovsky's Piano Concerto No. 1, a piece I had always liked. To my surprise, they're sat Young at the keyboard, playing to his heart's content. He looked up, ceased playing and said, "I haven't played for ten years, mate, but this one's for you." He recommenced playing, this time Chopin's Polonaise in A Flat Minor. I knew both pieces, as I had played the piano in my pre-teen years and although I had some liking for classical music, it was limited to Tchaikovsky, Chopin and Beethoven, the latter being my favourite composer.

However, I was more a sixties folk-music follower and, of course, the heady stuff of the rock 'n' roll of the seventies. Young surprised me with his musical talent, and told me that he had practised daily for years, but had given it all away, as many good musicians do. I was reminded of my father's brilliance as a piano player, and regretted that I had given up the practice. Dad really only ever played when he was in a melancholy mood or a little intoxicated. I preferred to be in the great outdoors rather than cooped-up in front of a piano, and I had stopped playing at the first opportunity. We were both greeted and joined by fellow pilgrims we had met on The Way, including the pretty, young German Julia who had planted a kiss on me in Burgos as we'd passed in a doorway. She swore that she did not remember the incident, and I believed her. I, too, often experienced black-outs when under the influence of alcohol in the past and found that I could not account for words or deeds during those times.

Young and I had secured the last two bunks available in the albergue. We knew that from here on it would be more difficult to obtain accommodation, as more pilgrims joined The Camino at Sarria, more a starting point for those wishing to walk the minimum of 100 km to receive a Compostela certificate in Santiago than a tourist attraction. It was now the beginning of the busy season and the character of The Camino experience from here would change drastically as beds became scarce and groups entered The Camino who were not yet familiar with pilgrim etiquette. The rush to grab supplies for the road, to prevent being delayed at café bars, was so different to my earlier experience. I looked forward to continuing my journey in more rural and relaxed surroundings. Like Young, I retreated to my bunk immediately after our albergue dinner. I climbed to the upper bunk and said good night to Julia, who was sharing the room with us and four others. Julia said her good night, adding that she felt privileged and honoured to be sharing a room with me. I did not understand why she felt that way and did not ask for her reasons. I just laughed, rolled over onto my side and went to sleep. The only incident during the night was when I rolled out of bed to go to the toilet and fell to the floor. I had forgotten that I was so high off the ground. Luckily, I was not injured and quickly climbed back into bed after going to the toilet. The very next morning, as I was repacking my backpack, Julia asked me what had happened during the night. I joked that I was climbing out of bed to visit her and fell. We both laughed, said "Buen Camino" and Young and I were back on the track before the light of day appeared.

"The moment you doubt whether
you can fly, you cease forever to be
able to do it. The reason birds can fly
and we can't is simply that they have
perfect faith, for to have faith
is too have wings."

Sir James M. Barrie

"As you breathe in, cherish yourself.
As you breathe out, cherish all beings."

The Dalia Lama XIV

CHAPTER 17.

OLD SYMBOLS & NEW SIGNS

Once again I was alone and my thought of my Sword of Discernment returned. This mythical symbol was evolving into something far more in keeping with the real Doug than the image of the Sword of St. James. The story of him riding a white stallion, leading the Christian warriors to drive the Moors from the distant glacial peninsula was folklore of the locals and undoubtedly a myth. Likewise, my quest was also a myth and although my true nature knew this, I was still determined to find some symbolic reward for my effort in walking the 800 km to Santiago. I thought of the biblical statement once more, "When I was a child, I thought like a child. I reasoned like a child. When I became a man, I put away childish things."

Yes, I had walked the path of my youth with my little band of brothers, played the games of youth with them along the track, enjoyed the fun, the laughter and the shared moments of introspection, remorse and pain. It had been good for them and good for me. I had experienced the pain of healing my inner child through isolation, being alone and writing a book of poems in the depth of depression. That was the past Camino in another life, grieving the wounds of my lost son and family.

This journey of behavioural patterns, acting-out of The Camino de Santiago, had cleared many emotional blocks. It was the slow inner search that leads to the release of shame, terror, pain and the feelings that still existed inside me. I was on the other side of the midnight of the soul and walking now into a new dawning. The old symbolic sword was fading like a crutch that supported a wounded man and the inner man and the inner Sword of Discernment were taking on new meaning; a meaning of new creative energy and a need of expression. I hurriedly journaled my thoughts for the day, thought about Young, who had long since gone ahead of me on the last leg to Santiago. A phone message from Robin said that he had caught-up with Dan and Young had caught-up with both of them. Roland, apparently, was not too far away and I assumed that he may have caught a train or bus to meet with his friends.

Each to their own on The Camino, I thought as once again I put aside my journal and tramped on alone. I had not fully let go and still held on to the idea that I would have my symbolic Sword of Discernment by the time I reached Santiago. The path up the mountain track to Hospital Alta da Cruz was constantly steep and exhausting. A tiny hamlet along the highway consisted of not much more than a new albergue and a hotel/restaurant. I sat in the beer garden with a fresh meat dish, some local vegetables and a cold bottle of tonic water. The weather was hot and dry, and I stayed only long enough to jot down the details of small hamlets and the distances I had walked that day. Continuing on, I traversed rolling hills, alternating between dirt tracks and quiet country lanes once more. If anything, The Camino Way, apart from distance, was no easy road to travel. The 800 km journey had more hard surfaces than any other walk I had encountered in my life. I surmised that perhaps that, more than anything, was the reason for my swollen feet.

I had left Ventas de Naron and the stories of a great battle between the Christians and the Moors in 820, and continued along the paved road to the high point of Sierra Ligone. On the way up the final slope, just before the downhill slope to Prebista, I again met Dominic, the Italian tiler. He was jogging down the hill, in the opposite direction, away from Santiago. We stopped briefly for a chat and I asked why he was going back, noticing that he was not carrying his backpack. He had realised that the princess whom we had met at our evening meal with him was not as expected. I visualized Robin and Young shaking their heads in agreement. He was returning to his Francesca, to be with her in her hour of need, and to help her on her journey to Santiago. I wished him good luck as he ran quite quickly and faded into the distance at the bottom of the slope behind me.

Just past the only house in Lameiros, with two coats-of-arms on the door and a small chapel to San Marcos, a saint who the locals believe protects crops from foul weather, I passed a stone marker, inscribed with the year 1672, where another chapel had once stood. Nearby, a carved wooden image of the Virgin Mary and child was especially poignant. Along this dry stretch of road the ruins of an ancient castle were detectable. I had stayed the night in Portos, in the only albergue, and had made an early start on my traditional continental breakfast.

The trail continued uphill along a paved road, through the hamlets of Lestedo and Rosari which, as the name suggests, was a site where pilgrims in past generations recited the Rosary. I would have had the opportunity there to do the same thing, but had lost my Rosary some days ago - the treasured beads of the pious Canadian school teachers who had parted with their sacred relic. It was really an excuse, by me, to not return to the tradition, at least not yet, I thought.

At Chascotes, just before Pals de Rei, The Camino passed two albergues, a municipal swimming pool with a large area of green grass where I sat and watched the locals playing in the water and sun-baking beside the pool. This was quite an unusual change from my usual days on the road. I stayed long enough to have my fill of cold tonic water with ice from the food and bar outlet, then continued with my journey on the unpaved roads of Palas de Rei. Only a few traces remained of the earlier Romanesque incarnation of the township. The town is mentioned in the Codex Calixtinus, an elaborate Medieval manuscript which includes sermons, homilies to St. James and a practical travel guide, leading it to be dubbed as the western world's first guide book. Apart from that, there is nothing there to elicit anything more than a passing glance from modern-day pilgrim.

The mostly dirt path took me to San Xulian, where there is a church retaining Romanesque elements, although it also shows a different architectural style, not having a slate or thatched roof that was predominant in all the other small churches I visited. The legend of St. Julian (Xulian in Galician) was particularly sad. On the night he was born, his father witnessed witches cursing the baby to one day murder his parents. In his youth, in a conversation with a deer whilst hunting, Julian was warned of his fate. In order to avoid completing his destiny, he travelled to Galicia to be as far as possible from his parents. Later, his parents went on The Camino pilgrimage to Santiago and, on the road, by chance, they were offered hospitality by Julian's wife. Julian was out hunting at the time, and returned to find two bodies in his bed. He assumed they were his wife and a lover, became enraged and

stabbed them both to death with his sword before discovering that he had unwittingly fulfilled his murderous destiny. In penance, he dedicated himself fully to the pilgrimage, building seven pilgrim hospitals along The Way. So many reminders of bitter battles, death and tragic events I encountered in stories, myths and legends during my Camino.

I continued on to Pontecampana, refusing the offer of a lift from the driver of a small bus who was encouraging pilgrims to come to his albergue off the beaten track by offering them a cheap meal and an overnight stay. Further along the paved road I crossed a cement bridge, the Porto de Bois, where a major 14th-century battle had been fought. The stream below the bridge is said to have run with blood. The Spanish of the north may well have told their stories of slaughter and fun to themselves, but they certainly saved their warrior history for the weary pilgrims. Mostly though, they keep to themselves in a serious sort of way and politely treated their Camino pilgrims with a great deal of respect.

I had been averaging between 28 and 30 km per day on my journey, and at last reached Melide, a busy modern town tracing its history of settlement back to prehistoric times. Melide and the surrounding area contained Neolithic dolmens and prehistoric casts, suggesting that the area was well-serviced as well as having been settled in those times. It was busy in its commercial hub, which had roots in the Middle Ages when it had four large pilgrim hospitals. Like many towns of The Camino, Melide has churches and monuments spread throughout. I spent much of my time there looking for a post office, and once again mailed some belongings to Santiago. I had jettisoned a total of 5 kilos and my backpack now weighed less than 10 kilos. I felt relieved as I put my lighter burden on my back and went in search of the Puperia Ezequil, the well-known local eating-house, to experience the best of Melide's famous Pulpo Gallego, boiled octopus. This was the one time I would have relished the local red wine with my meal, in the traditional way, but there was no way I was going to return to the drink for anyone or anything, and especially not for a single meal. I had already enjoyed an octopus meal in Samos, a few days earlier, but was eagerly anticipating repeating the experience. As I entered the great eatery hall, with its many scrubbed wooden table and bench seats, I was struck by the crowds of locals and pilgrims partaking of this ocean delight. The place was like a fish market with the distinct smell of salt, from pots boiling with octopus sat in the kitchen at the entrance to the premises. I ordered a large meal and began to search for a table. A distant voice from the crowd called me over to a spare bench; it was Dominic! He had arrived while I was looking for the post office and had come directly to the eating house. He had left his backpack here when he'd returned back along the track to Francesca the previous day.

Apparently she was still suffering with sore feet and had decided to catch a bus and train the rest of the way to Santiago, where she would be waiting with open arms for him when he finished his Camino. Dominic had jogged back to meet her, and then jogged back to Melide. Oh, the price of love for the Latin lover could not be expressed in words. We enjoyed our meal together, and he later joined me for a coffee on the outskirts of Melide. We wished each other "Buen Camino" and parted company as he quickly walked ahead of me, like a professional walker in a race.

It seemed a long way since leaving the albergue at Portos earlier in the day. I had roamed the earthern pathways, traversed rolling hills, dirt tracks and quiet country lanes, and enjoyed frequent stops in little villages along The Way. Now, after the busy but lovely Melide and its Galician delicacy in my belly, I walked the peaceful paths and commenced the long stage of the endless ups and downs to Arca.

I calculated that I had walked 20.4 km that day and, having looked at my map when leaving Melide, convinced myself that another 5.5 km to Boente would be quite enough walking for one day. This would leave only 47.5 km to Santiago.

The roads were becoming busy with many more pilgrims, as the two alternative routes, the Northern Camino Primativo and the Frances route had come together in Melide. I assumed accommodation would start to be more difficult to find the closer I got to Santiago, and made a mental note to arrange accommodation at the next tourist information centre.

As I climbed the last steep incline before Boente I passed a tall German woman who seemed to be making light work of the journey upwards as I increased my pace towards the top. Just before I reached the beginning of the slow descent to Boente, less than a kilometre below, I stopped to catch my breath and remove my boots to cool my feet. The lady of leisure, wearing cool-looking climbing gear, light boots and a neat, small backpack, passed me, wished me "Buen Camino" and remarked, "Take it easy, what's the rush?" I was once more reminded of Norm's words back home in Australia: "Doug, alcoholism is a hurry disease". I made up my mind to slow my pace, make stops more frequently, enjoy the hospitality, the Spanish food and accommodation and forget about things for a while.

On my way into Boente I got into stride with a Spanish family; the mother and daughter supported the father, who appeared to be having difficulty walking, suffering from a muscle and nerve disorder. He was really struggling, but seemed determined to continue. We stopped near a seat along the track for him to rest. They were from a local village and had been walking a section of The Camino every year; his goal was to complete the entire route to Santiago before he died. We talked about Australia, and he told me that when he was a young man he had wanted to go to Australia and cut down trees for a living. He had always been good with an axe from an early age, but life got in the way of his plan and he'd never been out of Spain. We parted with the understanding that people don't make a living swinging an axe any more, even in Australia.

My night's stay in the Boente albergue was enjoyable, to say the least. My final pilgrim's meal was a huge salad for an entrée, lamb with local vegetables for the main course, and a pear with ice cream for dessert. During the meal I enjoyed the company of the German lady whom I had met on the last steep climb before the descent to Boente. We were also joined by Karl and Peter, two middle-aged Austrian I had met and walked with for part of the way on the previous day. The German woman asked my age and, when I told her, she said, "You are Superman." In Burgos I had also heard this expression, used by a young German who admired my determination, despite my age, in climbing steep hills. I wondered if this had become an "in" term in Germany for when people did extraordinary things. The German lady, Peter and Karl talked as if I were not present. "This man is mad, like me", said Peter, and the German woman got into the swing of the good humour. It was nice to receive praise from fellow pilgrims; it made me feel I belonged on this walk and in their company. I told Peter, "I'm crazy, but what makes you believe that you are, too?" He replied, "I have been to Australia four times and I rode a push-bike across the deserts,

10,000 km in total. So I know I am crazy". "Yes, you are crazy", I replied, and we all laughed.

I was on the road the next morning at 6:00 am with my Austrian companions, but left them about 6 km along the track at a little café bar in Ribadiso de Baixo, where I had breakfast. It was there that I once again met my Italian friends, Marfuaus and Marcus. We talked about the then current economic crisis within the European Community as we walked the remaining 3 km to Arzua.

Marcus was worried about the future of his business in Italy, manufacturing fabrics for the clothing industry. Clothing material manufacture was once a big industry in Italy, and he was now the last of the traditional Italian manufacturers, supporting small business and keeping people employed. Because of the high labour cost in Europe, as in Australia, so many industries and businesses had moved offshore to China. The remaining large clothing manufacturers in Italy still supported him. He was holding-on and hoping to retain his clients, otherwise he would have to close down his business.

I left him with a worried expression on his face, and trusted he would get some answers on his Camino. He smiled as we parted, wished my "Buen Camino" and I shook hands with both of them before returning to the road. He and Marfuaus stayed behind to explore the remains of a Roman settlement near Arzua. I guessed something in their culture encouraged them to spend more time in that small village. Perhaps Marcus needed a distraction, and I thought he should count his blessings; with good health and beautiful Marfuaus by his side he should have been in seventh heaven.

I caught up with Kay, from Wichita, in the U.S.A. She seemed to be in her element and insisted that I make a note of her blog and email address, which she called her backpack full of dreams. I was not to know then that The Camino would prove to be my backpack of dreams. I walked on, promising that I would keep her posted of my progress, but never really found the time to do so. Stopping for a sandwich and a drink, I sat in a fragrant eucalyptus grove thinking of home, but quickly dismissed that thought and got back on the track after eating. After a long stage of 10.8 km I finally caught Karl and Peter in Salceda, where we sat for the best part of an hour talking with a Swiss lady. I excused myself, glanced back at their outlines on a sidewalk porch and walked on, thinking I had seen the last of them – but that was not the case. I stopped briefly for an afternoon snack at a popular lunch spot in Arca. The most impressive aspect of the town, which is bisected by a busy highway, is a large oak tree near the town hall in the centre of town. I also noticed plenty of albergues and essential businesses services there.

Despite having already walked a total of 27.5 km so far that day, I was determined to make it to Lavacolla by nightfall, another 12 km further. I knew it would be difficult, more because of the distance than the condition of the trail. The majority of pilgrims on this stretch of road seemed to be on a weekend stroll in the park; mothers walked their young children, all with matching backpacks. Some young women had stopped by the roadside and were painting their finger-nails and toe-nails. Others were dressed as if they were on a date, and others were walking so slowly, four abreast, making it difficult to pass them.

I thought of the Spanish man I had met in San Domingo, walking with his three sons, the eldest ten and the youngest five. I came across them a number of times at albergues and on the road during the first week of my walk. I never once heard those children complain or the father raise his voice to them. They all seemed to know what was expected of them as they made their way on The Camino, walking slowly, but with consistent consideration to those who wanted to pass them on narrow paths. Between Amenal and San Payo I realised that I had lost the hat I had purchased in Carrion at a camping-goods store. The same hat sold in Sydney for eighty dollars at a track and trail store, but mine had cost only fifteen. I cursed that I had lost it, as the sun on my head was beginning to burn. I stopped and dug deep in my knapsack to find the old peaked cap with which I had started the walk, put it on my head, shouldered my knapsack and walked on. It was useless to cry over spilt milk. I distracted myself by thinking of my evening in Carrion, singing with the guitar-playing singing nuns of the Santa Maria convent, the little chapel entry packed with young and old alike, all singing their favourite songs and many with their own instruments. It was a wonderful evening and a lovely place to be. It was unlikely that I would ever pass that way again, so I let the memory go and continued along the track. My thoughts were now occupied with living with higher awareness and with intuition. I needed to shift my body energy away from the pain and constant pounding of my feet on a hard surface, so I connected to information from within that related to more than the goal of claiming an outward Sword of Discernment, and allowed my mind to go to where the spirit of my nature guided it. I had become one with the road, weary but energized to complete the distance to Lavacolla before dark.

At the tourist information centre not far from Lavacolla, I booked two nights' accommodation in Santiago. I was now only 10 km from that final destination when I arrived at a hotel at the entry to Lavacolla. The place reminded me of the Spanish villas you see on postcards, and which occasionally appeared in foreign films of my youth. It seemed a good place to stay for the night before my final leg to Santiago the following morning. I'd had enough of albergue accommodation for this pilgrimage. The proprietor of the Hotel Casa de Amancio in Lavacolla stamped my pilgrim's passport and handed it back to me – with my hat! Karl and Peter had picked it up, noticing that I had left it behind after our chat on the café verandah 14 km back along the track. They had passed me while I was in the tourist information centre, and had left the hat here for me, assuming correctly that I would stay in the first hotel I found in Lavacolla. Their intuition was spot-on, and I was pleased to have my head-protector back again. Once again, letting-go and leaving matters to a higher power had proved effective.

CHAPTER 18.

SANTIAGO !

The final path to the city passes through eucalyptus forests and several small villages before reaching Monte de Gozo, from where the first glimpse can be had of the Santiago Cathedral's spires. The last 5 km into the city can often involve an atmosphere of jubilant pilgrims, singing and shouting their congratulations to others who have completed the Camino journey.

The atmosphere continues in the Plaza de Obradoiro, the large plaza facing the western façade of the cathedral, where pilgrims gather now as they did in Medieval times; there to meet once again, having come so far to reach their common objective, the Cathedral de Santiago. There they congregate by the hundreds, in time for the Pilgrims' Mass and to witness the "smoke belcher", the botafumeiro, the world's largest censer for spreading incense smoke. This ceremony is repeated daily, at noon, as it was in Medieval times. After the Mass, pilgrims visit the burial place of St. James, behind the main altars and touch the golden statue of Santiago. The final tradition is to obtain the Compostela Certificate for having completed the journey. Walking around the cathedral and marvelling at the greatness of the Romanesque architecture, visiting the museum and enjoying the food at the markets are all parts of the enjoyment and tradition of what is Santiago.

Lavacolla, on the outskirts of Santiago de Compostela, is possibly the last stop for pilgrims walking the French Way of The Camino. It was that for me, and I enjoyed my overnight stay and the hospitality shown by the proprietor, who was also chief cook and bottle-washer when it came to taking care of pilgrims' needs. He was a welcome mat for a weary pilgrim at the gates of the city. I enjoyed a deliciously-prepared lamb and vegetable meal and a

SIN beer in the company of Warfaus, another Austrian I had befriended along The Way some days earlier. We talked of our homelands, and his and my youth. He was a businessman like me, and now managed an international chair-lift company, which had installed chair-lifts for all Australia's ski resorts and many of the cable cars throughout the world. We talked a lot about the company's founder and his engineering feats, and I proudly told him of my father's ability as an engineer.

Warfaus loved the little private hotel where we stayed; he was staying for three nights, choosing to not attend the next day's cathedral celebrations, but preferring to enter Santiago a day or two later when there would be fewer people about. I guess he'd had enough of crowds, considering he was in charge of a very large number of employees in Austria. We said "Buen Camino" over our final drink together and I headed for bed. According to the brochure I glanced at before going to sleep, the origin of the town's name, Lavacolla, is "lavar", meaning to wash; pilgrims during the Middle Ages used to wash themselves in the stream that crosses the river at Lavacolla before entering the city and the Santiago Cathedral. This is one of the theories that the guides in the cathedral would relate later the following day. However, the name could also derive from the geography of the place, because the word "lava" can refer to a low pasture, and "colla" means a hill. Whatever the origin, Lavacolla still sees thousands of pilgrims every year, and has done since Medieval times; pilgrims like myself, getting close to their final destination, the Cathedral of St. James in Santiago de Compostela.

As I crossed the bridge over the stream, from the dirt path on which I had been walking, I thought of pilgrims of old, having their final wash before entering the city. It crossed my mind that perhaps not all of them washed, otherwise why was it necessary for the cathedral to install such a huge botafumeiro, the "smoke belcher" of sweet incense; a censer so large that it weighs 80 kg and stands 1.6 metres tall, requiring eight strong men with ropes and pulleys to swing it back and forth above the altar and across the pews to kill the stench of the unwashed pilgrims. These days, one would assume, pilgrims had showered at an albergue or hotel either somewhere near or in the city prior to the Mass celebration.

The censer is brought out only on special days; at other times, seeing it requires a donation of 3oo Euro. Perhaps that is why so many pilgrims, myself included, arrive on Sunday for the midday Mass, to witness the spectacle for free. These thoughts, and the magic and vibrancy of this city in the early morning light, engulfed me as, through the shadows, I caught sight of the cathedrals' spires from the last vantage point as I made my way in the early morning's semi-darkness. I thought of the expression of the apostle, Paul, "Looking through a glass darkly", given to mean that we do not see the end clearly, but we will do so at the end of our time here on this earth.

Historical evidence suggests that Santiago was once a Roman city, followed by Visigothic rule. Many stories of spiritual happenings, ghosts and witches accompany the myths in my mind: thoughts of the presence of the body of St. James; of the Knights Templar protecting The Way for Medieval pilgrims; the myth of St. James manifested to lead the Spanish army in battle to drive the Moors from the lands of Galicia. Still, my Catholic upbringing steeled me to celebrate the church ritual and pay homage to the Saint, irrespective of my personal opinions. It was, after all, written in the old Codex Calixtinus Compostela: "The most excellent city of the Apostle, complete with all delights, having in its care the valuable body of St. James, on account of which it is recognised as the luckiest and noblest city in all Spain".

I was about to enter the city of the kings of Galicia and of Leon who had been crowned here in the cathedral – the city that was to become the capital of Galicia; the town fortified in the 11th century after suffering a Muslim invasion from Al Andalus; the city of rich architectural heritage, with its role as the most important city in Galica and throughout the ages; the long-awaited city I was to encounter within the next 10 km, where I would receive my Compostela Certificate on the 25th August, 2013 after having walked 800 km across northern Spain on the path taken by thousands of pilgrims during and since Medieval times. This was the city at the end of The Way walked by St. Francis of Assisi; The Way of Napoleon, Charlemagne, Roland, and the man who started it all, St, James; The Way I had walked with so many of my new-found friends – my brothers and sisters of The Camino; the path to my Sword of Discernment; the way to letting-go of all imaginary things.

It was still dark when I had left Casa de Amancio private hotel in Lavacolla for the last 10 km to Santiago. I had an SMS conversation with Robin the night before, and we had arranged to meet at 9:00 am outside the front entrance of the Santiago Cathedral. The plan was to catch-up with all my young companions and, I hoped, others I had met along The Way, for a get-together after the midday Mass celebration. I knew that I had plenty of time before meeting my companions, and would stop somewhere on the city's outskirts for breakfast – the last of my usual orange juice, croissants and coffee. My headlamp served me well as I proceeded along a straight stretch of stone pathway with indications of a build-up of houses, typical of the approach to any large city. I passed the last of the forested bush land on my final leg to Santiago, where the final stamp in my pilgrim's passport, the "credential" document identifying me as a pilgrim, would be placed; documented evidence of my accommodation stays and sites visited along The Camino, and that I qualified for the Compostela de Santiago, the document awarded to those who complete The Way of St. James.

As I traversed the pathway near the forest I was aware of candle-lights appearing to come and go, although they did not threaten my progress. It was as if there were souls from a distant past, walking silently close by. In Galicia there are many myths which may date back as far as the middle stone age, when Homo Sapiens first migrated from Africa; a time when our great human ancestors roamed the ancient land and first exhibited symbolic thoughts and demonstrated creativity by telling strange myths; a time when legends were born. Myths and legends of witches and strange events seem to have reached fever pitch during Medieval times along The Camino, and some say witchcraft is still practiced widely in Galicia. The lights in the forest along this pathway are said to be a warning not to bump into the 'Santa Compana,' a procession of the dead, or restless souls, often sighted on country such as the one I was now on.

My guidebook had indicated crossroads particularly favoured by these spirits of the night, and explained that if I met them there I should draw a circle on the ground and step inside it to avoid being taken by them. It also warned to never accept a candle from one of them during their nightly recruitment drive for souls. I had noticed stone crosses placed strategically at crossroads along The Way, on which mementoes of pilgrims who had died were placed, and on which photos of the deceased walkers were now prominently displayed.

The last piece of advice in the guide book was, if all else failed, to drink aquerimada, a Galician fire-water made form a spirit distilled from wine, combined with lemon peel, coffee beans, cinnamon and sugar; setting this concoction alight while reading a magic spell would keep the bad spirits and witches away. I was not into drinking anything verging on alcoholic, nor did ghost stories scare me. I was more intent on my day's destination and catching-up with my friends of The Way than to be bothered by guidebook ghosts, advice on make-believe or crosses at crossroads and monuments I may encounter. Besides, my journey was more one of letting-go, searching for an outward symbol, my Sword of Discernment, which I felt would reach a climax in Santiago. Like Moses' forty years in the desert to reach The Promised Land, I had endured forty days on The Way, a time that would result in creative inspiration, renewed spirit and a later reminder of the experience of an unfamiliar land. I had ventured

from an inner parched desert of the soul to the waters of renewal. What need had I for ghost stories, witches and lost souls of the night. I was not afraid of those things, but did wonder, as I passed by those flickering lights in the forest, who or what there really were. As the night darkness slowly lifted, I cleared the forest and began the final 5 km into the city in the early dawning light. I had not walked far when, as dawn broke over the city of Santiago, I once more caught sight of the distant cathedral's spires above the sea of buildings in their shadow. The early morning sun's rays shone over the cathedral steeples among the grey silhouettes of buildings emerging from the darkness. The constant pounding of my feet on the cobble stones was in tune with the beat of my heart, a heart beating to the tune of my own drummer. From a side street emerged Karl and Peter, my Austrian companions of the previous day's walking. We talked once more of life, of common interest in personal adventure and our ever-onward life searching.
I left them and headed for a café for breakfast, with Peter's parting words still in my ears, "When I get to the cathedral Mass, Doug, I am going to pray that when I get to be as old as you are, I trust and hope to be as fit and healthy".

Soon afterwards, meandering through narrow streets I heard, from a side street another distant familiar voice calling, "Doug". I stopped and waited, and there appeared Dominic, the Italian tiler, who was staying nearby with Francesca, the lovely beauty who was still suffering with shin-splints from the walk and resting in a nearby private hotel before their final walk to the midday cathedral Mass. We exchanged email details and promised to communicate on return to our homelands.

Arriving at the Plaza de Obradoiro, the large open plaza outside the cathedral, I was greeted and hugged by a great many fellow pilgrims with whom I had walked at some stage along The Way; it was as if I was part of a unique family of brothers and sisters, a silent, loving group of angels, and as if I had entered heaven. I sensed the presence of Medieval pilgrims and many Knights

Templar surrounding me; and a man on a white steed waving a flaming red sword above his head. Also there was St. James of the myth and legends, the preacher for Christ, the fisherman turned apostle of Christ - the man whose body was supposed to be buried inside the cathedral I was about to enter.

The Cathedral was already packed with thousands of pilgrims for the midday Sunday Mass. The great weight of the botafumeiro, the "smoke-belcher", would be swung back and forth by eight men hauling ropes and pulleys so that the cathedral would fill with sweet-smelling incense. I remembered that it had been installed in Medieval times to offset the stench of all the unwashed pilgrims during the Pilgrims' mass – the same celebration that had taken place for centuries, and of which I was about to be a part. On this day, as in every modern spiritual service, the sweet-smelling incense smoke was symbolic of cleansing the world of darkness; to cleanse the souls of man – represented here by many pilgrims from far corners of the world. I thought that maybe, just maybe, it would cleanse my own soul of darkness to allow a new light to live, really live. My young brothers of the road were all waiting for me: Robin, Young, Dan, and even Roland, who had somehow managed to get ahead of me along The Way. We were soon joined by Anne Marie and her new-found friend, Alice. I was distracted by so many pilgrims I had met, and longed to converse with again – Lauren and her dad, Nino, and Nicole and so many others. Time did not permit but a few moments before the midday Mass service, so I had a brief chat with all except my brothers and the group with whom I had spent the most days on the road. We arranged to meet for a meal after the Mass.

The Cathedral was filled to capacity, with only standing room still available in the aisles but, as luck would have it, Nicole had saved a seat for me, as she was keen to meet with us all after the Mass and I had the directions to our meeting-point. The service was full of pomp and ceremony, with the bishop and priest dressed in finery for the occasion. I could not help thinking of the poor beggars at the cathedral door, on their knees all day begging some financial assistance from the church and from pilgrims. Like my fellow pilgrims, after the Mass celebrations I walked the few blocks from the cathedral to the pilgrims' office and waited in line to receive the Compostela attesting to my completion of the Camino Way to Santiago. I produced my stamped passport, and briefly recalled my childhood Catholic upbringing and receiving my confirmation, of being a soldier of Christ like the great soldier of myth, St. James the Greater.

I was led to collect my certificate of completion by Sandy, my old Canadian friend of the albergue in Leon, with whom I had shared a meal and who had shown me kindness during my stay in that city. I spent the afternoon wandering the streets of Santiago in a semi-daze, enjoying the laughter, love and conversations with my small band of Camino brothers and sisters, these special souls, with whom I had travelled so far alone and in groups. I knew something about the hearts of each of them and they, too, knew something about my own. We celebrated lunch and long conversations and later met again for a last supper together. We were invited by Anne Marie to a special restaurant she had discovered during an in-depth conversation with a Spanish police chief earlier in the day. Weariness had overcome me and had a sense of foreboding of the farewells to come after our meal. We enjoyed the meal and all hugged each other in turn. Like them, I promised to keep in contact and meet again some day.

With a final wave as I said farewell, I turned and walked away into the night, led by the light of the street lamps back to my hotel behind the cathedral. I climbed the stairs to the lower section that divided the square known as The Quintana of the Dead, was used as a burial ground as late as 1780, and continued up the stairs to the street and upper part, known as The Quintana of the Living; the shadows of the pilgrims of the past, ghosts and witches no longer haunting the night – at least not for me in the shadows now; I was more interested in the light and in living.

The next morning I walked the streets of Santiago alone, but was greeted by many more pilgrims with whom I had walked briefly along The Way. Back at the cathedral, which was relatively empty of pilgrims at this time of day, and in keeping with tradition, I followed the ancient ritual and climbed the small stairway to touch the golden statue of St. James. I hugged the statue but could not bring myself to say prayers of thanks, as is the custom. Directly under the statue is a crypt, into which I descended, where the bones of St. James and two of his followers are said to be buried. Somehow, the presence of the coffin and this place of homage found me on my knees on a nearby pew saying a prayer for guidance.

In truth, I knew the bones had been misplaced for more than three hundred years before being returned to the cathedral in the 16th century, and that there was no real proof that they were in fact the saint's bones, or that he had ever been in Spain at all. I put my doubts behind me and decided that if I wanted to get along, I should go along. In any case, what harm would it do to pray in such a solemn place, at a shrine to one who was known to have been an apostle of Christ Himself – even if he had not ever been to Spain?

Yes, I had laid-down so many burdens while walking the traditional way of so many pilgrims since the great Medieval pilgrimages, and needed to lay-down one more in my quest for a sword of Discernment. I was searching for the fulfilment of the myth, a symbolic Sword of Discernment, the sword of St. James the disciple of Christ, who probably never walked on Spanish soil, never mounted a white steed and never led a great military charge against the Moors. The historical facts disproved the myth, but the myth remains, and many other pilgrims throughout the centuries have been attracted to the story and ventured on the pathway to Santiago; pilgrims in search of their own heart's desire, laying-down burdens, letting-go, healing, in companionship, in a spiritual quest or just to do the long walk. Fact or fiction, the story of St. James remains and the journey itself is real for every pilgrim who takes to the road and lets their feet do the walking.

I had come to realise, and deep-down possibly knew it all along, that my search for a Sword of Discernment would be in vain. So I found my way to the market-place and purchased gifts for friends and family as mementos of my Compostela. Still determined to return home with an outward symbol of a sword, I settled for a black shirt with a red sword of the Knights Templar on the front; the sacrificial cross fleury of St. James, was the sword blade, making it the sword of a warrior. I had previously purchased a scallop shell with the same sword pictured its front – a shell I had encountered many times along The Way, hanging off pilgrims' backpacks as they made their individual yet collective journey to Santiago. I was not to realise at the time that my seed of creativity was in the heart of a lotus flower, a flower that nestled in my heart; a seed that would spring forth from the mouth of the dark dragon that now lay dead at my feet, pierced to its heart by the sword of the many steps I had taken to reach Santiago; the seed that would spring into creative verse, songs and books I would write as a result of my Camino. Yes, I would walk the Camino de Santiago again and I would produce an outward symbol of my Sword of Discernment, but it would come to be the pen that would prove to be mightier than the Sword. It would be creative expression that would be my Sword. It would be the love that would come to me like a Christ walking on the shattered stones of the marble of my heart - the light in the darkness that ventured towards me with pierced feet.

Santiago Travellers

There's a man walking The Camino Way,
he claims no earthly goods;
he lives on love for his fellow man,
carries his own cross.

By day and by night he helps the poor,
the lame, the blind, the lot;
yes, he is a Samaritan
on The Camino Way!

The poor are slowly starving
as they hold out their beggar tins,
and the unemployed cry out for help
to find a job for them.

The journey of The Camino ends
in the church at Santiago
where pilgrims flock in thousands
in their final letting-go.

The bishop in his mitre
praised pilgrims with a prayer,
preaching of the dark side gone
now that we are free to care.

Outside of the cathedral
the beggars line the doors
pleading for some help
from within the sacred walls.

The symbol of The Camino
Is but a scallop shell;
the many road maps on its back
have many tales to tell.

Oh! When you turn it over,
it turns into a hand…
the one that remains open
for our fellow man.

Santiago travellers,
doing their own thing

walking The Camino,
determined to be free.

Suffice to say, along the way
the poor, the lame, just beg,
whilst pilgrims on The Camino
see naught but what's ahead.

Santiago travellers
doing their own thing,
walking The Camino
for the freedom it will bring!

EPILOGUE.

An increasing number of pilgrims who reach Santiago choose to continue walking to Finisterre, where they cast-off possessions such as clothing, boots, or something they have carried for their entire Camino, by throwing them into the sea. I was reminded of Frederick, the young Danish actor and his father who carried a great metal Viking cross with the specific goal of casting it into the sea, to finally let-go of some psychological myth. I thought of Young, and walking with my band of youthful brothers, and trusted he would let-go of the dagger he carried within his chest – and the one in his backpack, the one with which he had planned to kill his mother. He was determined to pass this burden on to me, but I declined, knowing that he had to find his own way of getting rid of it.

Getting to Finisterre via Muxia from Santiago adds an additional 90 km walk to reach the coast and its seaside church. The wild ocean waves breaking onto the rocky coastline and he history of the place known as "the end of the world" apparently make the trip worthwhile. It is a custom for pilgrims to also burn a personal item of clothing at Finisterre as a further sign of letting go. The addition to the Santiago pilgrimage – an epilogue to The Camino experience - attracts pilgrims to gather in their hundreds in the summer heat at the lighthouse by the sea at Finisterre, at the end of their trial. There they watch the sunset, possibly signifying the end of their journey. Whilst tramping the tracks to Finisterre, consisting of easy walks while viewing hilly landscapes by the sea and visiting quaint villages may be an attraction, I had done all the letting-go I needed. Felix came to mind, the New Yorker with the tattoos and the ring in his nose, whom I had encountered on the trail, and I wondered if he had made it to Finisterre.

I had earlier come across Ollie, the young German I had met during my first day on The Camino; by chance, we had met on a street in Santiago, where we recalled our first day on the mountain and how we had searched together for water. He had just returned from Finisterre and had been thinking about me only that morning when he'd returned to Santiago. Ollie marveled at the strange happenings that occurred on The Camino and the coincidences of us thinking about each other and then actually meeting again. I had discussed our chance meeting with Karl and Peter, the Austrians, two nights previously, and had not expected to catch-up with Ollie again on my Camino; we had not met again after that first day's encounter. We discussed the Galician seafood and culture and he told me how he had relished the beauty of the coastal walk along the wild Galician coastline, with stunning glimpses of the sea and beaches. I had read about how the route passed tiny villages, beautiful gardens and stone hedges, and had listened to stories of the beauty of the beaches and walks through eucalyptus forests and picturesque hamlets. I said my goodbyes to Ollie and we exchanged email addresses, promising to keep in contact after we returned home. I had completed my Camino de Santiago, laid-down many a burden along The Way and was discovering a new-found vision for my future. I was a little too weary to bother walking some extra kilometres just to see something I could see every day back home in Australia. I had walked many a bush track surrounded by eucalyptus trees that reach great heights, and often walked on beaches. Swimming was also something normal for me in my home country, so I did not need to walk for another 90 km to the coast to relive an everyday Australian experience.

My Camino de Santiago was complete, and now I wanted only to return home, to smell the good old Australian gum trees, walk the busy tracks near my home and enjoy the springtime of Australia in my new-found freedom. I was more than mindful now of the final words of the priest in his homily during Pilgrim's Mass celebration at Santiago Cathedral just days before: "You have walked your dark night of the soul, the Camino de Santiago. Now you have stepped into the light and it's time to live, really live."

Author's Acknowledgements

The Camino de Santiago has become the benchmark for many who were, and are yet, searching for meaning, direction and vision for their future. It has been so for those who have traced the steps of St. James, the apostle of Christ who, supposedly, was in Spain in the 1st century AD. The French route has not always been followed for Camino pilgrimages; many ventured from what is believed to be the traditional path and walked from Paris, Munich, the Swiss Alps and even from Rome. Officially, there are nine traditional routes in Spain: the Camino Frances - the traditional "Napoleon route"; the Finisterre Camino - from Santiago to Finisterre and Muxia and return; Camino de Norte - Ir'un to Santiago; Camino Portugues - Lisbon to Santiago; Camino Aragones - Samport Pass to Puente la Reina; Camino de Levante - Valencia to Santiago; Camino Ingles Ferrol to Santiago; and Camino Primitivio Gig'ion to Melide.

There are four official French routes to Santiago, not counting the start of the French "Napoleon route" beginning on the French side of the border at St. Jean-Pied-de-Port. Three other French routes begin in Le Pur, Paris and Viezelay and end at St. Jean-Pied-de-Port. The fourth starts in Arles and ends at the Samport Pass. There are, no doubt, other Camino routes with equivalent meaning in the historic world of Christ's earthly kingdom, all equally as enlightening to spiritual and cultural adventure. Other official Camino pilgrimages considered to be as significant as The Camino de Santiago are to walk the way of the cross of Christ in Jerusalem; to follow the Jesus trail in Israel's Galilee region; or to follow the steps of St. Peter to his ultimate martyrdom in The Colosseum in Rome.

Other pilgrims take the walk to The Wailing Wall in Jerusalem, to touch the spirit of the ancient ways of the Jewish faith, whilst still others make the pilgrimage to Mecca (the Haj) to visit the holy places where Mohammed the prophet once walked. These places are considered essential for pilgrims of those particular faiths; journeys to be experienced at least once in a lifetime. Pilgrims of other faiths, or of no faith at all, curious to know more of the history, the culture, and to learn what is myth, legend or reality, make to journey to Mecca or The Wailing Wall. Whilst the majority of the world's population believe in some God of a particular faith or doctrine, a smaller number believe it's all scientifically based; others have an agnostic view. It is not for me to judge, for in truth none of us still living on this side of the curtain of life knows what is or what is not – and perhaps we are not meant to know. All I know is that The Camino de Santiago was, for me, the catalyst for my renewed yearning for adventure and a turning point in my choices of lifestyle for the future.

This book could not have eventuated if not for the journey I took, the enlightenment, the strange happenings I encountered and the friendships forged along The Way. The book, although begun a year ago now, was interrupted by my need to complete the book of prose and poetry that was also a consequence of my Camino journey. So, the book of prose, "From Darkness to Light", was actually completed before I returned to finish this work. Coupled with that, I was also inspired to write songs, and recorded an album prior to returning to complete this tale of my adventure. No excuse is made here for any repetition of poems which are included in the book of prose, for they are an intricate part of my story and the catalyst for my recording more songs and stories of my Camino in the future.

It is my belief that there is a power greater than me, a guiding light, if you will, but I choose to not preach of this to others, for I do not try to define this power, but just trust in its guidance. I only know that wherever the teller of this tale can get out of the way, amazing events transpire. I am equally certain that my Catholic upbringing – although I choose to not practice that faith any longer – has left some of the scaffolding of that belief, irrespective of my new-found philosophy of letting-go and trusting that I will be led wherever that spirit of my inner power dictates. My logical mind denies my heart, and would have me follow the religion of my Irish ancestry. You may find this in my Camino journey here, as I lay down my burdens. Should I now return to practice that faith, it would, I am sure, have me return to my head, not to my heart.

I now choose to follow the one whose secret is within my heart, and trust that you have already discovered your God in yours. If you have not, then I hope you gained either some benefit from my Camino experience, or a desire to step out there – thus making this little work worthwhile. You never know, our paths may cross along some future Camino road, or maybe in another life. I trust the story inspires you to use your talents to the full, be they one, five or ten.

Namaste.

"Pilgrims poor or rich, whether coming or going to the place of St. James, must be received charitably and respected by all peoples. For whoever will take them in and diligently provide hospitality for them will be hosting not only St. James but even the Lord Himself."

Extract from the 12th century Codex Calixtinus. (Attributed to the writings of Scriptor I, Amyeric Picaud – 12th century French scholar.)

About The author.

Doug McPhillips adventurer and founder of caminoway.com.au, commenced this journey of discovery over a decade ago as a result of life-changing experiences. The broad and expansive journey of his Camino is more than a geographical excursion.
The many tracks he has traversed back to the reality of personal health, wealth and happiness led him to hike The Camino de Santiago.

The people he met along The Way and the inward discovery on his 800 km trek from St. Jean-Pied-de-Port in France to Santiago in Spain has resulted in his book of poetry, CD of songs and this novel of life experiences inspired by the journey.

www.caminoway.com.au

Doug has written seven books in all since walking the Camino three times between 2013 and 2017. He has also written and recorded two album of songs which he credits as being inspired by walking The Way.

Printed Internationally at Ingram Sparke Publications
Australia, New Zealand, Canada, Europe and the U.S.A.

Printed in Australia.
Milling Printers
C/- Fine Impressions
69 Granville Street,
Pymble 2073.

All Rights reserved by
Douglas McPhillips
ABN 84 482 105 053

26/4/21. DJM

www.ingramcontent.com/pod-product-compliance
Lightning Source LLC
Chambersburg PA
CBHW070250010526
44107CB00056B/2409